The Pastoral Epistles

An Exposition of
First & Second Timothy
and
Titus

MICHAEL L. GOWENS

Sovereign Grace Publications
Shallotte, North Carolina

THE PASTORAL EPISTLES: *An Exposition of First & Second Timothy and Titus*
Published by *Sovereign Grace Publications*
Post Office Box 1150
Shallotte, North Carolina 28459
Email sovgracepublications@gmail.com
www.sovgrace.net

ISBN 978-1-929635-29-0

Scripture quotations, unless otherwise noted, are from the *King James Version*.

Printed in the United States of America.

Contents

Introduction to the Pastoral Epistles   1

The First Epistle to Timothy

1   Salutation to Timothy   7
2   Timothy's Job Description   11
3   The Apostle's Doctrine & Its Effect   15
4   The Right Use of the Law   21
5   Paul's Exemplary Ministry   25
6   The God We Worship   31
7   A Charge to Faithfulness   35
8   The Church at Prayer   41
9   Lifting Up Holy Hands   49
10 The Christian Woman's Testimony   53
11 The Church's Leadership: Elders   59
12 The Church's Leadership: Deacons   67
13 What is the Church?   73
14 The Coming Apostasy   77
15 A Good Minister of Jesus Christ   81
16 The Profit of Godliness   85
17 Exemplary Ministry   91
18 Qualities of an Excellent Minister   97
19 Interpersonal Conduct in the Church   103
20 "Family" Financial Responsibilities   109
21 The Church's Relationship to its Ministry   115
22 Slaves & Masters in the Church Family   119
23 Godliness & the Truth   123
24 Godliness & Contentment   127
25 Paul's Final Charge to Timothy   131

The Second Epistle to Timothy

Introduction to 2 *Timothy*   147
1   Paul's 'Swan Song'   159
2   Stir Up the Gift of God   163
3   Ashamed of the Gospel   167
4   Partaking of Gospel Afflictions   171

5 Be Faithful   175
6 True Apostolic Succession   179
7 The Nature of the Gospel Ministry   183
8 Reasons to Persevere   187
9 An Approved Workman   193
10 Vessels of Honor   199
11 Dealing with Contentious People   203
12 Dangerous Days Ahead   207
13 More Cultural Dangers   213
14 Surviving the Last Days   221
15 The Shepherd's Charge   235
16 The Dying Apostle's Epilogue   257
17 Come Before Winter   271

The Epistle to Titus

1 Introduction to *Titus*   281
2 Doctrine & Duty   285
3 The Priority of Godly Leadership   289
4 Christian Relationships in the Home   297
5 Grace Promotes Godliness   309
6 The Christian in Society   315
7 Paul's Doctrine of Salvation   319
8 Final Admonitions   325

Introduction to the Pastoral Epistles

Paul's two letters to Timothy and one to Titus are popularly known as the "pastoral epistles" because they are addressed specifically to pastors who had oversight of New Testament churches. Timothy was pastor of Ephesus Church, and Titus, the church on the island of Crete.

He refers to each man as his *son in the faith* (1 Tim. 1:2; Titus 1:4), a very intimate expression that bespeaks the close personal relationship that existed between Paul and these friendly associates in ministry. That close bond is exhibited in the very practical and forthright content of these three letters. Paul speaks to them like a father would speak to a son, offering counsel, encouragement and warning.

Beside *Philemon,* the pastoral epistles are the only New Testament letters addressed to individuals. Written near the end of Paul's earthly life, these epistles offer a more personal portrait of Paul the Aged than his more formal letters to churches.

Historical Background

The three letters were probably penned within a few years of each other. *First Timothy* and *Titus* were written in *circa* A.D. 63-64, and 2 *Timothy,* in *circa* A.D. 66-68. When Paul revisited the churches he had established, he left Timothy at Ephesus (1 Tim. 1:3). He proceeded to Macedonia, from whence he penned the first epistle to Timothy, offering counsel designed to assist him in dealing with some of the issues he faced. The letter to Titus, who was ministering on Crete, was also written at this time. A few years later, Paul was arrested again. While awaiting execution, he wrote 2 *Timothy*, his "swan song." Tradition records that shortly after the completion of 2 *Timothy*, the apostle Paul was beheaded just outside the city of Rome.

Similarities

The three epistles are similar in terms of the fact that they deal with practical matters of church life and function. First Timothy 3:15 summarizes Paul's purpose in these epistles: "*But if I tarry long, that thou mayest know how thou oughtest to behave thyself in the house of God, which is the church of the living God, the pillar and ground of the truth.*"

So, these letters are written to provide specific instruction regarding proper conduct of church members in the daily affairs and activities of the church. In them, Paul discusses such practical topics as the qualifications of church officers, the role of women in the church, the important connection between the pastor's personal devotion and public ministry, the protocol for addressing sin in the church, the care of widows bereft of family support, the importance of holiness in a world of ungodliness, the peril of loving money and the importance of using wealth for the glory of God, and many more.

The practical nature of the pastoral epistles does not mean, however, that there is no doctrine here. Although the elaborate doctrinal arguments of the epistles of *Romans* and *Ephesians* are missing (for here, Paul is writing to two fellow-ministers who are already theologically established), yet there are a number of references in the pastoral epistles to the fundamentals of the faith. In fact, 2 Timothy 3:16 contains what is arguably the clearest statement concerning the inspiration of Scripture in the Bible. Also, Titus 3:3-7 and 2 Timothy 1:9-10 affirm the great doctrinal truth that salvation is by grace alone. Titus 2:13 speaks of both the deity of Christ and His second advent, while 1 Timothy 2:5 describes the basic and fundamental doctrine of Jesus' mediation between God and men.

Differences

These similarities notwithstanding, the three epistles differ in terms of their respective intent and purpose. *First Timothy*, it appears, primarily targets the problem of Judaizing teachers in the church at Ephesus. The many references to false teaching in *1 Timothy* are likely aimed at the Judaizers, as 1 Timothy 1:7-10 suggests. Of course, the influence of Judaism on the early church was a perennial and pervasive problem. Evidently, the Ephesian church in Asia Minor was not immune to the troubling influence of this perversion of the gospel, though the problem was more pronounced in the region of Galatia. Paul writes to remind Timothy of the need to guard the gospel from the corrupting influence of false teaching.

In contrast to *1 Timothy*, *Titus* is primarily concerned to deal with the problem of cultural influence on the church. Crete was a very pagan, licentious, and ungodly environment, and the church felt the sting of that sinful influence. Paul writes Titus with advice concerning the proper response to the cultural challenges facing the church.

Second Timothy has yet a different focus. This personal letter is specifically geared to encourage Timothy to be faithful and not to lose heart. Evidently, Timothy was becoming discouraged by the relentless opposition and persecution the church faced. Paul's tender and tactful reminders of his own fidelity to Christ in the midst of great adversity are clearly aimed at buttressing Timothy's faltering faith.

Summary

Of course, Paul intends his counsel to these colleagues in ministry to be passed on to the church. The pastoral epistles, in other words, are not "for preacher's only." In fact, it is my studied opinion that every church member should familiarize himself/herself with these letters.

A study of these epistles will serve at least two purposes: (1) It will enhance understanding and shape expectations, both for those who stand in the pulpit and those who sit in the pew, of the nature of pastoral ministry; (2) It will inform the believer concerning the details of how the Lord intends his church to function and the organizational structure of the local church.

The
First Epistle
to
Timothy

1
Salutation to Timothy

Paul, an apostle of Jesus Christ by the commandment of God our Savior, and Lord Jesus Christ, which is our hope; Unto Timothy, my own son in the faith: Grace, mercy, and peace, from God our Father and Jesus Christ our Lord. (1 Timothy 1:1-2)

Paul begins his letter to Timothy with a description of his Divine commission and apostolic credentials. In many ways, this is typical of Paul's manner of greeting, or saluting, his readers. Like the other Pauline epistles except *Hebrews*, Paul first identifies himself as the writer. Next, he identifies the intended recipient of the letter, i.e. Timothy. Finally, he offers a benediction, or blessing. Several specifics are noteworthy in this particular salutation, however, in spite of its typical similarities to other Pauline greetings.

Apostolic Authority (1:1)

First, notice that Paul's self-description is marked by a special tone of authority. He evidently wants those who would hear this letter read in public to know that his words carry apostolic authority. The situation Timothy faced in Ephesus was such that he needed the backing of full apostolic authority.

So, he identifies himself as *"an apostle of Jesus Christ."* The Greek verb *apostello* means "to send on a specific mission as one's personal representative." An apostle, therefore, was an envoy or ambassador, whose word carried the same weight and authority as the one he represented.

Whom did Paul represent? He writes as an apostle *"of Jesus Christ."* Paul was an apostle, in other words, in the official sense of the term. Although *apostolos* is sometimes employed in a more general sense to describe someone who was sent to represent the church,[1] yet the primary use of this term in the New Testament describes those original disciples to whom Jesus said, *"As my Father hath sent [apostello] me, even so send [apostello] I you"* (Jno. 20:21; cf. Lk. 6:13).

Perhaps someone will object that Paul is not listed among the original "apostles" of the Lord. That is correct. He was, by his own admission, "one born out of due time" (1 Cor. 15:8)—a "Johnny-come-lately," so to speak. For that very reason, his apostleship was constantly called into question; nevertheless, each of the necessary criteria by which a genuine apostle of the Lord Jesus Christ was to be judged were present in Paul.

First, the apostles were personally chosen by Jesus Christ. Paul was no exception (cf. Acts 9:15). Secondly, the apostles received direct revelation from the Lord, not second-hand education from other men (cf. Mt. 16:17). Again, Paul meets this criteria (cf. Eph. 3:3; Gal. 1:11-12). Third, the apostles were eyewitnesses of the risen Christ (Acts 1:21-22). Paul qualified here as well, for he saw "Jesus Christ" on several occasions (cf. 1 Cor. 15:8; 1 Cor. 9:1; 2 Cor. 12:1-4; Acts 22:18; Acts 23:11). Finally, the apostles possessed the supernatural ability to work miracles and signs (cf. Heb. 2:3-4). Again, Paul also exhibited *"the signs of an apostle"* during his ministry among the saints at Corinth (2 Cor. 12:11-12).

Further, Paul indicates that he was an apostle of Jesus Christ *"by the commandment of God."* Ordinarily, he uses the word **"will"** *(thelema)*, but here he employs the stronger term *"commandment"*

---

1 See Romans 16:7 where Andronicus and Junia are listed as "apostles"; 2 Cor. 8:23 where the brethren traveling with Titus are called the *apostolos* of the churches; and Phi. 2:25 where Paul calls Epaphroditus "your messenger *[apostolos]."*

(*epitage*). *Epitage* speaks of a mandatory, royal edict. When a king issues a command, there is no room for negotiation (Ecc. 8:4). By the use of this word, Paul acknowledges that he is a man under orders to the sovereign God.

He does not deem his apostolic commission, however, a grievous burden. Instead, he is delighted to obey this "command" from the Sovereign of the universe. We know this fact by the way he describes the One who commissioned him: "*...by the commandment of God our Savior, and Lord Jesus Christ, which is our hope.*"

"*God our Savior and Christ our hope*"... These titles signal Paul's awareness of God's grace both to himself and to all of His people. It is gratitude for grace that actuates him to faithful service. He is a man constrained by the love of Christ. Paul writes and speaks plainly and truthfully because of all that God through Christ had done for him. Though Nero called himself "*Soter*" [Savior] of Rome, Paul ascribes this title to God alone. He thinks of his apostolic commission both in terms of what God had done for him in the past, i.e. salvation, and of what the Lord Jesus Christ meant to him as touching the future, i.e. hope.

By connecting the Father and the Son as the source of his apostolic commission, Paul implies the fundamental Christian doctrine of the Deity of Christ. If 1 Timothy 3:16 implies (as some commentators suggest) that this doctrine was being challenged by some of the false teachers at Ephesus, then Paul, by linking the Son with the Father in his opening remarks, intends to reestablish this foundational truth at the very outset of his letter.

Personal Affection (1:2a)

The second, noteworthy feature of Paul's salutation is the personal affection he expresses for Timothy. He calls him "*my own son in the faith.*"

The blending in this salutation of the apparently opposite concepts of authority and affection reminds us that Paul's apostolic authority was not the authority of a tyrant, but of a loving parent. That parental affection is now directed toward Timothy, Paul's personal apprentice in the gospel. His words express a tenderness and warmth, emotions that had no doubt intensified through many past seasons of rich fellowship in the gospel of Christ.

Like any parent, Paul was anxious for Timothy's welfare and spiritual progress. He writes this epistle to assist Timothy with some of the issues now facing him at Ephesus. Further, he writes to affirm and encourage Timothy. The adjective *own* means "true" or "genuine" and refers to a legitimate, as opposed to an illegitimate, child. "Timothy," Paul says, "you are a genuine follower of Christ." What rich affirmation!

Pastoral Addition (1:2b)

The final feature of Paul's salutation that is noteworthy is his use of an additional term in the customary formula of benediction. In each of his other letters, Paul greets his audience by saying *Grace and peace be unto you*, but in the pastoral epistles, he includes a third term—the word *mercy*: "*Grace, mercy, and peace from God our Father and Jesus Christ our Lord.*"

Why does he include the word *mercy* in his benediction to fellow ministers of the gospel? The answer to that question, in general terms, arises from the nature of the minister's calling, and in more particular terms, to the present challenges Timothy faced at Ephesus.

Gospel ministers need much mercy, principally because they themselves are unworthy sinners. They also need mercy because they handle an exceptionally valuable treasure as the truth of God with frail, fallible, and frequently clumsy hands: "*...we have this treasure in earthen vessels...*" (cf. 2 Cor. 4:7). Further, mercy is needed because the pressures of the pastorate are significant. It is only by virtue of Divine mercy that any mortal man is enabled to fulfill such a monumental calling as gospel ministry (cf. 2 Cor. 4:1).

2
Timothy's Job Description

As I besought thee to abide still at Ephesus, when I went into Macedonia, that thou mightest charge some that they teach no other doctrine, neither give heed to fables and endless genealogies, which minister questions, rather than godly edifying which is in faith: so do. (1 Timothy 1:3-4)

The Pastoral Epistles are so named because they are concerned with the pastoral care and oversight of local churches. A case can be made, therefore, that Paul intended *1 Timothy* to be read by the church as a whole, though the letter is personally addressed to Timothy. One piece of evidence for the premise that *1 Timothy* is more than a mere private communication is Paul's official, detailed description of his apostolic authority (1:1-2), a feature that would not be necessary if Timothy was intended as the sole audience of the letter.

Further, if this epistle was, in fact, intended for the eyes of others beyond its apparent and immediate audience, then Paul's frequent affirmations of Timothy take on a new relevance. When Paul says, for instance, that Timothy is his *"own* [lit. *genuine] son in the faith"* (1:2), or when he calls him a *"man of God"* (6:11), or reminds him that he had *"professed a good profession before many witnesses"* (6:12), he is not merely trying to encourage Timothy. Instead, he aims to reinforce Timothy's authority in the church at Ephesus.

Five primary topics are of concern to Paul in this epistle: (1) The church's *doctrine* (ch. 1); (2) The church's *testimony* to outsiders (ch.

2); (3) The church's *leadership* (chs. 3-4); (4) The church's *responsibility* to its own (ch. 5); and (5) The church's *goal* (ch. 6).

First Timothy is written, then, as a sort of manual for pastoral ministry. The themes it addresses are relevant to the church in every generation.

Historical Background

First Timothy 1:3-4 establishes the historical backdrop for the letter. Timothy had been left at Ephesus to correct a number of growing problems in that local church: *"As I besought thee to abide still at Ephesus, when I went into Macedonia, that thou mightest charge some that they teach no other doctrine, neither give heed to fables and endless genealogies, which minister questions, rather than godly edifying which is in faith: so do."*

The letter contains indications of several problems plaguing the church. Some in the church who aspired to a position of leadership (1:7) were disturbing the flock by their aberrant teaching (1:3). If the Ephesian Church functioned as some Bible students suppose, meeting in "house" churches or small groups at various intervals during the week and coming together as an entire congregation on Lord's Day morning,[1] the situation would have been ripe for maverick interpretations of God's word. Smaller groups assembling in various homes throughout the course of each week would make it virtually impossible for the pastor to manage everything that was being taught.

Chapters 3 (vs. 1-13) and 5 (vs. 17-25) of this letter indicate a similar problem. Paul's detailed list of qualifications for church officers suggests that the church had relaxed the high standards necessary for spiritual leadership and allowed unqualified men to occupy these offices.

---

1   Probably, Paul's reference in Acts 20:20, i.e. "publicly and from house to house," supports this premise.

This letter also contains hints of other problems that were troubling the church, such as the usurpation of spiritual leadership by some of the women in the church (2:9-15), the influence of the *Gnostic* heresy (4:1-5), confusion concerning the church's financial responsibilities toward its own members (5:3-16), and the dangers of coveting material possessions (6:6ff). In fact, it is likely that Paul's lengthy treatment of the subject of money in chapter 6 was intended, at least in part, to identify the faulty motives of the aforementioned false teachers.

These were some of the issues Timothy faced at Ephesus. It was for this very reason that Paul asked him to stay behind to correct the decaying situation there. Such a smorgasbord of problems would prove challenging for any gospel minister; nevertheless, Paul has confidence in Timothy's integrity and godly wisdom.

The contemporary church is really no different than the church at Ephesus in the first century. In fact, the deficiencies Timothy encountered at Ephesus still challenge us today. The need for godly, qualified, and faithful leadership in the local church, therefore, cannot be exaggerated.

Elder Joseph Holder poignantly notes that the dominant lesson of *1 Timothy* is that "wise and qualified church leaders [act as] a major insulator against and antidote to error within the local church community." I agree. The sheep tend to scatter when leadership fails. A Timothy on the scene, however, proclaiming truth in the face of falsehood, and modeling by means of personal godliness the message he proclaims is frequently the very thing that is needed to turn around the sad situation of a church in declining spiritual health.

3

The Apostle's Doctrine and Its Effect

As I besought thee to abide still at Ephesus, when I went into Macedonia, that thou mightest charge some that they teach no other doctrine, neither give heed to fables and endless genealogies, which minister questions, rather than godly edifying which is in faith: so do. Now the end of the commandment is charity out of a pure heart, and of a good conscience, and of faith unfeigned... (1 Timothy 1:3-5)

Firance *irst Timothy* spells out the details — the "nuts and bolts," if you please — necessary to a *sound* church. In fact, that word *sound* is arguably the key word of the pastoral epistles (cf. 1 Tim. 1:10; 2 Tim. 1:7, 13; 4:3; Titus 1:9, 13; 2:1, 2, 8). The Greek word gives us the English word "hygiene" and refers to that which is *healthy, wholesome,* and *well,* i.e. free from illness. According to Paul in 1 Timothy 1:3ff, the first thing necessary to a healthy church is *sound* or wholesome doctrine (cf. 1 Tim. 1:10).

The Importance of Sound Doctrine

Perhaps the greatest threat to the health of a local church is unsound doctrine. Paul wastes no time addressing this threat in his letter to Timothy. He reminds Timothy that correcting the spreading infection of false teaching among the saints at Ephesus was the primary purpose he asked him to stay there: *"As I besought thee to abide still at Ephesus...that thou mightcst charge some that they teach no other doctrine"* (v. 3).

The term *charge* means "command" and harks back to Paul's claim that he was an apostle by the *commandment of God* (v. 1). Timothy could speak with apostolic authority, therefore, commanding some to *"teach no other doctrine." Other* is the Greek word *heterodidaskaleo.* The prefix *heteros* means "different," and the root *didasko* refers "teaching." Timothy was authorized to insist—yea, even demand—that some in the church at Ephesus stop teaching a different doctrine.

Different from what? Different from the apostle's doctrine. Apostolic doctrine is the standard by which truth is measured (Acts 2:42; Lk. 22:30; 1 Tim. 2:2; 2 Ths. 3:14). Teaching that deviates from this norm undermines the integrity of the church.

Just as the Galatians had embraced *"another [heteros] gospel"* (Gal. 1:6) and the Corinthians were in danger of being beguiled by *"another [heteros] Jesus, another spirit, and another gospel"* than they had received from Paul (2 Cor. 11:4), so the Ephesians were now troubled by teaching that was qualitatively different from the true gospel. Paul says that the things these men are teaching comprises a significant alteration from apostolic teaching.

It is significant that Paul did not commission Timothy to simply labor with those men who were promoting ideas contrary to apostolic doctrine. He did not advise him to implore them to stop, or to gently suggest that they stop. Instead, Timothy was to command them to "cease and desist" at once.

Is the content of teaching in a local church really that important? Yes, it is. In fact, it is basic and fundamental to the health of the church. Corrupt doctrine, like infection in the body, weakens the church. Sound doctrine is health-giving, just like a well-balanced diet promotes health in the physical body, to the body of Christ.

Specifics of the Ephesian Problem

What particular form did the "different doctrine" take in the congregation at Ephesus? Who were these teachers of different doctrine, and what were they teaching? Verse 7 calls them *teachers of the law* — perhaps Jewish Christians in the Ephesian Church who retained their loyalty to the priority of the Mosaic Law. Of course, there is nothing wrong with teaching the law, but these men were not *using it lawfully* (1:8).

In what sense were these false teachers using the law improperly? Verse 4 provides the answer: "*Neither give heed to fables and endless genealogies which minister questions, rather than godly edifying which is in faith.*"

If the two terms *fables* and *endless genealogies* are to be taken together, as some commentators suggest, the reference is probably to the *Haggada* or rabbinical tradition. Apparently, some Pharisees retold Old Testament history in a document dated about 100 B.C. This rewrite of Jewish history emphasized the indestructibility of the Law with a special focus on elaborate genealogies and various legends associated with the patriarchs. The genealogical emphasis was apparently designed to stress the importance of a pure, Jewish pedigree.

Paul discounts the speculation as frivolous, charging it with *ministering questions rather than godly edifying*. He means that the only way it ministers to or serves people is to make them uncertain of the truth. Instead of clarifying truth, it clouds the mind with confusion. This emphasis, he says, does not remove doubts nor build up the church; it creates them and undermines the foundation of faith.

Sound doctrine, on the other hand, does "edify," or build up, the saints in a godly way. It makes the church strong and resilient. It strengthens the believer for godliness. For the express purpose of reestablishing sound doctrine in the face of these Jewish aberrations, then, Timothy was left in Ephesus.

The Goal of Apostolic Teaching

In contrast to the fanciful speculations of these false teachers and the confusion their teaching engendered, the apostle's doctrine that Timothy is charged to preach produces a better effect: *"Now the end of the commandment is charity out of a pure heart, and of a good conscience, and of faith unfeigned"* (1:5).

Again, Paul's reference to the *commandment* is a reference to the apostolic message. The message of the false teachers encourages controversy, he says, but the apostolic message encourages charity, integrity, and sincerity.

The word *end* is the Greek word *telos,* meaning "goal" or "target." For what goal does the apostolic message aim? What outcome is it designed to produce? What is the intended effect when the truth is proclaimed? He answers with a three-fold response.

First, the apostle's doctrine is designed to produce *"charity out of a pure heart"* in the lives of those who receive the message. The primary goal of gospel preaching, Paul says, is to foster love for God and for others in the hearts of believers. The message of Christ's self-sacrifice should prompt those who hear it to a life of the same kind of sacrificial love. Such a life of love, untainted by pretense or false motives, adorns and beautifies the gospel message.

Secondly, apostolic teaching aims at cultivating *"a good conscience"* in those who hear the message. Where the pure gospel is proclaimed and received, the believer possesses not only a loving heart but a healthy mind. He lives with a sense of pardoning mercy for past sins, and labors to maintain a conscience void of offense toward God and man (cf. Acts 24:16). The impact of God's revelation is witnessed by a growing integrity in the believer's daily conduct.

Thirdly, the apostolic message seeks to develop *"faith unfeigned."* The adjective *unfeigned* means "unpretentious, without hypocrisy, sincere." A real and genuine faith in God and the Lord Jesus Christ, sustaining the soul in the midst of the pressures of life, is one of the primary goals and outcomes of the apostle's doctrine.

What we have in this passage, then, is a contrast between the outcome of false teaching and the product of the true gospel. False teaching promotes confusion and controversy, undermining the spiritual health of individual believers and the local church as a whole. Truth, on the contrary, edifies the church—that is, it builds up believers on their most holy faith (cf. Jude 20). It makes God's people loving (both toward God and man), holy, and trusting. It fosters within their lives charity, integrity, and sincerity. Sound doctrine, in other words, is foundational to a sound and healthy church.

4

The Right Use of the Law

Now the end of the commandment is charity out of a pure heart, and of a good conscience, and of faith unfeigned: from which some having swerved have turned aside unto vain jangling: desiring to be teachers of the law; understanding neither what they say, nor whereof they affirm. But we know that the law is good, if a man use it lawfully; knowing this, that the law is not made for a righteous man, but for the lawless and disobedient, for the ungodly and for sinners, for unholy and profane, for murderers of fathers and murderers of mothers, for manslayers, for whoremongers, for them that defile themselves with mankind, for menstealers, for liars, for perjured persons, and if there be any other thing that is contrary to sound doctrine; according to the glorious gospel of the blessed God, which was committed to my trust. (1 Timothy 1:5-11)

Paul's summary in verse 5 of the effects of apostolic doctrine expresses a striking contrast to the effects of false teaching. False teaching promotes an ethical climate of controversy (v. 4), but true doctrine cultivates an ethical climate of love toward God and man, personal integrity, and genuine godliness (v. 5). Thus, doctrine is judged by its fruit.

But *some* at Ephesus had *swerved* from the apostolic message and *turned aside unto vain jangling* (v. 6). Paul's reference to this unnamed group that he calls *some* is identical to the group mentioned in verse 3, i.e. "charge *some* that they teach no other doctrine."

These false teachers were probably *Diaspora* Jews— Jewish people who had been dispersed throughout the Graeco-Roman world but who maintained loyalty to the tenets of the Mosaic Law. And their emphasis on the Law was off target from the gospel proclaimed by Paul. They were missing the true mark and engaging in empty speculation, i.e. *vain jangling*. These self- proclaimed instructors in the Law, while aspiring to a role of spiritual leadership in the church, did not even understand the Law they presumed to teach in such dogmatic terms (v. 7).

At first glance, one might conclude from his language that Paul is against the Law — namely, that he is an *antinomian*. But Paul's complaint is against the maverick interpretations and doctrinal innovations of these false teachers, not the Law *per se*. Is there any place, then, for the Law in the apostolic message?

Yes, there is. Paul insists that there is a sense in which the Law is still useful. His point might be summarized by the formula, "The lawful use of the Law is for the lawless":[1] *"But we know that the law is good, if a man use it lawfully; knowing this, that the law is not made for a righteous man, but for the lawless and disobedient, for the ungodly, and for sinners, for unholy and profane, for murderers of fathers and murderers of mothers, for manslayers, for whoremongers, for them that defile themselves with mankind, for menstealers, for liars, for perjured persons, and if there be any other thing that is contrary to sound doctrine"* (1:9-10).

Paul's point, stated simply, is that the Law still functions as a regulating authority, or an ethical standard. And it is the sinner, not the saint, that is the Law's target.

The primary purpose (and ongoing purpose, even during the Gospel dispensation) of the Law is the restraint of evil. The Law spells out God's moral absolutes and, thereby, functions as a means to the preservation of society.

In this day of moral relativism, when the concepts of right and wrong are primarily determined by individual preference, it is important that Christian people understand and affirm the right

---

1   John R. W. Stott, *The Message of 1 Timothy & Titus*, p. 46.

use of the Law. Though the ceremonial Law has been abrogated, the Law as a moral code has not. The God who gave it has not changed His mind about sin. It is still His will that mankind worship Him as the only true and living God, keep their vows and promises, observe a rhythm of work and rest, and respect the sanctity of life, property, truth, and marriage.

When these objective, ethical standards are replaced by personal tastes and whims, society disintegrates. No community can survive long where lawlessness, i.e. sin, is not restrained.

Of course, there is one thing the Law cannot do. It cannot change an individual's heart. It may deter sin by threatening shame and punishment, but it cannot make a sinner love what is right and good. Only the efficacy of Divine grace can change the heart.

What kinds of lawlessness are curbed by the Law? The first six terms — the *"lawless... disobedient... ungodly... sinners... unholy... profane"* — are general terms employed to describe those who live sinfully. The remainder of the listed categories, however, are more specific. *"Murders of fathers...and mothers"* refers to a breach of the fifth and *"manslayers"* of the sixth commandment. Both *"whoremongers"* and *"them that defile themselves with mankind"* refer to sexual promiscuity, whether heterosexual or homosexual in nature, and suggests a breach of the seventh commandment. *"Menstealers"* speaks of kidnappers and slave traders and refers to the worst kind of thievery, a breach of the eighth commandment. *"Liars"* and *"perjurers"* refer to a breach of the ninth commandment. The Law is given to restrain all of these.

Paul summarizes his list of sins curbed by the Law by a "catch-all": *"...and if there be any other thing that is contrary to sound doctrine"* (v. 10b). This reference indicates that the moral implications of the apostolic message are no different than the moral implications of the Law.

Paul's point in this context, then, is that the particular emphasis these false teachers were placing on the Law was misdirected. They were purporting to be teachers of the Law, but failed to comprehend the proper use of the Law. Paul, and *the glorious gospel of the blessed God* that he preached, did not dismiss the importance of the Law. Rather, he understood that the Law has its place as a restraint to ungodly behavior. Any use of it as a vehicle for eternal salvation comprises a deviation from apostolic doctrine.

5

Paul's Exemplary Ministry

According to the glorious gospel of the blessed God, which was committed to my trust. And I thank Christ Jesus our Lord, who hath enabled me, for that he counted me faithful, putting me into the ministry; who was before a blasphemer, and a persecutor, and injurious: but I obtained mercy, because I did it ignorantly in unbelief. And the grace of our Lord was exceeding abundant with faith and love which is in Christ Jesus. This is a faithful saying, and worthy of all acceptation, that Christ Jesus came into the world to save sinners; of whom I am chief. Howbeit for this cause I obtained mercy, that in me first Jesus Christ might shew forth all longsuffering, for a pattern to them which should hereafter believe on him to life everlasting. Now unto the King eternal, immortal, invisible, the only wise God, be honor and glory for ever and ever. Amen. (1 Timothy 1:11-17)

Paul now turns his focus away from the false teachers at Ephesus to his own ministry and the gospel he preached. It is a very personal passage in which Paul presents himself as a model for believers, but not in an arrogant way. Instead, his point is that God, so to speak, had "made an example" of him. "My case," he seems to say, "is an object lesson to everyone else of the transforming power of Divine grace."

The key thought is in verse 16: "*...that in me first Jesus Christ might show forth all longsuffering, for a pattern to them which should hereafter believe on him to life everlasting.*" The word *pattern* suggests the idea of a model or an example. The Greek word literally means "to draw a sketch; to write a first draft," and suggests the image of an artist beginning a picture.

God made Paul an example of saving grace, in other words, changing his heart and *"putting [him] into the ministry"* (v. 12). Paul, in turn, committed himself to herald that *"glorious gospel"* (v. 11) of grace the rest of his life. In contrast to the false teachers and their emphasis on the Law, Paul championed Divine Grace as the only message for sinners.

Paul, An Example for Sinners

This passage begins with a reference to the fact that God had entrusted Paul with a message he calls *the glorious gospel of the blessed God* (v. 11). He does not use these terms lightly, for the gospel message is indeed glorious. It is glorious because it is a message of good news to sinners. Paul knew that fact first-hand. His life is an example of the fact that God is able to change the greatest sinner and tender the hardest heart.

This passage, recounting Paul's personal story in very detailed terms, both begins and ends with an expression of praise to the Lord Jesus Christ. At the beginning he says, *"I thank Christ Jesus our Lord"* (v. 12); and at the end, *"Now unto the King eternal, immortal, invisible..."* (v. 17). Paul never got over the fact that grace had rescued and transformed his life.

For what is he thankful? Two blessings, in particular, comprise his doxology: (1) First, *"I thank Christ Jesus our Lord, who hath enabled me..."* (v. 12a). Paul traces his usefulness to its source in God's enabling grace; (2) Secondly, *"I thank Christ Jesus.. for that he counted me faithful, putting me into the ministry"* (v. 12b). It is obvious that Paul does not mean that his apostolic commission was due to any inherent trustworthiness in himself. He does not mean that he deserved to be an apostle. On the contrary, the second part of verse 12 follows closely on the heels of the first. It was because of God's "enabling" that Paul was equipped for service. Instead of touting his own worthiness for the office, therefore, Paul is actually ascribing praise to Christ for qualifying him to serve in that capacity.

It is clear from the language employed that Paul deemed gospel ministry a privilege. He thanks the Lord Jesus Christ for giving him the opportunity to serve. Such a grateful perspective and humble attitude befits every God-called minister.

One practical lesson that may be gleaned from Paul's words is the importance Christ places on faithfulness among His ministers. Faithfulness to the One who calls and commissions men to serve is the ultimate measure of a successful ministry.

Because of his sinful past, Paul is amazed at the grace that would rescue him from a self-centered life and place him into this high and noble office: *"Who was before a blasphemer, and a persecutor, and injurious; but I obtained mercy because I did it ignorantly in unbelief. And the grace of our Lord was exceeding abundant with faith and love which is in Christ Jesus. This is a faithful saying, and worthy of all acceptation, that Christ Jesus came into the world to save sinners; of whom I am chief"* (1:13-15).

Blasphemer speaks of his sinful words against the Lord Jesus Christ. *Persecutor* suggests his sinful deeds against the church of Jesus Christ. *Injurious* speaks of his sinful thoughts of deep-seated hostility, animosity, and hatred. The Greek word translated *injurious (hubristes,* from which we derive the English *hubris)* suggests a desire to see people hurt. Paul actually found pleasure in persecuting Christians.

So great did Paul consider his sins that he calls himself *" the chief of sinners"* (v. 15). Interestingly, the word *chief* means "prototype" or "model." Paul says here that was an exemplary sinner—a model sinner. He felt that his old carnal heart embodied the very essence of sin and depravity. He considers himself a prototype of the depth to which a sinner—any sinner—might sink.

But not only does he consider himself to be the prototype of sinners, he also considers himself to be the original model of God's abundant mercy: *"...but I obtained mercy, because I did it ignorantly in unbelief. And the grace of our Lord was exceeding abundant with faith and love which is in Christ Jesus..."* (v. 13b-14).

"But I obtained mercy..." He mentions the fact again in verse 16. Paul's story is not a tale of human merit but a memorial of Divine mercy. *"Because I did it ignorantly in unbelief"* (v. 13) does not indicate that his sins were excused because of ignorance; rather, that mercy was necessary because of his ignorance and unbelief.

Let me illustrate. If I were to say, "I obtained a new coat because I left my old coat at home," you would not conclude that forgetting my coat merited the new one. Instead, you would understand that because I had left my coat, I needed another. This verse literally means, "Because I committed these sins of blasphemy, persecution, and animosity in an attitude of ignorance and unbelief, I needed mercy from God."

Because of the Lord's *"exceeding abundant"* (lit. overflowing) grace, then, Paul's life was transformed from a life of animosity toward Christ and others into a life characterized by *"faith and love"* (v. 14). The language suggests the image of a river flooding its banks. Just as the overflowing of the Jordan River produced a fruitful harvest on either side, so God's overflowing grace has produced the fruit of faith and love in my life, says Paul. His life, once characterized by unbelief (v. 13) is now marked by faith (v. 14). His heart, once distinguished by hatred and animosity, is now characterized by love.

A marvelous transformation has occurred in me, says Paul, and Christ gets all the credit. He proceeds to state that this principle is the very heart and soul of the gospel message: *"This is a faithful saying, and worthy of all acceptation, that Christ Jesus came into the world to save sinners; of whom I am chief"* (v. 15). This poignant summary of the *"glorious gospel of the blessed God"* which Paul preached forms the first of five *"faithful* (lit. trustworthy) *sayings,"* or Christian maxims, in the Pastoral Epistles.

Paul indicates in verse 16 that Christ showed him mercy for a purpose: *"...that in me first Jesus Christ might show forth all longsuffering, for a pattern to them which should hereafter believe on him to life everlasting."* The word *first* is not an adverb meaning "first in time," but an adjective meaning "foremost in importance." Paul is saying that he is the premier or foremost example of saving mercy, just as he was the *chief,* or foremost example, of sinners.

Paul wants people to conclude from his story that if Christ can save a sinner like him, then there is hope for every sinner. The *longsuffering* God demonstrated toward Paul was a withholding of judgment. Such Divine patience to sinners is a reason to hope in the grace and mercy of the Lord.

When he speaks of *"them which should hereafter believe on him to life everlasting,"* does Paul mean that man's belief produces eternal life? He cannot mean that, for that would contradict passages that teach that regeneration precedes faith, like 1 John 5:1 and John 5:24. Instead, Paul is simply making the point that belief is an evidence of everlasting life. The preposition "to" literally means "with reference to" and describes the content of faith, *vis a vis* what is believed. The text means that all future believers will be able to trace the reason for their change to precisely the same source as Paul's transformation—the abundant grace and mercy of God.

No wonder Paul concludes with doxology in verse 17: *"Now unto the King eternal, immortal, invisible, the only wise God, be honor and glory forever and ever. Amen."* His whole life is marked by thanksgiving for God's grace in salvation, and for the privilege of being Christ's servant. May believers today follow his pattern of gratitude and never tire of hearing and believing the glorious gospel of God's grace.

6
The God We Worship

Now unto the King eternal, immortal, invisible, the only wise God, be honour and glory for ever and ever. Amen. (1 Timothy 1:17)

This autobiographical passage (1 Tim. 1:12-17), suggests at least three practical lessons. First, like other autobiographical sections in the Pauline epistles, this one is designed to draw attention, not to Paul but, to Christ and His amazing grace. Paul never talks about himself in order to satisfy his own ego (cf. 2 Cor. 4:5). Instead, he wants others to get the message from his case: "If God can have mercy on a sinner like me, then there is also hope for you."

Further, this passage indicates that Paul wants his readers to understand his motivation in ministry. He is compelled to preach this gospel of grace because it is the only message that explains his own experience. "This is what happened to me," he says, "and I cannot rest until I tell others what great things Christ has done for me." There is no more powerful incentive to speak for the Lord Jesus Christ like a conscious awareness of His pardoning mercy to someone like me, says Paul.

Thirdly, this passage implies an important Biblical principle, namely, a personal experience of grace in the life of every man who would proclaim the gospel message is a necessity, not a luxury (cf. 2 Tim. 2:6). Not only did Paul's personal experience motivate him in ministry, it also equipped him for ministry. Such a personal experience with Christ is a necessary prerequisite to a ministry that edifies the church of God. Perhaps this explains the historical practice during ordination proceedings of asking a prospective minister to recite his spiritual experience. The public reiteration of the candidate's own experience of grace informs the presbytery that he has personally tasted, or existentially grasped, the very gospel message he is charged to proclaim.

Having used himself as the prototypical sinner transformed by the grace of God, Paul utters one of those spontaneous doxologies that are so common to his letters: *"Now unto the King eternal immortal, invisible, the only wise God, be honor and glory forever and ever. Amen."* It is a paean of praise that has much to say about the God we worship.

The first and most basic thing Paul celebrates is the fact that God is *the King*. This speaks of the attribute theologians call *the sovereignty of God*. I am intrigued by Paul's sudden transition from a personal reference to God's pardoning mercy to the more transcendent attribute of Divine sovereignty. Both immanence and transcendence are true of our God and we must always be careful to maintain this dual emphasis.

Sovereignty simply means that God rules and reigns with absolute authority. It depicts Him as a great God who works His will and whose purposes cannot be thwarted (cf. Dan. 4:35; Job 23:13; Ps. 115:3). He "reigns" (Ps. 97:1; 99:1), as "a great King above all gods" (Ps. 95:3b). He is King of the nations (Ps. 22:28) and King of saints (Rev. 15:3). From His throne high in the heavens, His kingdom rules over all (Ps. 103:19). He is almighty over all, superlative to everyone and everything else that exists.

Paul now lists four characteristics of God the King. First, He is *eternal*. Literally, He is "King of the ages," transcending history. The fluctuations of time do not affect Him.

How salutary to the soul to know that time cannot change God! The God who created the universe is still the same today—undiminished in glory, unimpaired in power, and undisturbed in purpose. Scripture frequently cites the attribute of God's eternity as a "city of refuge" for the child of God (cf. Deut. 33:27; Ps. 90:2).

Secondly, He is *immortal.* The word means "not subject to decay and death; imperishable." Later, Paul will again refer to God as the One *"who only hath immortality"* (cf. 6:16). Death will never interrupt His sovereign reign.

Thirdly, He is *invisible.* He *"dwells in the light which no man can approach unto, whom no man hath seen nor can see"* (cf. 6:16). Such splendor and glory exudes from His presence that "no man can look upon Him and live." Just a glimpse of his glory left Paul blinded for three days (cf. Acts 9:9). Of course, the Lord Jesus Christ is *"the image of the invisible God"* (Col. 1:15), so that to see Him is to see the Father (Jno. 14:9).

In the fourth place, He is *"the only wise God."* He alone is God (cf. Is. 45:18), and He alone is ultimately wise. His wisdom is demonstrated in creation (cf. Ps. 104:24; Jer. 10:12), but most vividly in redemption (cf. Eph. 3:10; 1 Cor. 2:7). Paul exults in the Lord for the wisdom displayed by this unique God in his own story of salvation.

This is the God we worship. He is the God of grace — the God and Father of our Lord Jesus Christ. He is the God who changed Paul, and Paul is careful to give Him all the glory: *"...be honor and glory forever and ever. Amen."*

The chief end of man is the glory of God. We exist to give Him glory. Salvation from sin is the great impetus to the act of glorifying God. Paul is happy to devote his whole being to the glory of the One who loved him and had mercy on his poor soul. May all who have experienced similar grace devote their every energy to render to Him the honor and glory that is His due.

This thrilling text praising the sovereign King of heaven and earth is the inspiration for the popular Christian hymn by Walter Chalmers Smith. May we, with him and Paul, celebrate our great King.

Immortal, invisible, God only wise,
In light inaccessible hid from our eyes,
Most blessed, most glorious, the Ancient of Days,
Almighty, victorious, thy great name we praise.
Unresting, unhasting, and silent as light,
Nor wanting, nor wasting, thou rulest in might;
Thy justice like mountains high soaring above
Thy clouds, which are fountains of goodness and love.
To all, life thou givest, to both great and small;
In all life thou livest, the true life of all;
We blossom and flourish as leaves on the tree,
And wither and perish — but naught changeth thee.
Great Father of glory, pure Father of light,
Thine angels adore thee, all veiling their sight;
All praise we would render: O help us to see
'Tis only the splendor of light hideth thee."

7

A Charge to Faithfulness

This charge I commit unto thee, son Timothy, according to the prophecies which went before on thee, that thou by them mightest war a good warfare; holding faith, and a good conscience; which some having put away concerning faith have made shipwreck: of whom is Hymenaeus and Alexander; whom I have delivered unto Satan, that they may learn not to blaspheme. (1 Timothy 1:18-20)

With the contrast between the false teachers at Ephesus and Paul's own apostolic ministry, Timothy is now urged to make a choice between the two: *"This charge, I commit unto thee, son Timothy, according to the prophecies which went before on thee, that thou by them mightest war a good warfare; holding faith, and a good conscience, which some having put away concerning faith have made shipwreck: of whom is Hymenaeus and Alexander; whom I have delivered unto Satan, that they may learn not to blaspheme."*

Paul, however, does not leave Timothy in question as to which path to choose. He "commits a charge," similar to the trust a depositor places in a bank when depositing money, to Timothy. "Timothy," he says, "I have entrusted you with a very precious asset—the truth of God. Now I exhort you to guard this truth."

This *charge* to Timothy contains a number of important insights concerning faithfulness in gospel ministry. Let's consider them one-by-one.

Faithfulness: The Goal of Ministry

Paul calls Timothy to be faithful—to *"war a good warfare."* The challenge facing him in this particular situation at Ephesus was the same challenge he faced at every stage and in every venue of his life and labors as a gospel minister, i.e. to be faithful to the Lord Jesus Christ, his Commanding Officer (cf. 1 Cor. 4:2).

This metaphor of "warfare" implies a double thought. First, the minister's task, as well as the task of every believer, is not easy and comfortable. Just like the life of a soldier in combat is not easy, the gospel ministry is a life of conflict, tension, and struggle. The imagery is deliberately employed to suggest the thought of hardship and privation, circumstances that tend to discourage even the most resilient people (cf. 2 Tim. 2:3). Paul's reminder that the goal before him was to *"war a good warfare"* and to *"fight the good fight"* (1 Tim. 6:12), then, is calculated to encourage Timothy to faithfulness.

Secondly, Timothy is not at liberty to operate his ministry according to personal preference, but is, like a soldier, subject to the authority of another. The false teachers at Ephesus were mavericks and innovators, but the primary obligation of a soldier is to please his Commander. Paul wants Timothy to remember this fact.

As an incentive to faithfulness in ministry, Paul reminds Timothy of two important facts. First, by the reference to him as *"son Timothy,"* Paul reaffirms his own love and affection for him. This kind of positive peer pressure serves a very important role in the life of the church. When fellow-believers couch admonition in the endearing terms of brotherly love, reminding another of the Christian relationship they share, they exercise a powerful leverage for good on the conduct of their brethren.

Secondly, Paul reminds Timothy of his ordination: *"...according to the prophecies which went before on thee, that thou by them mightest war a good warfare..."* The reference to *"the prophecies"* that were previously reported concerning Timothy is undoubtedly a reference to the charge given to him by the presbyters at his ordination (cf. 1 Tim. 4:14). Paul wants him to remember the things the other ministers said to him, and the sacred responsibility he assumed on that occasion. Thinking back to his ordination day would serve as a powerful incentive to faithfulness in ministry.

The Criteria of Faithfulness

What constitutes "faithfulness" to the sacred trust of the gospel? Paul mentions two criteria: "*...holding faith and a good conscience...*" Both are essential (cf. 1:5; 3:9).

Though there is no definite article before the word *faith*, the Greek includes the definite article later in the sentence: "*...which some have put away concerning [the] faith have made shipwreck...,*" indicating that Paul is thinking about *faith* here as "the body of Christian truth." Hence, the criteria by which faithfulness is judged involves both an objective standard (apostolic doctrine) and a subjective one (a good conscience). Both the academic (or intellectual) and the ethical dimensions of gospel ministry are equally essential.

The false teachers had failed to hold on to the faith; hence, they had not been faithful to the apostolic message. Doctrinal soundness is crucial in the life of every gospel minister. Christ's soldiers are not at liberty to redefine the Captain's orders.

But ethical godliness is equally crucial in the minister's life. How many otherwise faithful ministers have so long disregarded the voice of conscience warning of some stubborn disobedience in their lives until they ultimately ruined their testimony! Gospel fidelity is measured by both heartfelt belief and holy behavior, not one without the other. Both conviction and conscience, the head and the heart, are important.

The Tragedy of Unfaithfulness

Paul now cites two people (with whom Timothy was undoubtedly familiar) as object lessons of unfaithfulness: "*...which* *some having put away concerning faith have made shipwreck: of whom is Hymaneaus and Alexander; whom I have delivered unto Satan that they may learn not to blaspheme."*

Like the false teachers at Ephesus, Hymaneaus and Alexander had erred in terms of doctrinal faithfulness. Perhaps they were moral men, conducting their lives with a view toward maintaining "a good conscience"; nevertheless, they failed in the first of these criteria, i.e. they did not *"hold faith."* It is likely that Hymaneaus is the same man mentioned in 2 Timothy 2:18 who taught that the resurrection was past already. Maybe Alexander was an accomplice in this doctrinal aberration. Whatever was their particular error, Paul calls it *"blasphemy."*

So serious was it that they were expelled from the church. To be *"delivered unto Satan"* is to be thrust back into the world, beyond the protection of the fellowship of the local church (cf. 1 Cor. 5:5, 13). Expulsion, however, was not intended to be punitive, but remedial — not permanent, but temporary. Paul clearly expects that they may be recovered: *"...that they may learn not to blaspheme."* How blessed it is to see one previously disciplined return to the fellowship of the church with a repentant attitude!

John R. W. Stott, in his commentary on *1 Timothy*, nicely summarizes this first chapter:

> In this first chapter, which concerns the place of doctrine in the church, Paul gives valuable instruction about false teaching. Its essential nature is that it is *heterodidaskalia*, a deviation (*heteros*) from revealed truth. Its damaging results are that it replaces faith with speculation and love with dissension. Its fundamental cause is the rejection of a good conscience before God.
>
> What then should Timothy do in such a situation? Paul does not tell him to secede from the church, which would have been an extreme reaction. But neither may he remain silent in the face of heresy, let alone compromise with it, which would have been the opposite extreme. Instead, he was to stay at his post, and to fight

the good fight of faith, both demolishing error and contending earnestly for the truth. [1]

1   Stott, *The Message of 1 Timothy & Titus*, p. 58.

8
The Church at Prayer

I exhort therefore, that, first of all, supplications, prayers, intercessions, and giving of thanks, be made for all men; for kings, and for all that are in authority; that we may lead a quiet and peaceable life in all godliness and honesty. For this is good and acceptable in the sight of God our Savior; who will have all men to be saved, and to come unto the knowledge of the truth. For there is one God, and one mediator between God and men, the man Christ Jesus; who gave himself a ransom for all, to be testified in due time. Whereunto I am ordained a preacher, and an apostle, (I speak the truth in Christ, and lie not;) a teacher of the Gentiles in faith and verity. I will therefore that men pray every where, lifting up holy hands, without wrath and doubting. (1 Timothy 2:1-8)

In chapter 1, Paul was concerned with the church's doctrine; now, in chapter 2, he shifts focus to the church's testimony to outsiders. The two exhortations concerning the function of the church contained in chapter 2—the exhortation to prayer, and the exhortation concerning the role of women—directly affect the church's public testimony in popular culture.

It is evident that Paul wants the church to be sensitive to the fact that they are being watched. He wants them to function, consequently, in a way that will promote and not hinder the gospel. His point in 2:9-15 is that confusion concerning the authority structure in the church is a testimony to the world that is counterproductive to the gospel. And his point in 2:1-8 is that prayerlessness on the part of believers complicates social life, thereby limiting opportunities to live a truly Christian life.

A Matter of Primary Importance

"I exhort therefore, that, first of all, supplications, prayers, intercessions, and giving of thanks, be made for all men..." (2:1). Paul exhorts the church to prayer *first of all*, that is, as a matter of primary importance. Of all the functions of the local church, none is more vital and fundamental than prayer. The church of the Lord Jesus Christ should be, first and foremost, a praying community (Is. 56:7).

Prayer was one of the primary characteristics of the early church. With no bank account to finance them, no military to defend them, and no governing body to protect them, the early saints waited on the Lord by means of prayer, and they prospered.

The *Acts of the Apostles* is the record of a people who believed in the power of prayer. Prayer was one of the four distinguishing marks of the Apostolic church (cf. Acts 2:42). While they tarried at Jerusalem, waiting to be baptized with the Spirit, they "continued...in prayer and supplication" (Acts 1:14). Prayer was made for guidance in the decision concerning an apostle to replace Judas (cf. Acts 1:24). When Peter and John were threatened by the authorities to speak no more in the name of Jesus, instead of being intimidated to the point of abandoning their efforts, they reported to the disciples all that had happened to them and the entire church lifted up its voice in prayer to God (cf. Acts 4:24).

Because of the escalating attention needed to handle the church's material concerns, the apostles soon recognized the need for deacons to handle these time-consuming yet important matters, so that the apostles would be free to give themselves "to prayer and the ministry of the word." The apostles saw prayer as a matter of primary importance (cf. Acts 6:1-7).

Later, following the example of his Lord, Stephen prayed for his persecutors as they stoned him (cf. Acts 7:60). Further, the report given to convince Ananias that Saul had undergone a radical change was, *"Behold, he prayeth"* (Acts 9:11). At the bedside of Dorcas, Peter prayed (cf. Acts 9:40). Cornelius was said to be a man who *"prayed to God alway"* and whose *"prayers...came up for a memorial before God"* (Acts 10:2b,4b). In the same account, notice that it was when Peter had gone on the housetop *"to pray"* that he saw the vision and was sent to Cornelius (cf. Acts 10:9). Then, when Peter was imprisoned, *"prayer was made without ceasing of the church unto God for him"* (Acts 12:5). Later, Paul and Silas, imprisoned in Philippi, *"prayed and sang praises to God"* at midnight (Acts 16:25).

Let this suffice to prove that prayer played an integral role in first-century church life. Further, let it suffice to remind the modem church of the priority of prayer in all that we are called to do.

Four Kinds of Prayer

Paul urges Timothy and the Ephesians to devote themselves to four specific kinds of prayer: *"...supplications, prayers, intercessions, and giving of thanks..."* The use of these four closely-related words for the act we call "prayer" is probably intended to teach the importance of a well-rounded and balanced emphasis on prayer in the life of the church.

Balance is needed because of the tendency to form a habit in which only one kind of praying, say supplication, is practiced. Paul urges the church toward spiritual maturity in every aspect of the discipline and privilege of prayer.

These four terms should probably be considered in terms of the familiar "genus and species" distinction. Just as there are a number of "species" of the dog "kind" (e. g. coyotes, wolves, German Shepherds, Poodles, Bulldogs, etc.), so there are specific forms of the general activity of "prayer." *Supplications* means "requests for specific needs" (cf. Phi. 4:6). *Intercessions* suggests the thought of making petition on behalf of another. *Giving of thanks*, of course, is the act of recounting God's blessings and expressing gratitude for them.

Paul wants the church to be a people who depend on God for their every need, who cry out to Him for others, and who are careful to render to Him the glory for the riches of His grace. When prayer is practiced in such a comprehensive and balanced way, the church will have the resources it needs to give a viable testimony to outsiders.

The Scope of Prayer

Paul next specifies the scope of the church's prayer life: *"...for all men; for kings, and for all that are in authority..."* (vs. lb-2a). The phrase *for all men* can either mean "all without exception" or "all kinds, categories, and classes of men."

Which definition is intended here? Is Paul calling upon the Ephesian Church to pray for every human being? Would such an injunction even be practical? I suggest that the expression *all men* is explained by the next verse: *"...for kings, and for all that are in authority..."* He intends the church to pray for those in positions of leadership, like Presidents, Governors, Mayors, Council Members, Senators, Congressmen, Police Officers, etc.

The Objective of Prayer

Why must the church pray for public officials and those in places of authority? *"...that we may lead a quiet and peaceable life in all godliness and honesty"* (v. 2b). Paul urges the church to pray for civil authorities so that an environment conducive to Christian living may be developed. The greater good, in other words, is the progress of the kingdom of God. Prayer for public leaders is a means to that end.

If there has ever been a time when prayer and supplications for those in authority was needed, lest the cause of Christ be hindered and the lives of Christian people be complicated, now is that time.

The topsy-turvy value system of popular culture has set the stage for serious persecution of the church unless God would intervene. The recent redefinition of marriage by modern revisionist judges in the Commonwealth of Massachusetts (together with a number of equally alarming trends in public morality) poses a significant threat to the moral fabric of America, and consequently, to the climate in which the church seeks to live out its faith. May we, as the church of the Lord Jesus Christ, recommit ourselves to fervent prayer, that the cause of Christ we seek to promote, would not be hindered.

Prayer with an Aim to Fulfilling the Church's Mission

What motivates the church to pray for civil authorities? If you answer "The church intercedes on behalf of ranking officials for her own safety," then you are correct (v. 2b), albeit only partly so. Though it is not wrong to pray for our own comfort, yet the church's prayer-life is not primarily self-concerned. It is rather Christ-centered and focused on the prosperity of the kingdom of God. Her prayers for public officials are ultimately evangelistically motivated: *"For this is good and acceptable in the sight of God our Savior; who will have all men to be saved, and to come to the knowledge of the truth"* (vs. 3-4).

The reason Paul cites for prayer that extends beyond the scope of personal needs, in other words, is the evangelization of others to the knowledge of the truth. This should be the supreme objective of the church's prayers. Through prayer for civil authorities, Paul urges, circumstances for the advancement of the gospel will be enhanced, and conversions, thereby, may be multiplied. Paul insists that this is God's goal, and it should be ours as well.

Universal Salvation?

When Paul says that God our Savior *"will have all men to be saved,"* does he intend to suggest the view commonly called "universalism"? First Timothy 2:4 is a favorite verse of those who espouse the position known as "general atonement," the idea that Christ died for the entire human race in general, the salvation of which depends ultimately on each individual's decision to accept him as Savior. But does this verse suggest that it is God's desire that every human being who has lived, lives now, or will live in the future be saved?

Verse 6 seems to give credence to the universalist's claim: "*Who gave himself a ransom for all, to be testified in due time.*" But does the pronoun *all* mean "every person without exception"?

If so, then we are left with only two possibilities. Either every human being will ultimately be saved, or the Lord Jesus Christ failed to secure a ransom.

The first possibility is unreasonable, for Scripture declares that some men will indeed suffer eternal judgment (cf. Rev. 20:10ff; Mt. 25:41ff; Dan. 12:2; Mt. 7:23). The second possibility is unthinkable, for Scripture proclaims the finished work of Jesus Christ, the successful Savior (cf. Jno. 19:30; 17:6; Heb. 1:4; 9:12; 10:14).

Those who espouse general atonement suggest that Christ merely made salvation possible, but that the final outcome is contingent on the sinner's response to the gospel. God wants everyone to be saved, they say, and Jesus Christ died to make it available, but all will be thwarted if the church fails to get the gospel to the sinner and the sinner fails to respond believingly to it.

But such a view makes the will of the sinner determinative in final salvation. If he fails to respond, everything that God the Father and God the Son have done is nullified.

How does such a view reconcile with passages stating that eternal salvation depends on God's will, not man's (cf. Eph. 1:5; Heb. 10:10; Jno. 1:13; Rom. 9:16)? Obviously, the popular interpretation of this passage to suggest the idea of a general (or even universal) atonement is fraught with problems.

What, then, does the passage mean? The first thing that needs to be said is that *the context defines the phrase "all men" in terms of "all classes or categories of men," not every person without exception.* If prayer is to be offered for *all men* (v. 1), a phrase qualified by Paul's explanation in verse 2 *("...for kings and all that are in authority...")*, then it is appropriate that we understand Paul's use of the same phrase just three verses later in the same way.

In addition to the immediate context, the preponderance of Biblical evidence indicates that the scope or extent of the atonement is special, definite, and particular, not general, indiscriminate, and vague. Consider, for example, verses such as Matthew 1:21; Psalm 111:9; Isaiah 53:8; John 10:11; Matthew 20:28; John 17:2; etc.

The second thing that should be said about this passage is that *verse 4 defines the "salvation" in view in terms of gospel conversion, not regeneration: "...to be saved, and to come to the knowledge of the truth."* That the term *salvation* is used in Scripture in more than one sense is an indubitable fact. Sometimes, the term is employed in the ultimate sense—i.e. to speak of eternal deliverance from the consequences of sin—and sometimes, it describes some form of temporal deliverance.

For example, later in this chapter Paul says that the woman *"shall be saved in childbearing, if they* [that is, her children] *continue in faith and charity and holiness with sobriety"* (1 Tim. 2:15). In chapter 4, he urges Timothy to *"Take heed unto thyself, and unto the doctrine; continue in them: for in doing this, thou shalt both save thyself, and them that hear thee"* (4:16).

Like these and many other New Testament passages, Paul employs the term *saved* in our text in the more general sense of some kind of deliverance. The particular nature of the deliverance in view is defined by the specific phrase *"to come to the knowledge of the truth"* (see Rom. 10:1-3 for a parallel passage).

What does he mean then? Paul urges the church to pray for national leaders so that an environment conducive to the propagation of the gospel might be cultivated with a view toward the conversion of all kinds of men to the truth of the gospel.

This passage applies to the church today, just as surely as it applied to the original recipients of Paul's letter. We must guard against an elitist attitude that limits gospel blessings to "us four and no more." If the church of the Lord Jesus Christ becomes ingrown and focused on its own self-preservation, it will cease to function as the Lord intended. It exists to promote the good news of Christ and Him crucified and to win converts to the truth. Yes, such a goal is beyond the pale of human strength; hence, we must heed Paul's exhortation to prayer. Brethren, let us pray.

9
Lifting Up Holy Hands

I will therefore that men pray every where, lifting up holy hands, without wrath and doubting. (1 Timothy 2:8)

Paul concludes the first half of chapter 2, a chapter dealing with the theme of the church's testimony to outsiders, with another injunction to pray. His previous discussion concerned the evangelistic purpose of prayer; now, he is concerned with the necessary criteria for acceptable and effective prayer.

Interestingly, verse 8 not only serves as the summary of verses 1-7, but also as a bridge of transition to the balance of the chapter. The phrase *"In like manner also..."* that introduces verse 9 indicates that Paul intends Christian women to display the same kind of piety in public deportment that Christian men demonstrate in public acts of worship to God. Paul's point is clear: *internal attitudes rather than an external display is to mark the believer in both public worship and public witness.*

Prayer is an Act of Worship

The first and most basic thing we may learn from this text arises from the image Paul employed to describe the act of prayer. Prayer is a matter of *"lifting up [the] hands."*

I suspect that this is a euphemism suggesting a spiritual truth, instead of a prescribed bodily posture for prayer.[1] This word

---

1 See the use of the image in the poetical books of the OT (e. g. Ps. 28:2; Lam. 3:41; Ps. 63:4; 134:2; 143:6)

picture conveys the idea of worship. Before the believer's "hands" are ready to reach out in service to others, they must first reach up in worship to God. The image suggests the further image of total dependence and personal vulnerability and openness. There is no greater expression of dependence on the Lord than the act of genuine prayer.

Three Criteria for Public Prayer

Paul's focus in this verse seems to be on public, in contrast to private, prayers. This observation arises from the fact that Paul encourages men to pray *every where*, that is, in all places. This is in keeping with his theme in this chapter regarding the believer's testimony to the world. Though prayer is essentially an act of private devotion, yet Paul conceives of occasions when Christian men will find it necessary to pray even in a more public setting.

It is not inappropriate for men to pray in public, so long as the inward motives are right. Of course, ostentatious displays of piety, like the Pharisees who prayed *"for to be seen of men,"* are never acceptable to God (cf. Mt. 6:4-8). But when the heart is right, prayer offered before a meal at a restaurant, or before an audience in a secular gathering, or on behalf of the congregation in public worship, or on behalf of a sports team before a game is not only appropriate, but a means by which the Christian gives testimony of his faith to people outside the community of the church. Paul does not forbid, but encourages, public praying.

In that light, Paul emphasizes three criteria for acceptable public prayer — holiness, love, and confidence. If we frame the point negatively, he emphasizes three hindrances to prayer — sin, anger, and unbelief. Let's consider each.

The first thing necessary is that the hands we lift toward God in prayer be *"holy hands."* No doubt, Paul has in mind Psalm 24:4 where *"clean hands and a pure heart"* are listed as necessities in one's approach to God. Unconfessed sin hidden away in the heart hinders the acceptability of our prayers to God, whether privately or publicly (cf. Ps. 66:18). To publicly pray, giving the appearance of piety, while the life is defiled with sin that has not been repented of, is unacceptable to the Lord. Not only will such prayers go unanswered, but they will injure Christian witness by virtue of the hypocritical nature of the very act of presuming to be pious.

Secondly, acceptable public prayer must be marked by *love for others.* Jesus taught that reconciliation must precede worship (cf. Mt. 5:23-24); therefore, it is impermissible to presume to pray in public when the heart is filled with animosity toward others. Prayer is to be *"without wrath."* An attitude of love is indispensable to acceptable public prayer.

Why? Because *wrath* (the word here means "anger as a settled state of mind") is a poor testimony for the gospel with its emphasis on the love of God. An angry man is easy to identify. Public praying from such a one in the name of Christ, consequently, is a sad advertisement for Christianity.

Thirdly, public prayer should be characterized by **confidence.** The word *doubting* refers to "doubtful reasoning" (cf. Lk. 24:38 where the same word is used). Prayer is not to exhibit any hint of uncertainty or distrust in God, else Christian testimony to those outside the church will be undercut.

All in all, this passage teaches that Christian men are encouraged to pray in public. They must at the same time, however, be sensitive to the fact that the attitudes and behaviors that mark their lives will influence the effectiveness of their public prayers. The believer must never forget that the spirit he exhibits in public directly reflects on the Christ he represents.

10
The Christian Woman's Testimony

In like manner also, that women adorn themselves in modest apparel, with shamefacedness and sobriety; not with broided hair, or gold, or pearls, or costly array; but (which becometh women professing godliness) with good works. Let the woman learn in silence with all subjection. But I suffer not a woman to teach, nor to usurp authority over the man, but to be in silence. For Adam was first formed, then Eve. And Adam was not deceived, but the woman being deceived was in the transgression. Notwithstanding she shall be saved in childbearing, if they continue in faith and charity and holiness with sobriety. (1 Timothy 2:9-15)

Paul continues his theme of the Church's testimony to outsiders in what is arguably the most controversial passage of the Pastoral Epistles. It is controversial primarily because it is a gender-specific passage concerning the role of women in the church.

New Testament passages like this one have spawned criticisms suggesting that Christianity is responsible for the repression of women. But there is nothing derogatory or denigrating toward women here. Just because the Christian woman is prohibited from occupying a teaching/leadership role in public worship does not indicate that she has no sphere of ministry at all. Neither does it mean that her Christian witness is any less significant than the man's.

In fact, Paul's focus in this passage concerns the Christian woman's public testimony to those outside the church and the importance of conducting her life in a way that will honor Jesus

Christ. His point is that she gives testimony to Christ and His gospel by means of her dress and deportment, her contented and submissive attitude toward her God-given role, and dedication to the lives of her children.

Her Dress & Deportment

"In like manner also, that women adorn themselves in modest apparel, with shamefacedness and sobriety; not with braided hair, or gold, or pearls, or costly array. But (which becometh women professing godliness) with good works" (2:9-10). The connective *"In like manner also..."* suggests a continuation of thought. Just as Christian men were to be mindful of the fact that outsiders were watching them, so Christian women must always be aware that they too represent the church in public.

What, then, does it mean to be a Christian woman in the public arena? It involves, first of all, the understanding that the manner of dress must be commensurate with her Christian profession. The principle here is unmistakable: *The manner in which a person dresses sends a message to others.* Believers, consequently, must be sensitive to the Christ they represent even in the way they dress.

Positively, Paul specifically states that Christian women are to adorn themselves *"in modest apparel, with shamefacedness and sobriety"* and *"with good works."* On the negative side, the Christian woman is to avoid the kind of ostentatious display that calls attention to oneself or accommodates cultural fashions that may prove to be an impediment to the gospel message.

Now, *modest apparel* does not mean drab, unattractive clothing. Paul does not forbid Christian women from looking nice. This passage does not prescribe a specific "Christian" fashion concerning hair-styles, cosmetics, or clothing, as some have erroneously concluded. Instead, it offers a general principle for determining what is and what is not appropriate for a woman professing godliness. The criteria for making this determination are three: (1) It should be modest, not ostentatious; (2) It should be inexpensive, not extravagant; (3) It should be discreet and chaste, not suggestive.

Paul expects Christian women to be cautious lest they dress in ways that are designed to attract attention to themselves. Obviously, the believer (whether male or female) should aim to draw attention away from self to the Lord Jesus Christ in every area of life. Christian women, then, are not to advertise themselves by a wardrobe that is seductive, suggestive, or extravagant, but to dress modestly, with decency (*shamefacedness*) and propriety (*sobriety*). For Christian women in Ephesus, this meant that they were not to dress in ways that tended to remind onlookers of the temple prostitutes at the goddess Diana's temple.

They are also to adorn themselves with *good works*. A Christian woman's beauty, in other words, is not primarily physical, but ethical and moral. A woman who cultivates the character of Christ and displays such in ministry to others exhibits a beauty of soul and life with which mere physical beauty cannot compare.

Her Attitude of Submission

"Let the woman learn in silence with all subjection. But I suffer not a woman to teach, nor to usurp authority over he man, but to be in silence. For Adam was first formed, then Eve. And Adam was not deceived, but the woman being deceived was in the transgression" (2:11-14).

Another way in which the Christian woman gives testimony to others concerns her public role in the life of the church. The word *silence* means, literally, *quietness*, and refers to an attitude of inner contentment. The role of Christian women in the public assembly is to be that of learner, not teacher. When she is content to occupy that role, she gives a powerful testimony to others for the glory of Christ.

Paul cites two reasons for male headship and female subjection in the worship of the church. First, this hierarchy originates in *the order of creation — "...for Adam was first formed, then Eve."* God Himself designed this authority/submission dynamic in creation, and just as redemption does not negate this principle in the context of the Christian home (cf. Eph. 5:22ff), neither does it nullify it in the function of the Christian church. This does not mean that women are less important, intelligent, gifted, or spiritual than men. It is a matter of function and hierarchical structure, not personal worth.

Second, the prohibition of female leadership in the church is due to the *nature of the Fall: "And Adam was not deceived, but the woman being deceived was in the transgression."* The Fall confirmed the wisdom of God's design. God had ordered every dimension of his world — even the marriage relationship — according to a hierarchy, and the Fall of man resulted from the violation of God's appointed roles for the man and the woman. Adam abdicated his responsibility and Eve, stepping out from under the man's protection, acted independently. The violation of God's order led to disaster.

The Godliness of Her Children

Does this mean, then, that Christian women have no sphere in which they may function in a teaching ministry? It doesn't mean that at all. Later in the Pastoral Epistles we will learn that the *"older women are to teach the younger women"* certain things. And here, Paul insists that there is great fulfillment to be found in the training of children: *"Notwithstanding, she shall be saved in childbearing, if they continue in faith and charity and holiness with sobriety"* (2:15).

The Christian woman's congregation, in other words, is her children. She is the primary teacher in the home. Though one of the consequences of the Fall was *"sorrow in bringing forth children,"* the godly mother may reverse the personal pain of child rearing when her children grow up to be godly. Instead of pain, she will find a deep sense of pleasure and fulfillment — a "salvation," if you will.

Further, when her children grow up to be godly, she gives testimony through them to a watching world. All in all, when the Christian woman occupies the role that God has given her to fill, she finds a personal sense of fulfillment and enjoys a usefulness in the life of the church that far outweighs any perceived benefit outside of God's design. Christianity aims not to oppress the woman, therefore, but to satisfy God's original design for her.

11

The Church's Leadership: Elders

This is a true saying, If a man desire the office of a bishop, he desireth a good work. A bishop then must be blameless, the husband of one wife, vigilant, sober, of good behaviour, given to hospitality, apt to teach; not given to wine, no striker, not greedy of filthy lucre; but patient, not a brawler, not covetous; one that ruleth well his own house, having his children in subjection with all gravity; (For if a man know not how to rule his own house, how shall he take care of the church of God?) Not a novice, lest being lifted up with pride he fall into the condemnation of the devil. Moreover he must have a good report of them which are without; lest he fall into reproach and the snare of the devil. (1 Timothy 3:1-7)

From instructions concerning the church's doctrine (ch. 1), and the church's testimony to outsiders (ch. 2), Paul now turns in chapter 3 to the important subject of the church's leadership. The criteria by which those who hold an official capacity in the church are to be measured is a tall order, indeed; nevertheless, compliance here is crucial to the health of the church.

Preliminary Considerations

"*This is a true saying, If a man desire the office of a bishop, he desireth a good work*" (v. 1). The titles "Bishop" and "Elder" (cf. Titus 1:5,7) refer to the same office—the former speaks of the function of the pastor as overseer *(episkopos[1])* of the church, and the latter *(presbyteros[2])*, the dignity of his office.

This passage teaches that pastoral ministry is integral to the function of the church. When Paul and Barnabas visited the churches in Lystra, Iconium, and Antioch, they *"ordained them elders in every church"* before taking their leave (Acts 14:23). And when Paul left Titus in Crete, he instructed him to *"appoint elders in every city"* (Titus 1:5). Pastoral ministry, then, is essential to the function of the local church.

Further, the passage suggests that the office of a bishop is a desirable office: *"...If a man desire the office of a bishop, he desireth a good work."* Evidently, some brethren in the church at Ephesus had aspirations for the ministry, and Paul refuses to scold them for or discourage them in such a desire. The gospel ministry certainly has its share of responsibilities—so much so James felt compelled to challenge Christian men to think seriously before aspiring to such a role in the church (cf. Jas. 3:1-2). But it also has its share of joys and blessings. The work of a minister is *"a good work"*—a noble, worthwhile, and honorable endeavor. Further, the office carries with it a special dignity and esteem by virtue of the very nature of the work (cf. 1 Ths. 5:12-13).

Perhaps Paul refers here to those he mentioned in chapter 1 who *"desired to be teachers of the law"* (1:7). If so, it is important to note that he does not complain that they had a desire for the office. He wants them (and the whole church) to know, however, that the desire itself is not enough to qualify a man for gospel ministry. Other criteria, principally in the area of personal integrity and godly conduct, must also be met.

So, while Paul is careful lest he discourage someone who has aspirations for the ministry, he is equally cautious lest he sanction

---

1   The term is Greek in origin and indicates the superintending nature of the pastor's ministry.
2   The term is Jewish in origin and indicates a position of seniority and dignity, like the elders in a Jewish synagogue.

the kind of maverick mentality exhibited by some in the church at Ephesus. Gospel ministry is not for freelancers and innovators; it is a character profession. Further, the various criteria by which a man is qualified to be a minister are not negotiable.

A further thought concerning the nature of the pastor's work should be emphasized here. The *bishop* functions in the church as an overseer, or superintendent. It is not, however, the superintendence of a master over a slave, but that of a shepherd over his flock. Just as a shepherd looks over his flock for their good and protection, so a pastor is charged with the responsibility to oversee the church. His work involves providing for their spiritual nourishment, protecting them against potential dangers, and leading them forward in the walk of faith. It requires, indeed, hard *work*, but it is a *good* work.

The church, in turn, is charged to follow and submit to their spiritual overseers: *"Obey them that have the rule over you, and submit yourselves: for they watch for your souls, as they that must give account, that they may do it with joy, and not with grief: for that is unprofitable for you"* (Heb. 13:17). When a shepherd-hearted man takes the oversight of a church, and a tender-hearted membership submits to his lead, the stage is set for the church to function as Christ set it up.

Finally, we may learn something of the three things necessary to the making of a minister of the gospel: (1) the call of God (cf. Acts 13:1; 20:28); (2) an inner compulsion and desire for the office (cf. 1 Tim. 3:1); (3) the conscientious screening and confirmation of the candidate's life and character by the church (cf. 1 Tim. 3:2-7). It is to that third matter that we now turn.

The list of qualifications for gospel ministers is daunting. Never do I review the list but I feel to be woefully inadequate. But though most gospel ministers will feel that they fall short of meeting the criteria perfectly, yet these characteristics serve as a benchmark by which spiritual leaders should be selected by the church.

Note that all but one of the sixteen criteria Paul cites has to do with personal character. The only exception is *"aptitude to teach,"* which refers to ability instead of character. The gospel ministry is primarily a character profession. A lapse in this area may very well jeopardize a man's right to lead the church.

Qualifications for Office of Bishop

What qualities, then, are necessary for those who would lead the church as Elders or Bishops? First, Paul mentions the basic and general requirement of *blamelessness: "A bishop then must be blameless..."* (3:2a). The word literally means "above reproach" and describes "one who has nothing which an adversary could seize on which to base a charge." Obviously, the word does not mean "flawless," else no one would be qualified for the office of bishop. It means, however, that the minister's public and observable conduct must be irreproachable. From this general platform, Paul now proceeds to list ten particular areas to be screened by the church in its search for spiritual leaders.

The first area is *the minister's marriage: "...the husband of one wife."* Various interpretations have been given to these words. Some have suggested that Paul is teaching that a gospel minister must be married. But it is doubtful that Paul himself was married on the occasion of writing these words. His words do suggest that a gospel minister must be male—for a female cannot be the husband of one wife—but they do not stipulate, in so many words, that a minister must be married.

Others suggest that these words aim to disqualify polygamists from the pastorate. It is true that polygamy was practiced in the Graeco-Roman world, but doubtful that it was common enough among Christians for Paul to mention it as a reason for disqualifying a man from the ministry. If, in fact, Paul is stating the obvious point that gospel ministers must not be polygamists, does he also intend to condone it for non-office-bearing believers? The very idea is incredible.

Still others argue that Paul intends to ban anyone who has ever been divorced/remarried from the pastorate. But Jesus allowed divorce/remarriage to the party victimized by the sexual sin of another (cf. Mt. 5:31-32; 19:9). Further, no Biblical or moral precedent exists for punishing the victim for the sin of the perpetrator—an inevitable dilemma if these words constitute an absolute ban on pastoral ministry for anyone who has ever been divorced/remarried.

The most plausible explanation, and the one that best fits the context, is that a minister of the gospel must be faithful to his wife —a "one-woman man," if you please. He must exhibit fidelity and dedication to his wife to the exclusion of every other woman in the world. He must not be a philanderer. He must not be flirtatious. He must not have a roving eye. His commitment and fidelity to his marriage vow validates him as someone who can be trusted to keep his word.

Next, Paul employs three terms that have to do with *the minister's self-discipline: "...vigilant, sober, of good behavior."* Spiritual leaders must be men who demonstrate self-mastery. *Vigilant* and *sober* are closely akin concepts, referring respectively to temperance and self-control. When a man rules his own inner attitudes and thought-life, his outward behavior will be respectable.

The third category has to do with *the minister's hospitality: "...given to hospitality."* He must be ready and willing to accommodate visitors in his home and to share his substance with those who are in need. The Greek word literally means "a lover of strangers." In the first century, itinerant preachers and fellow-believers who may be traveling from a distance would occasionally need lodging. The pastor would have ample opportunity, therefore, to personally practice the Gospel, incarnating its spirit of love and self-sacrifice.

Next, is *the minister's ability to teach: "...apt to teach."* Pastors are called to be teachers of God's word. An essential qualification of the ministry, therefore, is the ability to communicate truth in an intelligible way so that the people under their oversight may learn and grow in knowledge. The church is not authorized to recognize for ordination a man who lacks the ability to teach.

In the fifth place, Paul mentions *the minister's drinking habits: "...not given to wine"* (3:3a). In the Old Testament, kings and magistrates were warned against the power of strong drink to impair judgment (cf. Pro. 31:4; Is. 5:22-23). It is appropriate, then, that Paul would require those who handle the word of God and lead the church to exercise self-restraint in this area. It is nigh impossible to disciple others when the teacher himself lacks self-discipline in terms of an addiction to alcohol.

The sixth area is *the minister's temperament: "...no striker...but patient, not a brawler."* The minister is to be gentle, not quarrelsome. Like the Lord Jesus Christ who was meek and gentle (cf. 2 Cor. 10:1), spiritual leaders must be patient even when dealing with obstinate and difficult people. A hot-tempered man who loves to fight and argue is seldom a good advertisement for Christ or example to the Lord's people.

The seventh has to do with *the minister's attitude toward money: "...not greedy of filthy lucre...not covetous."* The false teachers of Paul's day used positions of influence as a vehicle to make themselves wealthy (cf. 1 Ths. 2:5). Such a covetous spirit should be conspicuously absent in the lives of God's humble servants. Avarice and greed are fundamentally incompatible with the gospel and its keynote of giving (cf. Acts 20:33-35).

The eighth area concerns *the minister's domestic example: "...one that ruleth well his own house, having his children in subjection with all gravity; (for if a man know not how to rule his own house, how shall he take care of the church of God?)."* Obviously, this passage does not mean that a minister's family must be perfect—a popular misconception, but impossible standard to meet. It means, however, that a pastor must be someone who demonstrates leadership in his home before he is entrusted with a position of leadership in the church.

Do his children respect and obey him? Does he model the kind of disciplined love and loving discipline in his family relationships that will be so necessary in his relationship with the flock? This qualification reminds us that even though pastoral ministry should be characterized by a spirit of gentleness, yet a certain authority also attends it.

Next, Paul cites *the minister's spiritual maturity*: "*...not a novice, lest being lifted up with pride he fall into the condemnation of the devil*" (v. 6). *Novice* speaks of a recent convert. The responsibility entrusted to a pastor makes maturity essential. So does the status associated with being a pastor. If a man is not mature, his position may easily "go to his head" and he may fancy himself more important than he actually is. Such pride will bring the same kind of judgment on the minister that came on the devil.

Finally, Paul mentions *the minister's reputation*: "*...moreover he must have a good report of them which are without, lest he fall into reproach and the snare of the devil*" (v. 7). Not only does the minister risk the same kind of judgment that came on the devil, but he must also guard against the snares of the devil. One such snare is the disgrace of a bad reputation. Satan is eager to discredit the gospel by making caricatures of Christ's servants. Because he is such a visible figure, a smear on the pastor's reputation is a stunning blow against the Christian testimony of the local church.

12

The Church's Leadership: Deacons

Likewise must the deacons be grave, not doubletongued, not given to much wine,
not greedy of filthy lucre; holding the mystery of the faith in a pure conscience.
And let these also first be proved; then let them use the office of a deacon, being
found blameless. Even so must their wives be grave, not slanderers, sober, faithful
in all things. Let the deacons be the husbands of one wife, ruling their children
and their own houses well. For they that have used the office of a deacon well
purchase to themselves a good degree, and great boldness in the faith which is in
Christ Jesus. (1 Timothy 3:8-13)

Paul next discusses the qualifications for the office of deacon. Like the office of elder, personal integrity and godliness is the most basic criteria for selecting men to function in this capacity.

The office of deacon was a position born of necessity, according to Acts 6. The apostles were diverting energies from the ministry of the word to administrative concerns; hence, the church was urged to select several brethren to whom the apostles might delegate oversight of those concerns in order to free the apostles to function in their God-called capacity. This episode was the inception of what became the *diaconate*.

We might learn several lessons from this account concerning the difference between these two offices in the structure of the New Testament church. First, gospel ministers (or elders) are Divinely "called" (cf. 1 Tim. 1:12), while deacons are chosen and appointed by the church. Secondly, elders and deacons have essentially different functions. The elder is primarily responsible for the spiritual oversight of the church, while the deacon is primarily concerned with its administrative and social needs. Thirdly, the offices of elder and deacon, even though occupying essentially distinct roles in the function of the church, complement each other to the welfare of the entire church when each functions as it was intended. A pastor has no greater ally than godly deacon brethren who work hard to shoulder the load of responsibility so that he may devote his time and energy to prayer and the ministry of the word.

Finally, the brethren selected to serve as deacons are to meet certain qualifications. They are to be honest and reputable men, for the responsibilities that attend the office demand integrity. Also, they are to be spiritual, not carnal, men ("...*full of the Holy Ghost*"), for even though they function in a primarily administrative capacity, their labors are still concerned with an essentially spiritual entity — the church of the Lord Jesus Christ. Finally, they are to be wise men, for they will frequently face decisions that require the exercise of discernment, an understanding of human nature and temperaments, and the ability to make choices that coincide with the primary purpose and objective of the church.

In 1 Timothy 3:8-13, Paul embellishes on this list of qualifications. Like the list for elders, this one focuses principally on personal conduct and character. Eight particular areas are noted.

Behavior

"*Likewise must the deacons be grave...*" The Greek word means "venerable" and speaks of a kind of majestic and awe-inspiring quality that is inviting, not intimidating. There is a certain dignity about him, born not from pride or a sense of self-importance but rather from godly behavior, that commands respect.

Speech

"*...not double-tongued...*" The expression means "sincere," on the positive side, and "not speaking out of both sides of the mouth," on the negative. He is not a stereotypical "politician," but his word is his bond. He is a man who can be trusted to do what he says.

Use of Alcohol

"*...not given to much wine...*" Like the office of elder, the deacon is to be a man who exhibits self-mastery and moderation. He must be temperate in every area of his life, especially in those areas that could so easily gain control over his mind and reason.

Attitude toward Money

"*...not greedy of filthy lucre...*" Because much of his job description relates to the handling and disbursement of money, the deacon must be devoid of the spirit of greed and covetousness. All selfish concern should be conspicuous by its absence.

Doctrinal Integrity

"*...holding the mystery of the faith in a pure conscience...*" Though deacons are not required to be "apt to teach," yet they are required to be doctrinally sound. The *mystery of the faith* refers to the sum-total of revealed truth. The brethren who occupy this office are to hold on to that once-delivered faith with conviction. Though a deacon brother may or may not be able to articulate the doctrines as well as the preacher, he must still know what he believes and why he believes it, and be ready, as a matter of conscience, to stand in its defense. It is as much a mistake to put an unsound man into this office as it is to select an unholy man to serve.

A Probationary History

"*...and let these also first be proved; then let them use the office of a deacon, being found blameless...*" The word *also* refers back to what was previously said about elders ruling their own houses well. The thought is that leadership qualities must first be evident in other spheres of life prior to a leadership appointment in the church. This requirement of a prior track-record of leadership is based on the biblical principle, *"He that is faithful in that which is least will be faithful in much."* The church should be cautious to test and scrutinize the qualifications of a potential candidate for this office prior to entrusting him with it. Further, the deacon brother himself should remember that fitness to serve depends not only on past history, but future conduct: *"...then let them use the office...being found blameless."*

Spouse and Family

"...even so must their wives be grave, not slanderers, sober, faithful in all things. Let the deacons be the husband of one wife, ruling their children and their own houses well..." Elder Joe Holder comments insightfully on this verse:

> Often a deacon in the church, by virtue of doing his job well, becomes aware of personal information regarding members of the church. Occasionally he will share this information with his wife. Will the deacon and his wife become the church's gossip megaphones and broadcast private information that embarrasses and discourages members, or will they manifest a consistent disposition of confidentiality and grace that enables members to talk with them freely, knowing that their confidence is highly prized and protected? A gossiping deacon or deacon's wife will quickly destroy a sense of safety and spiritual trust in a church. Increasingly members will protect their private lives, often taking problems that the church's leadership could help them solve to other resources that often will do far more poorly than spiritually minded men in the church.

Like an elder, a deacon must be totally committed to his wife alone. He must be a "one woman man," and a man that demonstrates godly leadership in his own home.

Their Reward

"...for they that have used the office of a deacon well purchase to themselves a good degree, and great boldness in the faith which is in Christ Jesus." The deacon who faithfully serves will gain two things. First, he will *"purchase to [himself] a good degree."* The word *degree* speaks of a rank or grade and obviously refers to the kind of honor and respect enjoyed by one who is faithful to his office. He *purchases* this degree, not by money, but by *using the office well.*

Secondly, he will gain *"great boldness in the faith which is in Christ Jesus."* The word *boldness* means "freedom of speech" or "confidence." Faithful service produces a certain Christian confidence and uninhibited freedom before God and other people —a precious blessing indeed.

13
What is the Church?

These things write I unto thee, hoping to come unto thee shortly: but if I tarry long, that thou mayest know how thou oughtest to behave thyself in the house of God, which is the church of the living God, the pillar and ground of the truth. And without controversy great is the mystery of godliness: God was manifest in the flesh, justified in the Spirit, seen of angels, preached unto the Gentiles, believed on in the world, received up into glory. (1 Timothy 3:14-16)

This passage acts as a summary of all that Paul has said thus far. He has talked about the church's doctrine, witness to outsiders, and leadership. Now he sums up his purpose in these terms: *"These things write I unto thee...that thou mayest know how thou oughtest to behave thyself in the house of God..."* The purpose of his written instructions thus far has been to address the kind of conduct that Christ expects from both pastors and people in the church.

Why is the conduct of the church so important? It is important because the church is such a noble institution. This passage employs three very vivid descriptions concerning the nature of the church.

The House of God

First, the church is God's house. Earlier in the chapter, Paul spoke of the Elder's "house" (v. 4) and the Deacon's "house" (v. 12), meaning, of course, their families (or households). Hence, it is probable that this reference describes the church as the household of God (cf. Eph. 2:19). The church is a "home away from home" for the children of God.

But every child in God's family is not living in this house. Only those who *"obey the gospel of our Lord Jesus Christ"* (1 Pet. 4:17). We are members of His household *"if we hold fast the confidence and rejoicing of hope firm unto the end"* (Heb. 3:5-6).

What a rich image! As children living together in God's house, we enjoy great privileges. We experience fellowship and communion with God our Father through the Spirit (cf. Eph. 2:22). We feed on the nourishing fare our Father provides—*"the children's bread,"* if you please (cf. Jer. 15:16; Mal. 3:10). We enjoy the companionship of our brothers and sisters in Christ (cf. Heb. 2:12).

But there are also great responsibilities associated with living in the household of God. There is a code of conduct required of us. His word teaches us *"how we ought to behave ourselves in the house of God."*

The Church of the Living God

Paul further describes the church as *"the church of the living God."* The first thought suggested by this label is the Divine ownership of the church. The church belongs to God as His special possession. It is not the pastor's church, or the deacon's church, or any member's church. It is the church of the living God.

Further, this description speaks of God's presence among His people. God lives among His people (cf. Jos. 3:10). Hence, the church is *"the temple of the living God"* who dwells in its midst (cf. 2 Cor. 6:16).

It is this *living God* who has "called out" (*ekklesia*) His church from the world (cf. 2 Cor. 6:17). Unlike the idols who have mouths but speak not, our God is the living God. We hear His voice speaking to us in the preaching of His word. He makes Himself known to us in the breaking of bread.

The Pillar and Ground of the Truth

Finally, the church is described as *"the pillar and ground of the truth." Pillar* (Gr. *stylos)* speaks of a column that served to hold aloft the roof of a building. The church, says Paul, is the column that upholds the truth.

Ground refers to the foundation of a building. The foundation is essential to the stability of a building in a time of storm. Paul's point is that the church functions to hold the truth steady so that it doesn't collapse when it meets the stormy winds of heresy and false doctrine.

The point is simple. The church exists for the truth. It functions to uphold and to protect the integrity of the truth. It fulfills this dual function by declaring the truth, disseminating the truth, and defending the truth.

What is the content of that truth? Verse 16 answers in six particulars centering on the person and work of the Lord Jesus Christ. *"God was manifest in the flesh"* speaks of the dual natures of the incarnate Christ. *"Justified in the Spirit"* refers to his resurrection. *Seen of angels* indicates his ascension—an event witnessed by the heavenly host (cf. Acts 1:9). *"Preached unto the Gentiles"* and *"believed on in the world"* speak of the progress and successful expansion of his kingdom in the earth. *"Received up into glory"* suggests the fact that his ascension is the precursor for his second coming.

Thus, this synopsis of the "great mystery of godliness" includes the themes of the incarnation, resurrection, ascension, gospel kingdom, and second coming of the Lord Jesus Christ. It is this truth that the church is commissioned to uphold and defend.

14
The Coming Apostasy

Now the Spirit speaketh expressly, that in the latter times some shall depart from the faith, giving heed to seducing spirits, and doctrines of devils; speaking lies in hypocrisy; having their conscience seared with a hot iron; forbidding to marry, and commanding to abstain from meats, which God hath created to be received with thanksgiving of them which believe and know the truth. For every creature of God is good, and nothing to be refused, if it be received with thanksgiving: for it is sanctified by the word of God and prayer. (1 Timothy 4:1-5)

Paul continues the theme of the church's leadership in chapter 4. The eschatological, i.e. doctrine of future things, focus of verses 1-5 seems to favor the interpretation we offered concerning the final phrase of 3:16 (*"...received up into glory"*). We suggested that this expression refers to the second coming of the Lord Jesus Christ and indicates that the Savior's ascension anticipates His glorious return. Now, it seems that Paul, triggered to think in eschatological terms, continues this line of thought regarding another, less encouraging, facet of the last times.

Not only will Christ return again, he says, but the church will be challenged with strange doctrines which will lead to apostasy. Even in spite of the church's efforts to uphold and defend the truth (cf. 3:15), some will *depart from the faith* (v. 1).

"Now the Spirit speaketh expressly that in the latter times, some shall depart from the faith, giving heed to seducing spirits, and doctrines of devils; speaking lies in hypocrisy; having their conscience seared with a

hot iron..." (vs. 1-2). That this *departure* (lit. apostasy) will occur has been explicitly revealed by the Holy Spirit. When will it happen? Paul answers in *the latter times,* a phrase that speaks of the last days of human history (cf. 2 Tim. 3:1; 2 Pet. 3:3; Jude 18).

This intriguing expression in the New Testament, i.e. *last days,* sometimes refers to the entire gospel dispensation (e. g. Heb. 1:2). There is a sense in which the gospel dispensation is "the last days." More frequently, however, the expression as it appears in the New Testament refers to "the last days of the last days," i.e. a time frame at the end of the gospel dispensation just prior to the end of human history.

That the church will be troubled by apostasy near the end of time is also indicated in 2 Thessalonians 2:3: *"...for that day shall not come, except there come a falling away* [lit. apostasy] *first..."* Though the church has always been troubled by erroneous doctrines, together with the inherent tendency of these false teachings to lead people into apostasy, yet the last days will bring defections from the faith on an even wider and more massive scale.

Paul describes a scenario that, on the surface, seems common. False teachers are *"speaking lies in hypocrisy, having their conscience seared with a hot iron"* (v. 2). Some of their less discerning hearers are influenced by their teaching to abandon the faith. But there is more to this story than meets the eye. Paul indicates that there is a spiritual dynamic at work behind the influence of these false teachers: *"...giving heed to seducing spirits and doctrines of devils..."* (v. 1b).

I appreciate the comments on this passage by John R. W. Stott in his book on 1st Timothy:

> We tend not to take this fact sufficiently seriously. Scripture portrays the devil not only as the tempter, enticing people into sin, but also as the deceiver, seducing people into error...And the apostles regularly attributed human error to devilish deceit (2 Cor.

2:11; Eph. 6:11; 2 Ths. 2:9ff; 1 Jno. 2:18; 4:1ff; Rev. 13:14). Is this not why intelligent and educated people can swallow the fantastic speculations of the cults and of New Age paganism, some of the far-fetched doctrines of the ethnic religions, and the barrenness of atheistic philosophies? It is because there is not only a Spirit of truth but also a spirit of falsehood, who is able to delude, drug, bewitch and even blind people.[1]

These seducing spirits, further, employ human agents to spread their deceptions. When Paul describes them as *speaking lies in hypocrisy*, he charges them with the worst kind of demagoguery, for they do not themselves believe what they teach.

And when he says that their respective consciences have been *seared* [lit. cauterized] *with a hot iron*, he means that they have for so long stifled the warnings of conscience that they are now morally desensitized. Like Hymanaeus and Alexander who slipped into error because they silenced the warnings of conscience (cf. 1:19), these false teachers are easy prey for deception.

Paul's graphic explanation of how apostasy happens might be summarized as follows: (1) The teachers dismiss the voice of conscience until it is rendered ineffective; (2) Therefore, they become easy targets of seducing demons; (3) They teach ideas that they do not themselves believe; (4) The seducing spirits use them as instruments to blind and deceive unsuspecting hearers; (5) Those who are deceived abandon the apostolic faith.

What precisely is the content of the false teaching of which Paul warns? It consists primarily of a false asceticism: "*...forbidding to marry and commanding to abstain from meats*" (v. 3a). The idea being advanced is that physical abstinence is the path to holiness.

Now, on the surface, this particular emphasis may seem to be plausible. The Bible does teach that self-denial is integral to sanctified living. But theirs is a *forced* self-denial—the kind of

---

1   Stott, *The Message of 1 Timothy and Titus*, p. 111.

legalistic imposition of rules that the Lord Jesus condemned. Further, it consists of a revision of God's created order. It is likely that what Paul is describing is akin to the first century heresy of *Gnosticism* which regarded everything material as evil. Thus, these people believe that the renunciation of marital intimacy and the renunciation of eating meat is the path to true enlightenment.

One does not have to look very hard to see shades of these two emphases in the modem world. Though it sounds melodramatic, the modern feminist movement in America has spoken of the need to abolish marriage with its patriarchal constructs. Further, vegetarianism has gained tremendous popularity within the past two decades. What Paul is concerned with here is not people who practice vegetarianism for dietary reasons, but for religious reasons. They object to eating food from animals—food that God has created to be received with thanksgiving.

Paul's point is that celibacy and vegetarianism are not God's will for everyone; therefore, to patently forbid marriage and the eating of meat is tantamount to a serious departure from the created order. For man to redefine God's priorities in favor of his own rules and restrictions is the very essence of the serpent's lie in the Garden of Eden.

In creation, God instituted the covenant of marriage, and blessed it with Divine sanction. To despise and forbid marriage, then, is essentially a matter of rebellion and ingratitude toward God. And to despise certain foods which God has created to be received with thanksgiving is likewise a sign of unthankfulness. Hence, the Christian should appreciate all the gifts of the Creator. To reject them is to demonstrate ingratitude toward Him.

15
A Good Minister of Jesus Christ

If thou put the brethren in remembrance of these things, thou shalt be a good minister of Jesus Christ, nourished up in the words of faith and of good doctrine, whereunto thou hast attained. But refuse profane and old wives' fables, and exercise thyself rather unto godliness. (1 Timothy 4:6-7)

In contrast to the apostate teachers referenced in verse 2, Paul urges Timothy to be *a good minister of Jesus Christ* (v. 6). Of course, the Lord Jesus Christ has all kinds of ministers — some good, some bad, and some indifferent. But there is no higher aspiration for a minister of Christ than to be a *good minister*. Further, this is the kind of spiritual leadership the church deserves.

What then makes a minister *a good minister of Jesus Christ*? By what standard is a good minister measured?

He Faithfully Teaches the Truth

"If thou put the brethren in remembrance of these things, thou shalt be a good minister of Jesus Christ..." (4:6a). Paul makes it clear that Timothy would be a good minister if he is a faithful teacher; hence, the teaching of *good doctrine* (4:6c) is fundamental to being *a good minister*.

A good minister, therefore, is someone who faithfully teaches God's word. He *puts the brethren in remembrance* of the apostolic message, like a merchant presenting his merchandise to a customer. Even when the particular emphasis may be less palatable to his hearers — like warning God's people about an end-times apostasy, the emphasis of this passage—the good minister is primarily interested to present the truth faithfully.

Christ's servants are not only called to teach the essential gospel message, but also the whole word of God (cf. Acts 20:27). In the preceding few verses, Paul has highlighted the doctrine of creation, emphasizing how an understanding of the principle that everything God created is good is the secret to developing a grateful attitude toward life and a healthy conscience which allows a person to enjoy not only distinctively "spiritual" things, but all the blessings of life (cf. 4:3-5). To those *who believe and know the truth* (v. 3), even the realms of nature and art offer occasion to enjoy the goodness of the Lord. The hymnwriter John Ellerton captured this thought when he wrote:

> *Yet these are not the only walls*
> *Wherein Thou mayest be sought;*
> *On homeliest work Thy blessing falls*
> *In truth and patience wrought.*
> *Thine is the loom, the forge, the mart,*
> *The wealth of land and sea;*
> *The worlds of science and of art,*
> *Revealed and ruled by Thee.*

Likewise, George Robinson:

> *Heav'n above is softer blue,*
> *Earth around is sweeter green;*
> *Something lives in every hue*
> *Christless eyes have never seen!*
> *Birds in song His glories show,*
> *Flowers with deeper beauties shine,*
> *Since I know, as now I know,*
> *I am His and He is mine.*

Paul insists that Timothy would be *a good minister* if he is faithful to present these truths—not only the doctrine of redemption but also the doctrine of creation and its implications for daily life—to the brethren. A minister who aspires to be *a good minister* may attain that noble objective when he is faithful to teach the whole counsel of God.

He Faithfully Nourishes His Own Soul

"...nourished up in the words of faith and of good doctrine, whereunto thou hast attained" (v. 6). *A good minister*, secondly, is one who *nourishes* his own heart and mind with the word of God. The present participle *nourished up* means "to be constantly nourished," indicating the ongoing need to feed on the truth of God. The *good minister* is not only interested in communicating God's word to others, but also in feeding on God's word himself. He is a student, as well as a teacher, of the Scriptures.

An effective teacher is someone who has first personally digested the message he aims to communicate to others. Next to his prayer closet, then, the minister's study is the most important room in his house. When he walks with the Lord in secret, the Father which sees in secret will reward him openly.

In contrast to the wholesome nourishment of the word of God, Paul cautions Timothy to completely avoid (the word *refuse* means "to reject and having nothing to do with") *profane and old wives' fables* (v. 7). Like "junk food" to the physical body, these do not nourish, but, rather, sap spiritual strength.

Paul's use of the phrase *old wives' fables* is colloquial, not insulting. In the prevailing culture of Paul's day, females were not permitted educational opportunities as were males. Hence, their method of explaining events and circumstances often tended toward myths and legends. This term, then, came to be used for any viewpoint lacking credibility that appeals to the uneducated class. It is still used that way today.

He means, then, that Timothy should avoid wild speculation and personal opinions that may seem right to some, but have no basis in the word of God. For an Old Testament counterpart to this New Testament admonition, consider Jeremiah 23:16-32.

He Disciplines Himself in Godliness

"...and exercise thyself rather unto godliness" (v. 7b). Thirdly, *a good minister* not only faithfully teaches and personally digests God's word, but he also disciplines himself to be godly. In other words, there is an *ethical* as well as an *academic* and a *devotional* dimension that is intrinsic to excellence in the gospel ministry.

Here the metaphor changes from nutrition to athletics. Paul's use of the Greek word *gumnasio* (from which we derive the English noun "gymnasium") is intriguing. He wants Timothy to train himself to be godly like an athlete would train and discipline himself to compete in the various athletic competitions that were so popular in the Graeco-Roman world.

Godliness does not occur magically. It takes deliberate effort, intense training, and steady commitment. Even so, *a good minister* is someone who works hard each and every day to behave himself as a God-fearing person. He disciplines himself lest his daily conduct would dishonor the Lord and disqualify himself from the privileged position of leadership with which he has been entrusted. Like Paul, he *"exercises [himself] to have always a conscience void of offense toward God and toward men"* (Acts. 24:16).

16
The Profit of Godliness

For bodily exercise profiteth little: but godliness is profitable unto all things, having promise of the life that now is, and of that which is to come. This is a faithful saying and worthy of all acceptation. For therefore we both labor and suffer reproach, because we trust in the living God, who is the Savior of all men, specially of those that believe. (1 Timothy 4:8-10)

Of the fifteen times the word *godliness* appears in the New Testament, nine are in *1 Timothy*. The Greek word, *eusebia*, means "reverence." In secular Greek, *eusebia* refers to respect for rulers, parents, and those in places of authority. In the New Testament, the term is used with an ethical connotation and speaks of a lifestyle of pious devotion toward God.

Godliness—the Goal

Godliness is the goal of the Christian life, both for preacher and people alike. The godly individual lives his life with a keen awareness that God is real. That focus impacts his conduct at every level. I like the definition of godliness offered by Jerry Bridges, a respected Christian author. Bridges writes that godliness is "devotion to God that results in a life that is pleasing to Him."[1]

Another popular theologian insightfully defines godliness as "heartfelt devotion toward God." He is correct. The heart is involved.

---
1   Jerry Bridges, *The Practice of Godliness*, p. 20.

We might say that godliness is a way of life that arises from a heart that fears, loves, and desires God. The godly person, therefore, is not concerned with the sheer observance of certain rules and regulations. The Bible talks of people who have a *"form of godliness but deny the power thereof"* (2 Tim. 3:5). Instead, the godly individual lives to please God because he wants to. His heart bubbles up (see Ps. 45:1 margin) in love and reverence for the Lord, spilling over into his daily conduct and attitudes.

It is to such a life, springing from the inner resources of piety, that the man of God is called. And what a profitable life it is! Unlike physical exercise which only profits for a little while (v. 8a), spiritual exercise, or soul-work, if you please, is beneficial for the long-term. The individual who makes the practice of godliness his goal is involved in an activity that both benefits his life now (*"...having promise of the life that now is"*) and anticipates the blessings of his life in heaven (*"and of that which is to come"*).

For a summary of how godliness benefits life now, consider Psalm 37:4; Psalm 84:11; 145:19; Proverbs 14:26-27; Proverbs 19:23; and Psalm 31:19-20. But in what sense does godliness have promise of the life that is to come? Well, it should be obvious that Paul does not mean that a godly life *merits* eternal salvation, for he unequivocally affirms that salvation is by grace, not by human works. What, then, does he mean?

No doubt, Paul's words affirm that a godly life is an evidence of grace. The concept of "godliness" is employed, then, as an assurance of eternal salvation. But I maintain that Paul's reference to the long-term benefits of godliness refers to something even more basic and fundamental.

In saying that godliness has promise of the life that is to come, Paul indicates that the individual who lives to love and please God now is involved in the very same activity that will occupy his every thought and deed in heaven. To say it in other words, *God-centeredness* and heartfelt devotion to the Lord is the very nature and chief business of the life to come. To pursue that same goal in our lives now is to experience the days of heaven upon earth.

Discipline — the Means

How does a person become godly? Is godliness a virtue automatically communicated when a person is born again? Well, the capacity for being godly is certainly given in regeneration, but godliness itself can only be attained by rigorous and disciplined training.

Paul instructs the young preacher, *"Exercise thyself unto godliness."* *Exercise* refers to the kind of strenuous, dedicated training that an athlete undergoes in preparation for competition. Paul indicates that Timothy must expend the same level of energy and put forth the same kind of dedication for the purpose of godliness that a Greek athlete exerts at a physical level.

Godliness, in other words, does not come about by magic. It takes commitment and self- discipline (cf. 1 Cor. 9:24-27). If a person will be godly, structured effort to read, study, and meditate on God's word, to spend time alone with God in prayer, to participate in the common life of the people of God, and to worship the Lord with fellow believers, is a spiritual necessity. This truth is so basic and fundamental to Christianity that Paul calls it an axiomatic truth: *"This is a faithful saying and worthy of all acceptation"* (v. 9).

Paul — an Example

Paul did not require anything of Timothy that he did not also require of himself. It was this goal of godliness and the practice of spiritual discipline necessary to attain the objective that occupied Paul's life: *"For therefore we both labor and suffer reproach, because we trust in the living God..."* (v. 10a). Paul devoted his life to the pursuit of godliness, trusting in God, even though it brought personal suffering and persecution to his life.

Salvation — the Motive

Why would Paul, or anyone else (for that matter), pursue a goal that required so much effort and produced so much personal pain? The motive that drives the believer forward in the pursuit of godliness is God's gracious gift of salvation: *"Who is the Savior of all men, especially of those that believe"* (v. 10b).

The distinction he makes has baffled commentators for centuries. Why does Paul distinguish between a salvation for *all men* and a salvation in a special sense for *believers*? Every commentary in my library that deals with this passage expresses some level of bewilderment (and just as many opinions as various commentators) at this distinction.

What, then, is the answer? How should we make sense of this distinction between Paul's reference to salvation for *all men,* especially for *those that believe*? As we have previously noted, Paul employs the verb "to save" in this epistle both in its ultimate sense, i.e. salvation from eternal punishment (cf. 1:15), and its temporal sense, i.e. salvation in knowing the truth of the gospel (cf. 2:4,15; 4:16). In an eternal sense, God is the Savior of *all men*, that is, all classes or kinds of men, because he has an elect people *"out of every kindred and tongue and people and nation"* (Rev. 5:9).

But there is a further sense — a *special* sense — in which he is the Savior of believers, for they enjoy not only the gracious blessing of eternal life but also the gracious benefits of a gospel understanding. They enjoy, if you will, both *"life"* and *"life more abundant"* (cf. Jno. 10:10).

A similar passage from Paul's pen — and a verse that employs the same grammatical construction — demonstrates that Paul did, in fact, intend to distinguish between "eternal" salvation and "gospel" salvation. Consider this verse as a help in understanding 1 Timothy 4:10b: *"Do good unto all men, especially them who are of the household of faith"* (Gal. 6:10). Place the two verses side by side to see the similarity in sentence structure.

Did Paul in Galatians 6:10 intend to distinguish between two categories of people—i.e. those outside the church and those inside the church—in this verse? Yes, indeed. Even so, 1 Timothy 4:10 teaches that the Lord is the Savior of a people even beyond the company of believers, but that those who believe enjoy *salvation* in even a further sense and *special* sense. Understanding Paul's habit in his epistles of distinguishing between unconditional eternal salvation and conditional temporal salvation (via the act of *believing*) is basic to accurate biblical interpretation.

What favor has God extended to his children in that he has not only secured their salvation from eternal ruin but also provided deliverance from false doctrine, theological error, religious bondage, emotional despair, personal guilt feelings, and fear of final judgment to the believer in the gospel church! Such amazing grace and kindness of our *living, Savior God* should motivate everyone who hopes in His mercy to pursue godliness.

17
Exemplary Ministry

These things command and teach. Let no man despise thy youth; but be thou an example of the believers, in word, in conversation, in charity, in spirit, in faith, in purity. Till I come, give attendance to reading, to exhortation, to doctrine. (1 Timothy 4:11-13)

Paul continues his exhortations to Timothy in verses 11-13. He urges this young man to lead the church both by an authoritative word and a godly example. Both authority and example are intrinsic to a biblically effective pastorate.

The Minister's Authority

Spiritual leadership in the church carries with it a certain authority: *"These things command and teach"* (cf. Titus 2:15). Timothy, like every gospel minister, was called to assume the responsibility of communicating God's word to the church, not to wait for someone else to delegate authority to him. Peter said that elders are to *"take the oversight"* of the church, meaning simply that they are to take the lead.

Once a man has been publicly recognized as an ordained minister of Christ's gospel, there is no need to await further permission to function in that capacity. Intrinsic to a call to the ministry and ordination by a presbytery is a God-given authority to teach God's word and responsibility to function as a spiritual leader.

The two terms Paul uses, i.e. *command* and *teach*, indicate that preaching should be both authoritative and instructive. Timothy was to be bold and confident in his communication of God's word. He was not to merely make suggestions, but to courageously declare the truth of God.

The term *teach*, however, indicates that the minister's authority is not dictatorial, but didactic. His authority extends no further than the word of God (cf. Heb. 13:7). Paul prescribed that the saints at Corinth follow him, but only as he followed Jesus Christ (cf. 1 Cor. 11:1). Even so, the minister who steps beyond the context of God's word and proceeds to lead on his own authority presumes a posture to himself that belongs only to the Lord Jesus Christ (cf. Jer. 5:31).

The minister's authority is always a *delegated* authority and if he uses it as an authoritarian, thinking himself to be a boss (or, in biblical terms, "a lord over God's heritage") over the church, Christ may remove him from his position of leadership as he did the "idol shepherds" in Israel (cf. Zech. 11:17; Eze. 34:2-10)

"Let no man despise thy youth." Timothy's youthfulness, however, was an obstacle to authoritative leadership. It is likely that he was encountering resistance from some in Ephesus because he was so young. Perhaps some were jealous that such a young man had been put in charge over them. Others, perhaps, found it difficult to submit to someone who was deemed less experienced.

Youth is certainly an obstacle to effective spiritual leadership. How, then, can someone like Timothy overcome this formidable hurdle? By commending his ministry to their approval by exemplary conduct: *"...but be thou an example of the believers..."*

The Minister's Example

These words, i.e. *"...be...an example of the believers,"* are rich with meaning. Paul indicates that the minister is to model the message he communicates to others and so to win the right to lead with authority (cf. Titus 2:7).

In other words, the Lord Jesus Christ gave the ministry to the church as a living example of what it means to be a Christian, an object lesson in discipleship. The ministry is Christianity in miniature. It is a microcosm of the Christian life. When a believer looks at his pastor, he should see someone who personifies in his life, as closely as is possible in a fallen world, the very gospel he verbally proclaims on the Lord's day. Not only does our gracious God tell his church to live a life that is consistent with the gospel of Christ, but he also shows them *how* to live that life through the ministers He has given them.

The kind of life a minister leads will directly affect the effectiveness of the gospel he preaches. The Thessalonians received Paul's preaching *"in power, and in the Holy Ghost, and in much assurance"* (1 Ths. 1:4). Notice, however, the key to Paul's powerful message: *"For our gospel came not unto you in word only, but also in power...as ye know what manner of men we were among you for your sake"* (1 Ths. 1:5). Paul's gospel preaching concerning Jesus Christ took on a relevance and a credibility because of his own godly life and example that it would not have had otherwise.

What was the result? They *"became followers* [lit. imitators] *of us, and of the Lord..."* (1 Ths. 1:6). The right to occupy a role of leadership in the church of Jesus Christ does not depend primarily on charisma (that is, a person's giftedness) but on character (that is, personal integrity). Paul proceeds to list six areas in which the minister should model his message.

(1) Speech - *"Be an example of the believers in word..."* Preachers should be exemplary in their speech habits. Because the ministry is a microcosm of the Christian life, pastors should model self-discipline in the use of the tongue. Critical, sarcastic, abrasive, unkind, dishonest, vulgar and slanderous words from a minister set a precedent within a community of faith for the same. In this age of mass communication and pervasive social media influence, the

need for recovering a Biblical speech ethic among gospel ministers
is great.

(2) Conduct - *"Be an example of the believers...in conversation...."*
Conversation means "lifestyle, behavior, conduct." Ministers are
intended to lead the way for the Lord's people in terms of godly
conduct. They should regularly pray for wisdom to know how to
conduct themselves in every given situation. Since the pew tends to
imitate the pulpit, it is imperative for pastors to set the pace for
godliness by an exemplary demeanor.

(3) Attitude - *"Be an example of the believers...in charity...."* Agape, i.e.
charity, is essentially "a self-sacrificing commitment to the welfare
of another." In the New Testament sense of the term, love is not an
emotional infatuation or attraction, but an unselfish willingness to
give something up for the benefit of someone else. The epitome of
agape is the cross.

Ministers should embody this *agape* attitude of sacrificial service
in their respective ministries. Does a preacher preach the
importance of sacrificing one's time to serve Jesus Christ? Then he
should model his message by being totally committed to the
church. Does he preach the priority of giving? Then he should be
willing to set the pace by regular, sacrificial giving himself. Does he
warn the people he serves against covetousness, and encourage
them to be content with God's promise to provide the necessities of
life, then he should set the example by learning to be content with
God's provision, whether he is rich or poor.

Does he teach married couples that self-denial is the key to a
happy Christian marriage, then he must practice it himself. Does he
preach about the gracious Savior's compassion to the walking
wounded, then he must personify that same compassion to others
who fall. Love must be the dominant characteristic of his life, and
those under his ministry will follow suit.

(4) Disposition - *"Be an example of the believers...in spirit...."* A
gospel minister is called to be a living illustration of the difference

Jesus Christ can make in a person's general temperament. Though people are born with certain temperamental bents (e.g. sanguine, phlegmatic, melancholic, and choleric), Christ, through the Spirit's sanctifying influence, can remake those natural tendencies, minimizing the negatives associated with each and cultivating the positives of each personality type.

Jesus Christ can even transform a person's natural disposition, making him more Christlike and cultivating Christian character within his heart. He can take a person prone to irritability and crankiness and make him patient, kind, considerate, and gentle. He can transform cynics into encouragers and those prone to depression into cheerful, joyful Christians.

Solomon said, *"A man of understanding is of an excellent spirit"* (Pro. 17:27). A preacher's insight into the truth should manifest itself in such an exemplary disposition. A pastor who has a humble, gentle, servant's heart, will infect the church he serves with the joy germ, a contagion indicative of spiritual health.

(5) Devotion - *"Be an example of the believers...in faith...."* Faith is essentially a metaphysical concept. It deals with the question, "What is real?" To most people, reality is defined by the tangible world. Skyscrapers, freeways, automobiles, material possessions, other people—these are the things of which reality is made according to popular opinion. In other words, most people "live by sight." The Christian, on the contrary, is called to *"live by faith"* (cf. Hab. 2:4; Rom. 1:17; Gal. 2:20; 2 Cor. 5:8).

To the Christian who lives by faith, God, heaven, and angels are just as real as the tangible realities of earthly existence. Prayer, worship, and other devotional activities are supremely practical and realistic. Ministers must model such a conviction of God's reality by maintaining the spiritual disciplines of prayer, meditation, and Bible intake. In other words, pastors are called to be *"an example of faith,"* an object lesson that God is real.

(6) Morality - *"Be an example of the believers...in purity...."* Finally, the minister must be committed to moral purity. Nothing undermines a pastor's right to lead like moral impropriety. The late Scottish Presbyterian Robert Murray M'Cheyne once remarked, "A holy minister is an awful [awesome] weapon in the hand of God." The corollary is likewise true: an unholy minister is an anemic influence in the lives of the people he presumes to serve. How can an unholy man credibly insist that Christian people under his care and oversight live holy lives? Just as a bald man would not be a very effective salesman of hair restorer; and in the same way that personal trainer who is overweight and out of shape cannot expect to have much influence as a motivator of physical fitness, so a preacher of righteousness who lives an unrighteous and unholy life sabotages the very message he presents to others.

Thanks be to God he has given us gospel ministers who teach us His word, and then model that word in their own lives as living illustrations of Christianity. May we follow their lead, and then, mobilize to minister to others in the name of our blessed Lord.

18
Qualities of an Excellent Minister

Till I come, give attendance to reading, to exhortation, to doctrine. Neglect not the gift that is in thee, which was given thee by prophecy, with the laying on of the hands of the presbytery. Meditate upon these things; give thyself wholly to them; that thy profiting may appear to all. Take heed unto thyself, and unto the doctrine; continue in them: for in doing this thou shalt both save thyself, and them that hear thee. (1 Timothy 4:13-16)

Paul's exhortation to Timothy regarding the church's leadership concludes with a series of imperatives. Reading like an ordination "charge," Paul encourages this young preacher to pursue excellence in ministry. He addresses four particular areas — the minister's *focus, diligence, commitment,* and *personal and theological vigilance.*

The Minister's Focus
First, Paul reminds Timothy of the need to maintain a keen focus on the task before him: *"Till I come, give attendance to reading, to exhortation, to doctrine"* (v. 13). In the secular world, the primary cause of poor job performance is an inadequate job description. Likewise the minister who loses focus on the primary functions to which he has been called tends to divert his energy toward peripheral matters. Such a loss of focus necessarily produces a ministry that merely "treads water" or (if I may mix my metaphors) "spins its wheels."

What tasks deserve the minister's focused attention? First of all, *reading*. The personal intake of information through regular reading is vital to the gospel minister. "*Study to show thyself approved unto God*" (cf. 2 Tim. 2:15a) suggests that personal Bible familiarity, both of Scripture's content and theological meaning, is a spiritual necessity for every preacher, not just those who prefer academic pursuits. Consistent daily reading of God's word is as necessary to a gospel minister in this world as an oxygen tank is to a diver in the deep, blue sea. Reading good "*books and especially the parchments*" (cf. 2. Tim. 4:13b) of God's book is the preacher's life-supply.

The Greek word *anagnosis*, however, refers not merely to the private act of reading, but primarily to the act of reading aloud in public. Just as Ezra and the priests publicly read the Law of Moses (cf. Neh. 8:8) and Jesus publicly read from the prophecy of Isaiah (cf. Lk. 4:16), so Timothy's job description involved the regular, public reading of scripture.

It is sad that in the interest of time, many preachers today omit the public reading of God's word in public worship. Of course, the preacher seldom omits his sermon, but for some reason, he thinks that the reading of scripture is optional. I guess that in his mind, the sermon is more relevant than the word on which that sermon is supposed to be based. If anything is omitted from the worship format, however, the reading of God's word should be the last.

For some people, the public reading of the Bible may be the only exposure to the word of God they've had during the entire week. Of course, that should never be the case, but any man who has pastored for any length of time knows that sometimes it is. Further, the preacher need not read an entire book or even an entire chapter, but a salient paragraph consisting of ten or twelve verses, a Psalm, or a story from the life of Jesus in the Gospels is always appropriate. One thing is certain: the public reading of God's word is the only exercise of his public ministry in which the minister is speaking without the potential of error or mistake.

Secondly, he was to devote his attention to *exhortation* and to *doctrine.* Just as Ezra and the priests explained and applied the things they had read (cf. Neh. 8:8), so the reading of Scripture is to be followed by an exposition of the same. The word *exhortation* (meaning "verbal encouragement") suggests that Timothy was to use God's word to give pastoral encouragement to God's people. *Doctrine* suggests that he was to use Scripture to give didactic instruction to his hearers.

The point, then, is that the minister's primary focus is to be the communication of God's word. His job description consists of reading the word, then explaining, expounding, and applying it to his hearers. Maintaining a clear and keen focus on this primary objective is crucial to excellence in ministry.

The Minister's Diligence

Next, Paul warns Timothy of a danger facing every gospel minister: *"Neglect not the gift that is in thee, which was given thee by prophecy, with the laying on of the hands of the presbytery"* (v. 14). It is the danger of spiritual negligence.

This verse indicates that the ability to preach the Gospel is a *gift* from God. When God calls a man to preach his gospel, he equips that man with a spiritual speaking gift. Of course, the man is responsible for cultivating and improving the gift through personal education and opportunities to exercise his gift. But the talent itself is a gift from God. Like every God-called minister, Timothy was gifted with a special talent for gospel ministry.

The verse further indicates that others had officially recognized Timothy's gift *by prophecy* and *the laying on of the hands of the presbytery* — doubtless the clearest references to the official practice of "ordination" in Scripture.

But Timothy, and every gospel minister, faces a potential danger. Even though they have been gifted and sanctioned to function in a ministerial capacity by an official presbytery, ministers may, in fact, neglect their ministerial gift.

What is required to destroy a homestead? Must a person torch the house, sow salt in the garden, starve the livestock and poison the well? No, all he has to do is neglect it and it will destroy itself. Wind, weather, weeds and the wilderness will soon undo all the progress made to develop a functional residence if daily efforts to maintain it are relaxed (cf. Ecc. 10:18). Even so, neglect of his God-given gift via watching the television more than reading the bible, prioritizing a secular job over the call to preach, plowing to the neglect of praying, and surfing the web over studying the word is disastrous to ministerial effectiveness.

Instead, Timothy is to *stir up* his gift (2 Tim. 1:6) — that is, to fan the flames until it roars like a bonfire. Diligence to keep one's mind fresh and keen by consistent study of God's word is crucial for excellence in ministry.

The Minister's Commitment

Third, Paul urges Timothy to be totally committed to his ministry: *"Meditate upon these things; give thyself wholly to them: that thy profiting may appear to all"* (v. 15).

He wants Timothy to consciously and deliberately think about the important position he occupies. Further, he urges him to completely immerse himself in his work, devoting his whole heart and soul to it. Ministry is to be his all-consuming passion in life.

He adds an interesting incentive to this injunction: *"...that thy profiting may appear to all."* The word *profiting* means "pioneer advance." By throwing himself into the work of the ministry, others will notice Timothy's growth and progress, like a pioneer advancing mile after mile as he cuts a trail forward, and desire to follow his lead.

Instead of traveling in circles like a mule tied to a grindstone, the excellent minister is always moving forward. He never stops growing, learning, and improving his skills. His ambition for spiritual progress is not fueled by his own ego, but a holy passion to be more useful to the Master. He desperately longs to be the best minister he could possibly be, to deliver clearer and more powerful sermons, to set a more consistent example of godliness before the people he serves, to be more useful in making converts and witnessing the church in a state of spiritual vitality. He is, as George MacDonald said, "deathly afraid of personal, spiritual deterioration." He knows that "a man may sink by such slow degrees that long after he is a devil, he may still give the appearance of being a good Christian." And he knows that the only way to prevent the tragedy of a backslidden devotion and lackluster ministry is to continually press forward in personal growth.

Personal & Doctrinal Vigilance

Finally, Paul admonishes Timothy to ongoing vigilance: *"Take heed to thyself, and unto the doctrine; continue in them: for in doing this thou shalt both save thyself and them that hear thee"* (v. 16). Timothy is first exhorted to be personally vigilant—to take heed to himself. The minister's "self-watch," as C. H. Spurgeon termed it, is vital to Timothy's (and every man's) ministry. Every preacher must constantly guard his attitude, his thought-life, and his daily conduct. Failure in his calling as a minister almost invariably begins with the failure to take heed to himself.

Secondly, he is exhorted to be theologically vigilant—to *take heed to the doctrine*. He must be true to the truth, faithfully handling the word of God, guarding against perversions of the truth and efforts from this ungodly world to undermine the integrity of God's word.

Further, he is to *continue in them*, that is, to persevere in living and teaching the truth of God's word. He is not to give in to the temptation to quit or abandon the principles of the faith. Nothing artificial or man-made will substitute for the faithful teaching of

God's word—not special music, dramatic plays, motivational talks, or clever programs. The rule for gospel ministers is a long obedience in the same thoroughly-biblical direction of ministry, in spite of cultural trends. Continue, says Paul, to every preacher. Keep on keeping on. There is no need to invent something new. Consistency in faithful biblical exposition and personal godliness is the order of the day for Christ's servants.

In so doing, Timothy's ministry will exercise a saving influence both in his own life and in the lives of his hearers: "...*for in so doing, thou shalt both save thyself and them that hear thee.*" He will be saved from dishonoring the name of Christ and hindering the cause of Christ, and they will be saved from false doctrine, the ungodly influences of this world, and the loss of their Christian testimony. Again, this reference suggests that there is a *time salvation*, separate and distinct from *eternal salvation*, taught in the Bible.

This passage indicates that excellence in ministry depends on keeping a proper focus, maintaining diligence, being totally committed, and being vigilant to guard one's own heart as well as the integrity of the truth. May God bless His church with this kind of spiritual leaders.

19

Interpersonal Conduct in the Church

Rebuke not an elder, but intreat him as a father; and the younger men as brethren; the elder women as mothers; the younger as sisters, with all purity. (1 Timothy 5:1-2)

Chapter five begins a new theme in 1 Timothy — *the Church's Responsibility Toward Its Own*. The church has a responsibility not only to outsiders (ch. 2), but also, as this chapter indicates, to its own members.

Paul employs a familiar metaphor to teach about the cultural climate that should prevail in the church. He describes the church as a family unit in which interaction between members is governed by an existing relationship. Just as the family metaphor suggests the idea of intimate involvement in the lives of its various members, so there is an intimacy inherent in the relationship between church members.

When a church functions as a family, each member treats one another with respect and grace; nevertheless, everyone is not to be treated indiscriminately alike. Both the factors of age and gender dictate how a church family should interact among the various members that comprise it.

Seven categories of people are addressed in this discussion of the church's responsibility toward its own. Paul addresses *older men* (5:1a), *older women* (5:2a), *younger men* (5:1b), *younger women* (5:2b), *widows* (5:3-16), *preachers* (5:17-25), and *slaves* (6:1-2). It is significant that Paul does not segregate these various categories into their own groups, each as a separate class, but addresses them as integrated and involved in the entire life of the church. The focus is not on the needs of the group itself as if each merits special attention, but on Timothy's conduct toward each one.

It is doubtful, in other words, that Ephesus Church had an "older men's" group and a "younger women's" group. Instead, all were a part of the one group, the church. Yet Timothy is to recognize the particular circumstances of each demographic and adapt his approach to each based on the individual status and circumstances.

The modern habit of dividing people into classes by gender, age or marital status is foreign to the New Testament pattern for church life. The biblical pattern is whole families, men and women, married and single, adults and children, rich and poor, gathering in one body for the worship and service of God. There is no biblical example of a youth program, a nursery, a single's group, a women's auxiliary, or anything else that tends to foster a class structure within the body of Christ. New Testament church life according to the primitive, apostolic model was both age- and gender-integrated.

Older Men (5:1a)

"Rebuke not an elder, but entreat him as a father..." The word "elder" here does not refer to an "elder" in the official ecclesiastical sense, but to an older person who is mature in years. Paul envisions that Timothy will have occasion to confront an elderly person who may not be living up to his Christian responsibilities. How is he to handle such cases?

He is to show a certain deference to seniors, avoiding harshness. The word *rebuke* means "to strike verbally." Sharpness and harshness should be avoided when admonishing someone older than himself. The principle of respect due to the aged prescribed in Leviticus 19:32 still applies in the New Testament.

Instead of harsh rebuke, Timothy is to *entreat* his elder brethren in the church, like a son would plead with a *father*. A filial respect instead of an authoritarian spirit must mark his conduct toward his elders. Daniel's respectful appeal to Nebuchadnezzar recorded in Daniel 4:27 is an excellent example of this Christian principle.

Younger Men (5:1b)

"*...and the younger men as brethren.*" Timothy's treatment of people in his own generation is to be characterized by equality, not condescending superiority. Just as brothers in a family love each other, young men in the church should love each other. One is struck by the gracious spirit that Paul himself demonstrated to Timothy (cf. 2 Tim. 1:4; 1 Ths. 3:2). He treated him as an equal, not someone of inferior status. If an aged apostle like Paul engaged a man many years his junior with a spirit of collegiate respect and brotherly tenderness, a condescending spirit to younger brethren in the ministry and the church is always out of bounds by those with seniority of years or experience.

Older Women (5:2a)

"*...the elder women as mothers...*" Paul, again, models this principle in Romans 16:13. There he refers to the mother of Rufus as his mother also. Over the past four decades of Christian ministry, God has allowed me to benefit from the kindness and example of many "mothers in Israel" among the Old Baptists. What a treasure these godly women are in the church of the Lord Jesus Christ!

Younger Women (5:2b)

"*...the younger as sisters, with all purity.*" Timothy is to demonstrate love to both men and women in the church; nevertheless, he must be careful to insure that it is a holy love. When he treats the younger women as *sisters*, he is to do it "*with all purity.*"

When men must interact with young women in the church, discretion is of the essence. A deliberate effort to maintain dialogue that is distinctively spiritual and pure, not carnal and provocative, is crucial.

The Church as a Family

In the New Testament, the church is described by a number of metaphors. It is called a "flock," a "body," a "bride," a "priesthood," and a "kingdom." But no image is more descriptive of the relational nature of the church than this metaphor of a "family."

The church is not simply a glorified civic club. It is a family affair. The exhortation in our study passage to think of its various members as fathers, mothers, brethren, and sisters suggests this much.

This "family" model is the idea behind Peter's exhortation to *"love the brotherhood"* (1 Pet. 2:17), as well as that of the writer to the Hebrews to *"let brotherly love continue"* (Heb. 13:1). Paul again picks up the same theme in Romans 12:10, saying, *"Be kindly affectioned to one another in brotherly love; in honor preferring one another."*

The Lord Jesus taught that those who do the will of God are his spiritual family (Mt. 12:46-50). Though faithful discipleship sometimes comes at the high price of estranged natural relationships, our Lord has promised compensation within the church to those who leave all to follow him — compensation in the form of *"brethren, and sisters, and mothers, and children"* (Mr. 10:28-30).

Without doubt, John Fawcett knew something of this family relationship within the life of the church when he wrote:

> *Blest be the tie that binds*
> *Our hearts in Christian love;*
> *The fellowship of kindred minds*
> *Is like to that above.*
> *Before our Father's throne*
> *We pour our ardent prayers,*

Our fears, our hopes, our aims are one,
Our comforts and our cares.
We share our mutual woes,
Our mutual burdens bear,
And often for each other flows
The sympathizing tear.
When we asunder part,
It gives us inward pain,
But we shall still be joined in heart,
And hope to meet again.

20
"Family" Financial Responsibilities

Honor widows that are widows indeed. But if any widow have children or nephews, let them learn first to shew piety at home, and to requite their parents: for that is good and acceptable before God. Now she that is a widow indeed, and desolate, trusteth in God, and continueth in supplications and prayers night and day. But she that liveth in pleasure is dead while she liveth. And these things give in charge, that they may be blameless. But if any provide not for his own, and specially for those of his own house, he hath denied the faith, and is worse than an infidel. Let not a widow be taken into the number under threescore years old, having been the wife of one man. Well reported of for good works; if she have brought up children, if she have lodged strangers, if she have washed the saints' feet, if she have relieved the afflicted, if she have diligently followed every good work. But the younger widows refuse: for when they have begun to wax wanton against Christ, they will marry; having damnation, because they have cast off their first faith. And withal they learn to be idle, wandering about from house to house; and not only idle, but tattlers also and busybodies, speaking things which they ought not. I will therefore that the younger women marry, bear children, guide the house, give none occasion to the adversary to speak reproachfully. For some are already turned aside after Satan. If any man or woman that believeth have widows, let them relieve them, and let not the church be charged; that it may relieve them that are widows indeed. Let the elders that rule well be counted worthy of double honor, especially they who labor in the word and doctrine. For the scripture saith, thou shalt not muzzle the ox that treadeth out the corn. And, The laborer is worthy of his reward. (1 Timothy 5:3-18)

Paul continues his discussion of the church's responsibility toward its own by talking about two special areas of need: (1)

the financial support of *"widows indeed"* (vs. 3-16); (2) the financial support of pastors (vs. 17-18).

Widows Indeed (vs. 3-16)

The church bears a responsibility to minister to all widows (cf. Jas. 1:27),[1] but it has a special responsibility to godly widows who have devoted the remainder of their lives to serving the Lord by serving His people. *"Widows indeed,"* as Paul terms them, are female members of the church who are bereft of a husband and hence, of financial livelihood. They are either not interested in or not capable of future marriage, having devoted themselves for the rest of their days to the Lord. It is possible that Dorcas in Acts 9:36-41, was such a *"widow indeed."*

Paul indicates that such widows deserve the church's financial support, and that churches with such widows have a financial responsibility toward them. *Honor* involves more than mere personal respect and emotional encouragement. It speaks of making financial provision for another, as Jesus' interpretation of the word in the 5th Commandment suggests (cf. Mt. 7:10ff). The same word will later be employed to speak of the church's financial responsibility toward its pastor (v. 17).

Of course, widows in the first century were largely at the mercy of society. There were no government programs available to assist them, and when they were also bereft of an extended family, they were really in dire straits. The first century church, consequently, recognized the need and marshaled its resources for the aid of widows in the number.

But who qualifies to be maintained by the church as a *"widow indeed"*? Evidently the church was maintaining some widows who should have been supported by their families. Paul insists that only

---

1   The word *visit* in James 1:27 does not mean simply "to talk about the weather." It is a shepherding term, meaning "to visit with a view toward meeting a need," like a shepherd might visit each lamb in his fold, tailoring his ministry according to the individual need.

certain widows should be *"taken into the number,"* that is, placed on the registry for financial support.

The church's benevolence to widows, in other words, is not to be indiscriminate. Certain qualifications must be met before a widow is *"taken into the number"* of people who are financially maintained by the congregation.

First, she must be **destitute of family support**: *"But if any have children or nephews, let them first learn to show piety at home, and to requite their parents: for that is good and acceptable before God"* (v. 4). A widow who has surviving family members should be supported by her family, not the church. In fact, Paul says that family members who fail to provide for their own have *"denied the faith"* and are *"worse than an infidel* [i.e. unbeliever]*"* (v. 8; cf. also v. 16).

Such strong language indicates that it is not even the way of the world, in general, to neglect its own. Families who assume responsibility for the care of their respective widows relieve the church of an unnecessary burden (v. 16).

Family members should care for their own widows, for two reasons: (1) Because of gratitude for the care their parents gave to them—*"...to requite their parents"* (v. 4); (2) Because it is pleasing to the Lord—*"...for that is good and acceptable before God"* (v. 4b).

Secondly, she must be **godly and devoted to serving the Lord**: *"Now she that is a widow indeed and desolate, trusteth in God, and continueth in supplications and prayers night and day"* (v. 5). In contrast to her godliness, other widows *live in pleasure*, that is, they live for themselves rather than the Lord. Such widows, which Paul will further describe in verses 11-15, are not to be included in those whose income is supplemented by the church.

Thirdly, she must be **at least sixty years of age**: *"Let not a widow be taken into the number under threescore years old..."* (v. 9). Her seniority makes it unlikely that she would seek another husband, but would be content to devote her remaining years to the service of the Lord. Younger widows, by way of contrast, would be more prone to *"cast off their first faith"* (v. 12), that is, to disregard their previous pledge of total commitment to the church in lieu of their desire for a husband. Hence, Paul counsels the younger widows to *"marry, bear children, guide the house, give none occasion to the adversary to speak reproachfully"* (v. 14). This noble calling of homemaking will prevent the urge to idly wander about from house to house and involve themselves in other people's business (v. 13).

In the fourth place, a *"widow indeed"* must meet the criteria of **marital fidelity**; *"...having been the wife of one man"* (v. 9b). Faithfulness to her husband while she was married to him is crucial for the widow who is eligible for financial assistance from the church.

Fifthly, she must be **renowned for her good works**: *"Well reported of for good works..."* (v. 10a). What kind of *good works*? Specifically, Paul mentions *"bringing up children,"* either her own or orphaned children, *"lodging strangers,"* no doubt a reference to her hospitality toward travelers, *"washing the saints feet,"* action which displays her servant-hearted lifestyle and her concern for others in the church, *"relieving the afflicted,"* a reference to her charitable compassion and concern to minister to others, and *"diligently following every good work,"* a reference to her history of authentic Christian discipleship.

It is evident by the portrait painted of this kind of woman that she is totally devoted to the Lord and His people. Hers is a lifestyle of ministry and service to others. Such widows are a priceless blessing to the church and when they are in need, it is the church's happy privilege and solemn responsibility to come to their aid.

Gospel Ministers (vs. 17-18)

"Let the elders that rule well he counted worthy of double honor, especially they who labor in the word and doctrine." (5:17). Beginning with verse 17, Paul addresses the church's responsibility toward its ministers. That responsibility includes three parts: financial

assistance (vs. 17-18), respect for the office (vs. 19-21), and caution prior to ordaining a man to such a responsible position (vs. 22-25).

As we noted previously, the word *honor* speaks of financial remuneration. It is translated from *timés*, a Greek word suggesting the idea of an honorarium, or a gift in response to services rendered without charge.

That churches are responsible for compensating the servants of God for their labor is without question. Paul quotes from two passages, one in the Old Testament (Deut. 25:4) and one in the New (Mt. 10:10; cf. Lk. 10:7) to teach that ministers should be monetarily compensated for their spiritual labors (cf. 1 Cor. 9:7-11; Gal. 6:6; 2 Chr. 31:4).

But he specifies one particular group of ministers as those who are to be *"counted worthy of double honor."* No doubt, this expression speaks of a higher level of compensation than an ordinary love gift, and is probably a reference to full financial support (cf. 1 Cor. 9:14).

Two criteria are mentioned for those ministers who are worthy of being fully supported by the church. First, these are elders that *rule well* and secondly, that *"labor in the word and doctrine."* Notice that full support by the church is tied to the minister's work ethic, not to the sheer fact that he holds the office. Implied in this criteria is the fact that he must work sufficiently to merit the support.

But how does one measure and codify the subjective expression *"rule well"*? It is defined by the second phrase, *"those who labor in the word and doctrine."* The minister that *labors* with an indefatigable commitment to studying the Scriptures and teaching them faithfully and consistently to the people under His care is one that *rules* (the word means "leads") *well* and is *worthy of* — i.e. he deserves — full support.

Of course, small churches may lack the necessary resources to sustain a full-time minister. In such cases, the minister must be willing to "make tents," if necessary, in order to provide for his own. But obviously, the best case scenario is for the minister to give himself fully and completely to the work before him, and for the church to free his hands by rendering to him the due reward of his labors.

21
The Church's Relationship to its Ministry

Against an elder receive not an accusation, but before two or three witnesses. Them that sin rebuke before all, that others also may fear. I charge thee before God, and the Lord Jesus Christ, and the elect angels, that thou observe these things without preferring one before another, doing nothing by partiality. Lay hands suddenly on no man, neither be partaker of other men's sins: keep thyself pure. Drink no longer water, but use a little wine for thy stomach's sake and thine often infirmities. Some men's sins are open beforehand, going before to judgment; and some men they follow after. Likewise also the good works of some are manifest beforehand; and they that are otherwise cannot be hid. (1 Timothy 5:19-25)

In addition to the church's concern to liberate the hands of a dedicated minister from the distraction of secular employment so that he may devote himself entirely to the pastoral care of the church and the ministry of the gospel of Christ, Paul has two further admonitions to the church in respect to its responsibilities to gospel ministers.

Respect for the Office (vs. 19-21)

First, the church has a responsibility to show respect to the man who holds the office of elder. "*Against an elder receive not an accusation, but before two or three witnesses. Them that sin rebuke before all, that others also may fear. I charge thee before God, and the Lord Jesus Christ, and the elect angels, that thou observe these things without preferring one before another, doing nothing by partiality*" (vs. 19-21).

Paul wants them to hold their ministers in high regard—to *"esteem them very highly in love for their works' sake"* (1 Ths. 5:13). But what about the minister who needs to be confronted for some failure or sin? How is the church supposed to deal with this scenario? After all, the church's leadership is supposed to be accountable to the church.[1]

It is evident that Paul does not believe that elders are exempt from the church's ethical and theological standards. The church has a responsibility, however, to demonstrate respect for the office even when examination or confrontation is in order. This passage outlines the appropriate "grievance procedures" to follow in the event that someone in the church has a complaint against the minister.

Paul's counsel to Timothy is that he must never listen to gossip about a minister if it is made by only one person. Every charge must be substantiated by two or three other people before it is even considered.

What if the charge is proven true? Then, the erring minister, who refuses to repent (for the word *sin* is in the present tense meaning "to persist in sin"), is to be publicly rebuked. Though painful, such a step will prove to be a powerful deterrent to everyone in the congregation (v. 20). Paul urges Timothy to be faithful to address each case according to protocol and to do nothing by partiality.

Caution Before Ordination (vs. 22-25)

Further, the church has a responsibility to exercise caution prior to ordaining a man to the ministry: *"Lay hands suddenly on no man, neither be partaker of other men's sins: keep thyself pure"* (v. 22).

Sufficient time to make an informed decision regarding a candidate's call and qualification for ministry is essential. In fact, the church does an unqualified man no favors when it endorses him for the work, nor even a qualified man, when it hastens his

---

1   Unaccountable leadership is one of the characteristics of a cult.

advancement to this position of spiritual leadership before he has sufficiently matured in the faith, and exhibited a level of personal and emotional maturity that is conducive to a leadership role.

"Drink no longer water, but use a little wine for thy stomach's sake and thine often infirmities" (v. 23). Paul diverts in verse 23 to a bit of personal counsel to Timothy regarding his physical health, then returns to his thought of hasty ordinations in verse 24. Every minister who is truly serious about serving Christ should also be sensible in terms of his physical health. It is possible to so abuse the body that a man of God limits his usefulness in the church. The previously mentioned M'Cheyne remarked, when as a 29 year old minister he lay on his death-bed, "The messenger still has a message, but I've killed the horse." Learning how to apply the appropriate remedy to one's own peculiar maladies in order to maximize both the quality and the quantity of ministry opportunities is an important part of devotion to the Lord who has called us.

In verses 24-25, Paul resumes his thought concerning the danger of hasty ordinations: *"Some men's sins are open beforehand, going before to judgment; and some men they follow after. Likewise also the good works of some are manifest beforehand; and they that are otherwise cannot be hid."*

Paul indicates that some men's moral flaws are quite public and judgments about their character are clear and evident. Other men tend to be more private and introverted. In those cases, it may take longer to come to a conclusion about their fitness for office. In either case, whether the church considers for ordination an extrovert or an introvert, it is better to err on the side of caution when it comes to ordaining a man to the gospel ministry.

22
Slaves & Masters in the Church Family

Let as many servants as are under the yoke count their own masters worthy of all honor, that the name of God and his doctrine be not blasphemed. And they that have believing masters, let them not despise them, because they are brethren; but rather do them service, because they are faithful and beloved, partakers of the benefit. These things teach and exhort. (1 Timothy 6:1-2)

Paul addresses one final group in his instructions concerning the church family — *servants* (or slaves) and their *masters*.

The slaves Timothy is to instruct are clearly church members. In verse one, however, the Christian slave is yoked to an unbelieving master. In verse two, both the slave and the master are believers. I am intrigued that instead of counseling the church at Ephesus to lobby the Roman government for the abolition of slavery, Paul opts instead to counsel the individual slaves to apply a Christian ethic to their current situation. He wants them to learn to ask themselves this question at every turn — "What does it mean to be a follower of the Lord Jesus Christ in my current situation?"

Seeing that slavery has been largely abolished in America, how does this lesson apply to our modern Western culture? The principles enunciated here may apply to any hierarchical relationship, such as employee/employer, student/teacher, etc. The passage, then, holds the believer to a high work ethic as an expression of his faith in the Lord Jesus Christ.

Responsibility toward an Unbelieving Master

What does the gospel of Christ require of the believer who is accountable to an unbelieving master? Paul answers that the believer in an inferior position is to *honor* (lit. to highly value) the individual in the higher position. Of course, there is no prohibition against seeking to change one's situation if it is unpleasant. But "slaves" in the Graeco-Roman world did not generally have this option. Paul wants them, therefore, to be content with their station as a testimony to the gospel of Christ. Christian slaves can learn contentment with their unpleasant circumstances by remembering that though they are bound in a natural sense, yet they are free in Christ (cf. 1 Cor. 7:20-24).

Why should a believing slave consider and treat his master *worthy of all honor*? Obviously, because as human beings, they are worthy of respect, regardless of their conduct (cf. 1 Pet. 2:17a). But Paul gives them an evangelical incentive: *"...that the name of God and his doctrine be not blasphemed."* The Christian is to do everything with an eye to the impact his actions will have on the gospel he professes to believe (cf. Phi. 1:27; Eph. 4:1; Titus 2:10).

Responsibilities toward Believing Masters

In verse 2, Paul addresses the slave who has a believing master. His counsel is straight-forward — do not take advantage of them because they are brethren. Evidently, some of the Christian slaves were taking advantage of the fact that their respective masters were fellow believers. No doubt, this kind of abuse of privilege still occurs today when brethren work together in various business ventures.

Instead of taking advantage of them, they are to serve them even more diligently for two reasons. First, they are to be even better employees because their masters *"are faithful and beloved."* The relationship of oneness in faith and love is a powerful incentive for diligence on the job. Secondly, because they are *"partakers of the benefit*," that is, because of the common fellowship in the blessings of the gospel that believing slaves enjoy with believing masters. Instead of being an excuse for negligence then, their union in Christ should prompt Christian slaves and masters to an even greater level of service.

An Example

Paul's insistence that Christian slaves serve their earthly masters with honor and diligence as a testimony to the gospel they profess is vividly illustrated in the way he dealt with the runaway slave Onesimus. The book of *Philemon* recounts the story.

Though Philemon, the master, was a Christian, Onesimus, the slave, was not. Onesimus abandoned his responsibilities, doing some financial harm to Philemon in the process. In the interim between his escape and Paul's letter to Philemon, Onesimus encountered the apostle Paul and was converted to the faith.

As one of his first acts of importance, Onesimus is sent back to Philemon to make amends. It is significant that though Paul counsels Philemon to forgive him *"for love's sake,"* he also requires Onesimus to resume his responsibilities as an obedient servant. Just because he was now a believer, Onesimus did not have the right to skirt his responsibilities, nor did Philemon have an obligation to release him.

The thrust of Paul's counsel to servants and masters may be simply stated in the principle, *"Let every man abide in the same calling wherein he was called"* (1 Cor. 7:20). If a servant is obligated to a master at the time of his conversion, he should not assume that his newfound freedom in Christ liberates him from his extant moral responsibilities. Instead of seeking to escape his subordinate position, the slave should seek to implement the ethical principles of the gospel in both his job performance and his attitude to his master. And if a master has servants at the point of his conversion,

he should apply the spirit of the gospel to his employees, treating
them with Christian charity.

When both master and servant are believers, they should esteem
the brotherhood enjoyed within the family as paramount to even
their business arrangements. Any hierarchical structure that exists
between them in the workplace must be subordinate to the mutual
fellowship enjoyed within the church.

If each assumes personal responsibility for faithful treatment of
the other because he belongs to Christ and if neither permits the
dynamic of hierarchy to infringe on their fellowship in the gospel,
subordinates and superiors may each enjoy the full benefits of the
church family.

23
Godliness and the Truth

If any man teach otherwise, and consent not to wholesome words, even the words of our Lord Jesus Christ, and to the doctrine which is according to godliness; he is proud, knowing nothing, but doting about questions and strifes of words, whereof cometh envy, strife, railings, evil surmisings, perverse disputings of men of corrupt minds, and destitute of the truth, supposing that gain is godliness: from such withdraw thyself. (1 Timothy 6:3-5)

B eginning with 6:3, Paul addresses the fifth and final theme of *1 Timothy*: the church's goal. The key word in this section is *godliness* (vs. 3, 5, 6, 11). This important New Testament word suggests the thought of "heartfelt devotion toward God issuing in sincere service to others."

Paul indicates that godliness is the church's goal. And he highlights two threats to the pursuit of that goal: 1) false teaching; 2) covetousness.

False Teaching (vs. 3-5)

Verse 2 ended with the admonition to Timothy to *"teach and exhort"* the things Paul had communicated to him. Paul quickly adds that some men were teaching a different message: *"If any man teach otherwise and consent not to wholesome words, even the words of our Lord Jesus Christ, and to the doctrine which is according to godliness..."*

We have already been informed that the church at Ephesus was being troubled by false teaching (cf. 1 Tim. 1), and now Paul identifies the ungodliness inherent in every doctrinal deviation: "...*whereof cometh envy, strife, railings, evil surmisings, perverse disputings of men of corrupt minds, and destitute of the truth, supposing that gain is godliness.*" He speaks with candor—pulling no punches. In this day of cults and innovative, religious movements, it is essential that believers understand the dynamic behind false teaching. From the apostle's words, we may extract three tests of spiritual teachers: *the test of truth*; *the test of unity*; and *the test of motivation*.

1) The Test of Truth. The first mark of a false teacher is that he deviates from the truth. That there is such a standard of Christian orthodoxy is evident by Paul's reference to *wholesome words* (that is, healthy teaching), *the doctrine* (v. 3), *the truth* (v. 5), and *the faith* (vs. 10, 21).

That truth consists of "*the words of our Lord Jesus Christ,*" meaning not only the "red letters" in the four Gospels, but the entirety of apostolic teaching (cf. 1 Cor. 11:23a). Secondly, truth promotes *godliness*. It leads to devotion toward God, on a vertical dimension, and ethical holiness, on the horizontal.

The proper response to this truth is humility and submission. Those who deviate from this truth, Paul says, demonstrate their pride and ignorance. Rejecting the true gospel in favor of man-made opinions only reveals the teacher's own conceit and rebellion.

2) The Test of Unity. Secondly, the false teacher possesses an unhealthy interest in controversy: "...*doting about questions and strifes of words, whereof cometh envy, strife, evil surmisings...*"

The word *doting* suggests the idea of "sickness" and stands in stark contrast to Paul's use of the word *wholesome* (i. e. healthy) when speaking about the true gospel. Their speculations and quibbles over words do not promote spiritual health. Instead, they weaken and impair the health of the body of Christ. Few indicators of spiritual sickness in a congregation are as conspicuous as petty fussing, bickering, jealousy and suspicion.

In fact, the false teacher's interest in being novel tends to divide, not unify, the church (cf. Rom. 16:17). Paul says that the promotion of false teaching produces *envy* (resentment), *strife* (contention), *railings* (malicious talk), *evil surmisings* (suspicion), and *perverse disputings* (a state of constant irritability). Obviously, relationships are less than healthy when such divisiveness prevails.

He proceeds to identify heterodox teachers as men of "*corrupt* (or twisted) *minds and destitute of the truth.*" Strong words, indeed, but warranted by the seriousness of the issue.

3) The Test of Motivation. The third mark of a false teacher has to do with his motivation for ministry. Paul said that they "*suppose that gain is godliness.*" They operate, in other words, from a motive of personal profit in a monetary or financial way. They are hirelings and demagogues, exploiting their position as teacher as a means to personal wealth.

Ephesus was a very wealthy city. It was also a very religious city. The cult of the goddess Diana had once proved to be a very lucrative business, bringing the silversmiths no small fortune. People there were accustomed to marketing their religious wares and perhaps even charging a sum for religious instruction. It is likely that some of the false teachers with whom Timothy had to deal were exhibiting the same kind of greed that was once so common in the city.

In such a climate, Paul found it necessary to remind God's people that he did not operate from faulty motives (cf. 2 Cor. 2:17; 1 Ths. 2:5). Even today, many seek to commercialize the gospel, and to turn the house of God into a house of merchandise. Such a tendency should always be a flashing caution signal to God's people when it comes to evaluating the character of a man's ministry.

This scathing denunciation of false teachers, the divisiveness that they spawn, and the faulty motives from which they operate, is intended to teach the importance of doctrinal orthodoxy. False teaching is not a matter of insignificance in the church. Instead, it is extremely destructive. It weakens the health of the church, dividing the people of God and promoting disunity and confusion. What an ungodly thing, then, it is. Is it any wonder that Paul commanded Timothy to teach and exhort the wholesome words of our Lord Jesus Christ?

24
Godliness & Contentment

But godliness with contentment is great gain. For we brought nothing into this world, and it is certain we can carry nothing out. And having food and raiment let us be therewith content. But they that will be rich fall into temptation and a snare, and into many foolish and hurtful lusts, which drown men in destruction and perdition. For the love of money is the root of all evil: which while some coveted after, they have erred from the faith, and pierced themselves through with many sorrows. (1 Timothy 6:6- 10)

Not only is false teaching a threat to Christian godliness, but covetousness is as well. How many believers have fallen into the trap of covetousness and erred from the faith! Perhaps next to false teaching, the love of money is the number one reason that Christian people are tripped up on the path of discipleship. Both falsehood and covetousness are ungodly.

Notice Paul's intriguing play on words in verse 6. The false teachers claimed that financial *gain* was godly (v. 5b). But Paul turns the phrase and says, "No, gain is not godly, but *godliness with contentment is great gain.*" The truly wealthy person, in other words, is not the materially affluent, but the individual who is content to be godly. Spiritual gain, not financial, is real wealth.

Content to Be Godly

The false teachers thought that religion should yield dividends, and Paul concedes that it does, but only to the person who is content with what he has. The Greek word translated *content* was used in secular Greek culture to speak of a self-sufficiency that was independent of external circumstances. But as Christians, we know that the source of our sufficiency is not within but outside of ourselves. The Lord Jesus Christ is our sufficiency. The contented Christian, then, is a person who possesses such an inner sense of Christ's sufficiency that he is satisfied with his lot in life. Whatever his circumstances may be, he already possesses all in Christ; hence, he is at peace.

In verses 7-10, Paul contrasts two classes of people: (1) *the contented* (vs. 7-8), and (2) *the covetous* (vs. 9-10). The contented are people who realize that in terms of earthly possessions, their exit from this world will be exactly like their entrance into it: "*...for we brought nothing into this world and it is certain we can carry nothing out*" (v. 7; cf. Job 1:21; Ecc. 5:15). They have learned, consequently, the secret of traveling light during their pilgrimage here.

So, what should be the believer's attitude toward material things? He should be satisfied with the necessities of life: "*...and having food and raiment, let us be therewith content*" (v. 8).

Now, Paul is not promoting a lifestyle of asceticism. He is not prohibiting a person from possessing more than the bare necessities of life, for later he will say that "*God gives us richly all things to enjoy.*" He is, however, defining a "bare minimum" in which it is possible to live contentedly. If you have food, shelter, and clothing, says Paul, then you can (and should) live contentedly in Christ (cf. Mt. 6:32-33).

Oh, that as Christian people, we would be content to be godly! To make godliness the goal of our lives and to trust the Heavenly Father to supply the material necessities we need — that is the path to true and abiding peace.

The Peril of Covetousness

Covetousness is the opposite of contentment. It is the spirit that craves more than God in His providence has given. It was covetousness that fostered discontent with God's abundant grace in the hearts of Adam and Eve and compelled them to desire forbidden fruit. And it is the same discontented spirit that prompts us to every sin we commit in life (v. 10a).

"They that will be rich" is Paul's descriptive phrase for a covetous heart. These are people who *"love money"* and want to get rich. Solomon spoke of the inadequacy of silver to satisfy its possessor (cf. Ecc. 5:10), and Paul speaks of the dangers inherent in seeking monetary wealth.

He says that those who want to get rich *"fall into temptation and a snare* (lit. a trap)."* Covetousness is a trap for the unsuspecting soul. Though money promises happiness, it seldom (if ever) really delivers on its promise (cf. Ecc. 5:12).

Instead, covetousness brings *"many foolish and hurtful lusts which drown men in destruction and perdition."* The path of history is littered with lives brought to grief and temporal destruction through covetousness—Achan, Judas, Ananias, Sapphira, and many more. Such illicit desires, consequently, are *foolish* (i.e. irrational), and *hurtful* (i.e. destructive, not beneficial), says Paul.

John Stott writes, "The irony is that those who set their hearts on gain end in total loss, the loss of integrity and indeed of themselves. For, as Jesus asked, 'What good is it for a man to gain the whole world, yet forfeit his soul'."[1]

Some have even loved money to the extent that it became their god and they *"erred from the faith...piercing themselves through with many sorrows"* (v. 10b). It is not possible to serve God and mammon simultaneously. Those who make the pursuit of wealth their goal in life invariably depart from the faith.

---

1   John R. W. Stott, *The Message of 1 Timothy and Titus*, p. 152.

The multimillionaire Jay Gould is an example of the folly of covetousness. He died unlamented though his estate was valued at $100 million. It is reported that his last words were, "I'm the most miserable devil in the world."

Paul's warnings remind us that covetousness is an ungodly, and self-destructive sin. Contentment, however, is a beautiful and godly virtue. May we as believers learn to be content with the necessities of life while pursuing godliness as our life ambition.

25

Paul's Final Charge to Timothy

But thou, O man of God, flee these things; and follow after righteousness, godliness, faith, love, patience, meekness. Fight the good fight of faith, lay hold on eternal life, whereunto thou art also called, and hast professed a good profession before many witnesses. I give thee charge in the sight of God, who quickeneth all things, and before Christ Jesus, who before Pontius Pilate witnessed a good confession; that thou keep this commandment without spot, unrebukeable, until the appearing of our Lord Jesus Christ: which in his times he shall shew, who is the blessed and only Potentate, the King of kings, and Lord of lords; who only hath immortality, dwelling in the light which no man can approach unto; whom no man hath seen, nor can see: to whom be honor and power everlasting. Amen. Charge them that are rich in this world, that they be not highminded, nor trust in uncertain riches, but in the living God, who giveth us richly all things to enjoy; that they do good, that they be rich in good works, ready to distribute, willing to communicate; laying up in store for themselves a good foundation against the time to come, that they may lay hold on eternal life. O Timothy, keep that which is committed to thy trust, avoiding profane and vain babblings, and oppositions of science falsely so called: ehich some professing have erred concerning the faith. Grace be with thee. Amen. (1 Timothy 6:11-21)

With verse 11, Paul begins his final charge to Timothy regarding his ministry at Ephesus. First, he speaks a personal word by way of exhortation to Timothy (vs. 11- 16). Next, he counsels Timothy concerning his treatment of the wealthy in the church (vs. 17-19). Finally, he speaks a further personal word to Timothy (vs. 20-21).

A Personal Exhortation to Timothy (vs. 11-16)

The language resembles the kind of final instructions that a commander would give to his troops prior to battle. A tone of seriousness pervades the passage. He reminds Timothy of his position as a *man of God* (v. 11), a phrase used of people like Moses (Deut. 33:1), Samuel (1 Sam. 9:6), David (Neh. 12:24), and Elijah (1 Kings 17:18) in the Old Testament. He employs language that indicates the strenuous effort necessary to a faithful ministry, comparing the task before him to a battle and an athletic contest (v. 12). And he issues this charge "*in the sight of God...and before Christ Jesus,*" a sobering formula intended to impress Timothy with the solemnity of his calling. It is evident that Paul wants Timothy to realize the great responsibility upon him as a *man of God*. In lieu of that objective, Paul charges Timothy in three particular areas.

Ethics

"*But thou, O man of God, flee these things: and follow after righteousness, godliness, faith, love, patience, meekness*" (v. 11). Paul reminds him that in contrast to the false teachers, Timothy was a *man of God*. The goal he pursues, consequently, must be different from the money-loving religious hucksters. Timothy must *flee*, i.e. take evasive action, every other ambition, pursuing (*follow after*) instead a truly Christian ambition.

Paul defines the Christian's goal in terms of various character traits — *righteousness* (meaning "just dealings with others"), *godliness* (meaning "heartfelt devotion to God"), *faith* (meaning "trust in God to supply his needs"), *love* (meaning "a self-sacrificing life of service to others"), *patience* (meaning "endurance in difficulty"), and *meekness* (meaning "gentleness toward difficult people"). Just as people naturally run from threat and run toward attraction,

Timothy is to run from the threat of worldly ambition and to run toward the attractive goal of Christlikeness.

Doctrine

"Fight the good fight of faith" (6:12a). Secondly, Paul charges Timothy in the area of doctrine. The truth, Paul indicates, involves a battle. The devil is relentless in his attempts to confuse and delude God's people. The world assails the truth with a myriad of counterfeit philosophies and human ideas. Indeed, doctrinal integrity involves a fight.

But it is a *good* fight, the ultimate "just war." There is nothing dishonorable or ignoble about this *fight of faith*. In fact, it involves a good and noble objective—the glory of God. It is for a good cause—the cause of Christ. And we engage in it for a good and honorable purpose—the liberation of God's children from the bondage of this world. The gospel minister is not called to be a heretic hunter, but he is commissioned to be a freedom fighter. Such a role will necessarily involve an ongoing robust defense of the truth against false doctrine.

Timothy must not shrink in cowardice from the exacting demands upon him. He must not compromisingly sell-out in the hour of battle. Instead, he must fight for the faith, like a soldier in combat fights for his country. Paul's charge to Timothy reminds him that he must not only stand fast against evil, but also against error.

John Stott comments on this passage:

> Nobody enjoys a fight, unless of course the person is pugnacious by temperament. Fighting is an unpleasant business— undignified, bloody, painful, and dangerous. So is controversy, that is fighting for truth and goodness. It should be distasteful to all sensitive spirits. There is something sick about those who relish it. Nevertheless, it is a "good fight"; it has to be fought. For truth is precious, even sacred. Being truth from God, we cannot neglect it

without affronting him. It is also essential for the health and growth of the church. So whenever truth is imperiled by false teachers, to defend it is a painful necessity.[1]

Personal Experience

Thirdly, Paul charges Timothy in the area of personal experience: *"Lay hold on eternal life, whereunto thou art also called, and hast professed a good profession before many witnesses"* (6:12b).

"Lay hold on eternal life" is not a formula by which Timothy might be born again, for Timothy, the man of God, had already been quickened, as the language at the end of the verse indicates. This imperative, however, means "to seize, like a runner in the games grasping the ribbon at the end of the race." Paul exhorts Timothy to embrace and enjoy his eternal life, living it fully and completely. God had called him to Himself in regeneration. Now Timothy is to realize who he is and to live in the light of that Divine gift of grace.

What are the grounds for Paul's charge concerning faithfulness and integrity in ministry? Paul now offers Timothy and every gospel minister four incentives for faithfulness.

The Presence of God

The first motive to a faithful discharge of ministerial duty is the awareness that God is present. Paul's phrase *"in the sight of God"* expresses his ongoing awareness that all of life was lived before the Divine gaze. Paul practiced the presence of God (cf. Ps. 16:8). He lived with an inescapable sense that God was watching him.

For that reason, he did not feel at liberty to edit and parse the Scriptures according to personal preference (cf. 2 Cor. 2:17). He preached every sermon as if God was watching over his shoulder to hold him to account for how he handled holy scripture. And he wanted Timothy to remember that all of life is lived before the face of God.

---

1   Stott, *The Message of 1 Timothy & Titus*, p. 156.

The awareness that God is *"not far from every one of us"* (cf. Acts 17:27b) is a powerful incentive to faithfulness in ministry. May each and every servant of the Lord Jesus Christ make Hagar's exclamation — *"Thou, God, seest me"* — the motto of his life and labor.

The Example of Christ

Secondly, Paul cites the example of the Lord Jesus as an incentive to fidelity in ministry: *"...and before Christ Jesus, who before Pontius Pilate witnessed a good confession..."* Just as our Lord stood firm and steadfast in the face of opposition, so gospel ministers must stand uncompromisingly in spite of potential persecution for the truth's sake. We must never shrink in intimidated fear from the face of any man, regardless of his political power. Our Lord stood before Pilate in the knowledge that the truth could condemn him to personal suffering, yet he never flinched in his commitment to doing the will of His Father. What a sterling example of faithfulness!

The Return of Christ

Thirdly, Paul offers an eschatological basis for his appeal. He reminds Timothy that the Lord Jesus Christ is coming again. The word translated *appearing* in verse 14 is *epiphany*,[2] meaning "manifestation." One day the risen Christ will again appear (cf. Heb. 9:28). When he does, he will *show* (lit. reveal or manifest) *who is the only Potentate, the King of kings and Lord of lords.*

Though now the kingdom of God coexists with the kingdoms of this world, i.e. political empires, yet God has a plan. He intends to display His sovereign supremacy over all things, *in His times.* Then, every knee will bow and every tongue confess that Jesus Christ is Lord to the glory of God the Father (cf. Phi. 2:10-11).

That knowledge that we do not participate in a losing cause is, likewise, a powerful incentive to faithfulness in ministry. Our cause is not doomed for defeat or disaster, but destined for victory. God is

---

2   See the same term translated *coming* in 2 Thessalonians 2:8.

operating according to His time table. According to His plan, He will one day reveal the fact that He alone deserves to be glorified. Knowing this fact should spur on every minister in faithful obedience to the Savior, come what may.

The Character of God

Finally, Paul reminds Timothy of the ineffable character of God: *"Who only hath immortality, dwelling in the light which no man can approach unto; whom no man hath seen, nor can see: to whom he honor and power everlasting. Amen."*

A high view of God is a powerful incentive to faithfulness in ministry. It produces an attitude of reverential awe, like a subject would have for his king. Obviously such a spirit promotes a desire to please and obey one's master. To realize that the God we serve is the *high and lofty One that inhabiteth eternity* (cf. Is. 57:15), should cause every gospel minister to tremble at the very thought of displeasing Him.

Counsel Concerning Wealth (6:17-19)

In this final charge, Paul further charges Timothy concerning the wealthier members of the church: *"Charge them that are rich in this world, that they be not highminded; nor trust in uncertain riches, but in the living God, who giveth us richly all things to enjoy; that they do good, that they be rich in good works, ready to distribute, willing to communicate; laying up in store for themselves a good foundation against the time to come, that they may lay hold on eternal life"* (6:17-19).

Like the paragraph in verses 6-10, this one addresses the subject of money. The former passage, however, was directed toward people who were not rich but wanted to get rich. This paragraph is directed toward those who were already financially wealthy.

C. H. Spurgeon commented that the poor are the hallmark of the church (cf. Mr. 12:37), and it is true that the early church was largely comprised of people who were financially poor (cf. Jas. 2:5;

2 Cor. 6:10; 1 Cor. 1:26). Several references in the New Testament, however, indicate that many congregations consisted of some wealthy and influential people (Jas. 2:1ff; 1 Tim. 6:17). What sort of treatment should these wealthy Christians receive?

It is significant to note that Paul does not scold the rich for being wealthy. Neither does he insinuate that they should feel guilty because they are rich. Instead, he cautions them about the dangers of wealth then counsels them concerning the special responsibility they possess to use their wealth in a godly way.

The Dangers of Wealth

Wealth poses two particular dangers to those who possess it. First, riches tend to engender pride and a sense of self- importance (v. 17a). It is not uncommon for rich people to feel a sense of superiority to and to look down contemptuously on others. For this reason, Paul urges, "*Charge them that are rich...to be not highminded.*"

The Old Testament warned of the temptation to boast in wealth. The description of the king of Tyre includes this poignant observation: "*By thy great wisdom and by thy traffic hast thou increased thy riches, and thine heart is lifted up because of thy riches*" (Eze. 28:5). Further, the Lord warned Israel that when their gold and silver multiplied, then their "*heart [would be] lifted up, and [they would] forget the Lord*" (Deut. 8:13-14).

There is no justification, however, for pride of wealth. It is the Lord who gives a person "*power to get wealth*" (Deut. 8:18). Both "*riches and honor come*" from Him (1 Chr. 29:12). Even Job understood that to boast in pride over his wealth was tantamount to a denial of God (cf. Job 31:25, 28). "*Charge the rich not to be highminded.*"

The second danger wealth poses is a false sense of security: "*...nor trust in uncertain riches...*" People who are rich in this world tend, as a rule, to put their hopes in money. Psalm 49:6 indicates, however, just how futile wealth is as a source of help: "*They that trust in their*

*wealth, and boast themselves in the multitude of their riches; none of them
can by any means redeem his brother, nor give to God a ransom for him."*

Paul employs the adjective *uncertain* to describe the futility of
wealth as an object of trust. Riches are essentially transitory. They
tend to fly away—to perish with the using (cf. Mt. 6:19). Wealth is
uncertain.

Instead, Paul says, *"Charge them to trust in the living God, who
giveth us richly all things to enjoy."* Christians are not to exchange
materialism for asceticism, but to appreciate all God's rich and
abundant blessings in life.

The Godly Use of Wealth

Timothy is also to encourage the rich to use their wealth in a
godly way. The "rich" are to be *"rich in good works"*—to use their
financial resources to do good and noble things for others. They are
to be *"ready to distribute"* and *"willing to communicate."*

The word translated *distribute* suggests the thought of generosity.
Communicate comes from the Greek word *koinonia* meaning "to
share in common." The wealthy, then, are to overflow in the good
work of generously sharing their substance with others who are in
need. To use the resources with which God has blessed them in the
fellowship of giving is true ministry indeed.

Verse 19 suggests that the godly use of wealth is the best
investment an individual can make: *"Laying up in store for themselves
a good foundation against the time to come, that they may lay hold on
eternal life."*

Obviously, Paul does not mean that an individual's use of money
determines whether or not he goes to heaven when he dies. Neither
does he suggest that there is a class structure in heaven in which
some people live in a Main Street mansion while others live in a
single-wide mobile home on the other side of the tracks. He simply
means that using one's wealth to minister to others is a much better

investment than simply accumulating it for the sake of a personal nest egg for the future.

The wealthy who invest their resources in the service of God are laying up for themselves a spiritual treasure, the assurance that they have ministered to the saints, not a material one. Believers are taking hold of the life that is truly life when they prioritize the spiritual over the material.

A Final Plea to Preachers (6:20-21)

In his closing comments, Paul speaks a final, personal word to Timothy. It is a passionate and intimate plea, as the exclamation *O Timothy* suggests: "*O Timothy, keep that which is committed to thy trust, avoiding profane and vain babblings, and oppositions of science falsely so called: which some professing have erred concerning the faith. Grace be with thee. Amen.*" (6:20-21).

The Pastor as a Guardian

The pastoral epistles employ several metaphors to describe the nature of gospel ministry—i.e. a soldier, a farmer, an athlete—but none is more pervasive than the metaphor of guardian. Paul had left Timothy in Ephesus to guard the church against false teaching (cf. 1 Tim. 1:3), and Titus in Crete to protect the church against ungodliness (cf. Titus 1:5). From the pastoral epistles, consequently, a pastoral theology of the pastor as a Divinely-appointed guardian of a sacred trust emerges.

The pastor is God's sentinel, commissioned to protect God's truth from distortion. He is God's watchman, charged to protect the inhabitants of Zion against the threat of danger. He is God's shepherd, called to oversee the flock and defend them against potential predators.

The verb *keep* in verse 20 emphasizes this important pastoral responsibility. It originates from the Greek word *phulasso* (translated "keep" in 1 Tim. 6:20 and 2 Tim. 1:14). It means "to guard, keep watch, hold." Similar words in the pastoral epistles include:

- *tereo* (translated "keep" in 1 Tim. 5:22 & "kept" in 2 Tim. 4:7) = "to watch over, keep an eye on"
- *epecho* (translated "take heed" in 1 Tim. 4:16) = "to pay attention to"
- *antecho* (translated "holding" in Titus 1:9) = "to maintain possession of"

Now, the opposite of this commitment to pastoral vigilance is an attitude of carelessness, as Paul expresses in 1 Tim. 4:13-15, "*Neglect not...*" Paul is saying, "Timothy, don't be careless about your gift, but be careful to fulfill your pastoral duties." Now again, in his final charge, he reiterates the responsibility that rested on Timothy to function as God's spiritual sentinel.

The various images employed in Scripture to describe the nature of pastoral ministry also develop the thought of "guarding" and "overseeing":

- *episkopos* (translated "bishop" in 1 Tim. 3:2) = "one who oversees, or watches over"[3]
- *poimen* (translated "pastor" in Eph. 4:11) = "a shepherd; one who cares for the flock"

Both images are employed in Acts 20:28: "...over the which the Holy Ghost hath made you overseers [*episkopos*] to feed [*poimainei*] the church of God..." and in 1 Peter 2:25 with reference to the Lord Jesus Christ: "...the Shepherd [*poimen*] and Bishop [*episkopos*] of your souls." Christ is the ultimate "Pastor." He safely "keeps" his

---

3   Thomas Oden writes, "Bishop translates *episkopos*, which is derived from the family of Greek words referring to guardianship, oversight, inspection — accountably looking after a complex process in a comprehensive sense. *Episkopos* implies vigilance far more than hierarchy."

own (Jno. 17:11-12), watching over their souls and safeguarding their eternal life.

So, the pastor is commissioned to be a spiritual sentry. In his book, *The Minister as Shepherd,* Charles Jefferson compares the pastor's responsibility to protect the flock to an Eastern shepherd's duty:

> The Eastern shepherd was, first of all, a watchman. He had a watch tower. It was his business to keep a wide-open eye, constantly searching the horizon for the possible approach of foes. He was bound to be circumspect and attentive. Vigilance was a cardinal virtue. An alert wakefulness was for him a necessity. He could not indulge in fits of drowsiness, for the foe was always near. Only by his alertness could the enemy be circumvented. There were many kinds of enemies, all of them terrible, each in a different way. At certain seasons of the year there were floods. Streams became quickly swollen and overflowed their banks. Swift action was necessary in order to escape destruction. There were enemies of a more subtle kind—animals, rapacious and treacherous: lions, bears, hyenas, jackals, wolves. There were enemies in the air; huge birds of prey were always soaring aloft ready to swoop down upon a lamb or kid. And then, most dangerous of all, were the human birds and beasts of prey— robbers, bandits, men who made a business of robbing sheepfolds and murdering shepherds. That Eastern world was full of perils. It teemed with forces hostile to the shepherd and his flock. When Ezekiel, Jeremiah, Isaiah, and Habakkuk talk about shepherds, they call them watchmen set to warn and save.[4]

The pastoral epistles charge the gospel minister to exercise guardianship in three particular areas of life. First, the minister must *guard himself* (cf. 1 Tim. 4:16a; Acts 20:28a). John Stott comments: *"Only if pastors first guard themselves will they be able to*

---

4 As quoted in *Rediscovering Pastoral Ministry*, p. 341.

guard the sheep. Only if pastors first tend their own spiritual life, will they be able to tend the flock of God."

Paul has already talked about the importance of personal integrity in ministry in 1 Tim. 3:1-7. Spiritual gifts without personal godliness will not result in a fruitful ministry over the long term. There is no credibility in a man dressed in rags trying to sell name-brand suits, and there is no credibility in an ungodly man trying to tell others about the transforming power of God's grace in Christ. The minister must guard himself against immorality, impure motives, slothfulness, covetousness, fear and discouragement, bad attitudes, and many other potential pitfalls that await him.

Secondly, the minister must *guard the flock.* He must protect them from both internal diseases like personal ungodliness and external threats such as corporate disunity and worldly deception. The book of Titus will focus on this particular subject.

Thirdly, the minister must *guard the truth.* This emphasis is dominant in 1st Timothy (cf. 1:3-4; 4:1-5; 6:3-5). As a Divinely appointed sentry, the gospel minister is commissioned to maintain the integrity of apostolic doctrine (1 Tim. 4:16b) and to guard the treasure entrusted to his care.

Fulfilling this positive injunction to *keep the trust* will require Timothy, on the negative side, to *"avoid profane and vain babblings and oppositions of science falsely so called."* What is to be Timothy's response to the pseudo-intellectual arguments of those who simply want to attack God's word? He is to *avoid* them.

Speaking of this simple counsel to *avoid* worldly philosophy and false science, there is wisdom in the counsel of Romans 16:19: *"Be simple concerning evil and wise concerning that which is good."* Timothy is not to make the refutation of the church's critics his primary business, but to devote himself to guarding the truth from false teaching by faithfully and consistently proclaiming it.

Why is it dangerous for a believer to become too enamored with the pseudo-intellectualism of the world? Because it confuses the mind and diverts from the truth: "...*which some professing have erred concerning the faith*" (v. 21). Instead of catering to the world and its wisdom, Timothy and every gospel minister must make the safekeeping of the deposit of truth entrusted to them the number one priority of life. Such a charge is of paramount importance.

The
Second Epistle
to
Timothy

Introduction to 2 *Timothy*

S*econd Timothy* is Paul's "swan song." Tradition says that shortly after it was written, Paul was beheaded by Nero on the Ostian Way, outside the city of Rome. Writing from his Mamertine prison cell, Paul knows that his time is short. Though he had previously anticipated the potential of death during his first incarceration, he believed, as Philippians 1:19-26 suggests, that he would be acquitted. No such confidence is expressed in 2 *Timothy*.

In fact, Paul now writes to his young protégé in the faith as a dying man awaiting execution: *"For I am now ready to be offered [that is, to be poured out in martyrdom as a libation, or drink offering, before God], and the time of my departure is at hand. I have fought a good fight, I have finished my course, I have kept the faith: henceforth there is laid up for me a crown of righteousness, which the Lord, the righteous judge, shall give me at that day: and not to me only, but unto all them also that love his appearing"* (2 Tim. 4:6-8).

His mood is unusually reflective, the kind of death-bed reflection on the past that typically characterizes a person's last words. He speaks of his *forefathers* and his memory of Timothy's pious beginnings in life (1:3,5). He recalls the rejection of the believers in Asia (1:15) and the encouragement and affirmation of Onesiphorus, who was not ashamed of his chain (1:16). He remembers, albeit not with resentment or bitterness, the theological apostasy of Hymenaeus and Philetus (2:17-18), the defection of Demas (4:10), the hostility of Alexander the coppersmith (4:14-15), and the way the believers in Rome let him down at his *first answer* before Caesar (4:16; cf. Phi. 2:20-21).

He also reflects on his own past afflictions and persecutions, as well as the Lord's faithfulness to deliver him out of them all (3:11; 4:17). He looks back on his ministry with the contentment of a clear conscience and the satisfaction of a completed task (1:3; 3:10; 4:7).

Furthermore, Paul's tone is strangely tender and familiar – the kind of tenderness and compassion that a dying father exhibits toward his beloved son. Paul's final letter to Timothy, his *dearly beloved son* (1:2), is literally teeming with encouragement.

Even the most cursory reading of the epistle indicates that Timothy was discouraged. False teaching within the Christian community, and societal pressure and opposition without, were taking a toll upon Timothy's spirit. Evidently, Timothy was constitutionally weak and frail (1 Tim. 5:23). Perhaps, he possessed a personality that was prone to intimidation.[1] His youth, moreover, with its inherent lack of credibility, compounded the challenges he already faced (1 Tim. 4:12).

Prone to a bit of melancholy by nature, Timothy was beginning to weaken beneath the burden of persecution. With the wisdom and compassion of a father in the ministry, consequently, Paul writes to remind him of the need for unflinching courage and the importance of an unashamed fidelity in his confession of Christ (1:7-8). He affirms his younger brother by reminding him of his own personal love for Timothy (1:3-4), of Timothy's personal heritage (1:5), and of his call and ordination to the ministry (1:6).

Paul, further, reveals his own commitment to Jesus Christ, expecting, no doubt, that Timothy would be stimulated to faithfulness by his mentor's own courageous example (1:8,12; 2:10; 3:10; 4:17-18). Finally, Paul asks Timothy to come to him, bringing his coat, books, and parchments, and especially himself, that he *"might be filled with joy"* (1:4; 4:9,13,21). How significant that the aged, cold, and lonely apostle, in the face of certain death, would be

---

1 Consider Paul's stern warning to the ruthless Corinthians lest they flex their muscles against this sensitive man of God (1 Cor. 16:10-11).

more concerned to encourage a fellow-laborer in the gospel than for his own comfort and safety!

Paul's charge to Timothy, consequently, is unmistakably direct and clear. The dying apostle is not only reflective concerning his own life, and sympathetic concerning Timothy's need for encouragement and affirmation; he is also concerned for the welfare of the church once he is gone, both in his time and in every subsequent age. So, like a General charging his young Lieutenant in the faith, Paul's letter is filled with admonitions to faithfulness: "... *stir up the gift of God...hold fast the form of sound words...keep [that good thing which was committed to thee] by the Holy Ghost...be strong in the grace that is in Christ Jesus...commit [the things I've taught you] to faithful men...endure hardness as a good soldier of Jesus Christ...study to show thyself approved unto God...shun profane and vain babblings...flee youthful lusts...continue in the things which thou hast learned and hast been assured of...*" (1:6; 1:13; 1:14; 2:1; 2:2; 2:3; 2:15; 2:16; 2:22; 3:14).

He outlines the characteristics of an increasingly degenerate and godless culture (3:1-9) and of the inevitably of persecution from it (3:12-13). Finally, he lays down certain absolute essentials for Timothy and every successive pastor who would be faithful to his gospel commission in an environment that is antagonistic to the gospel of Christ (4:1-6). It is to these essentials that we now turn.

A Pastor Named "Timothy"

Second Timothy is one of three New Testament letters known as the "Pastoral Epistles," so named because they were written to pastors to instruct them in the dynamics of pastoral ministry. Whether or not he had been officially designated its pastor, Timothy was serving the church at Ephesus in a pastoral capacity (1 Tim. 1:3; 2 Tim. 1:16-18; 4:19).

Pastoral ministry is the act of shepherding the flock of God. In fact, the masculine noun "pastor" is derived from the Greek word (*poimen*) for "shepherd." The Christian *poimen* cares for God's sheep by providing for their spiritual nourishment, protecting them from predators, and overseeing their spiritual welfare.

His role is at the same time one of service (i.e. he exists to supply the needs of the flock) and leadership (i.e. he exercises oversight of the flock as one who must answer to the Great Shepherd for their condition). The pastorate is the personal, or the people, side of ministry involving actual day in and day out interaction, at a grass roots level, with real people who live in a real world.

For Timothy, and for every other pastor, shepherding means living with the consequences and ramifications of one's preaching in a real life, ongoing ministry. The pastor-teacher's primary responsibility is not to "*make disciples*" but to "*teach them* [i.e. the disciples who have already been converted] *to observe all things*" that the Lord Jesus Christ has commanded (Mt. 28:18-20).

In other words, pastoring is a matter of discipling the disciples. Unlike the evangelist, who makes and baptizes new converts, and then moves along to another field ready to harvest, the pastorate involves a long-term commitment to the flock over which the Holy Spirit has made him the overseer. God's plan is for evangelists to begin a work—to break the ground, if you please—then for pastors to stabilize and strengthen it by cultivating and tending the crop. Evangelistic ministry is initial, therefore, and pastoral ministry, perpetual and ongoing. Or to say it in other words, the goal of gospel ministry is initially evangelism, then edification.

As an apostle, Paul functioned as both an evangelist and a pastor. He both planted churches and remained active in their ongoing care and nurture. Second Corinthians 11:28 indicates that he exercised a pastoral authority and responsibility, by virtue of his apostolic office, over "*all the churches.*"

Neither I nor any other minister since the apostles possesses such a far-reaching authority or responsibility. Our commission is more akin to Timothy's than Paul's. We are shepherds, charged, like Timothy, with the care of local flocks, not apostles, entrusted with the authority to mandate and govern the cause of Christ in general. The apostle's charge to Timothy, consequently, is his charge to every pastor-teacher in every subsequent era of the kingdom of God.

Protecting the Sheep from Predators

Timothy ministered in a society not unlike our own. False teaching, just as Paul had predicted (Acts 20:29-31), had infiltrated the church at Ephesus. Some had already *swerved* from the faith (1 Tim. 1:6) and made theological shipwreck (1 Tim. 1:19-20; 4:1; 5:12,15; 6:3-5,21; 2 Tim. 2:16-18; 4:14-15).

Evidently, the false teachers were promoting a rhetorical controversy that left the Christians in Ephesus confused and befuddled (Notice the many references to "word battles": 1 Tim. 1:4-6 [*vain jangling*]; 4:2 [*speaking lies in hypocrisy*]; 4:7 [*profane and old wives' fables*]; 6:3-4 [*...wholesome words...doting about questions and strifes of words*]; 6:20 [*avoid profane and vain babblings*]; 2 Tim. 2:14 [*strive not about words to no profit*]; 2:16 [*shun profane and vain babblings*]; 2:23 [*foolish and unlearned questions avoid*]; 4:15 [*he hath greatly withstood our words*]).

Some of the most vocal of these self-proclaimed teachers were aspiring to the ministry (1 Tim. 1:7; 1 Tim. 6:3-5), necessitating Paul's reminder of the qualifications for gospel ministry in 1 Timothy 3:1-7. Some of the women in the church had even assumed a role of leadership, and others were contributing to the strife through gossip and slander (1 Tim. 2:9-15; 3:11; 5:1-16; 2 Tim. 3:6). In a word, the Ephesian church was in a state of theological chaos and confusion.

How was Timothy to deal with this confusion? He faced, in a very real sense, a battle, a fight of faith, a spiritual war, not only against a pagan culture but also against the infiltration of the world's unbelief into the church. The relentless pressure was taking a toll on his enthusiasm. He was beginning to lose focus. He was weakening beneath the heavy load.

What did he possibly have in his pastoral arsenal that would counteract the false teaching of these wolves and diseases that threatened to scatter the flock? Was there an antitoxin to the cancerous poison of false doctrine (2 Tim. 2:17)? Could the church at Ephesus be saved from apostasy?

It was against this dark background of intellectual chaos in Ephesus that Paul charged the young pastor, "*Preach the Word.*" The Word, which he had been commissioned to proclaim and teach at his ordination, was the one and only weapon capable of defeating the enemy's falsehoods (1 Tim. 1:18).

"*Words of faith and of good doctrine*" would work not only to Timothy's, but to the church's salvation from error (1 Tim. 4:6,16). By "*laboring in the word and doctrine,*" Timothy could "*fight the good fight of faith*" (1 Tim. 5:17, 6:12).

Over and again, Paul urges his comrade in arms to "*hold fast the form of sound* [healthy and health-giving] *words*" (2 Tim. 1:13), to "*commit* [the things Paul had taught him] *to faithful men*" (2 Tim. 2:2), to "*study*" and "*rightly divide the word of truth*" (2 Tim. 2:15), to resist the temptation to argue, but to "*be gentle, apt to teach, patient, in meekness instructing those that oppose themselves lest God peradventure will give them repentance to the acknowledging of the truth...that they may recover themselves out of the snare of the devil...*" (2 Tim. 2:24-26), to "*continue in the things which [he] had learned and had been assured of, knowing of whom he had learned them*" (2 Tim. 3:14), and to "*preach the word*" (2 Tim. 4:2).

The word! The word! "Timothy," Paul says, "rediscover the tools of the shepherd; you have a rod and a staff in your possession; use them to protect the flock from predators." This word, Paul reminds Timothy, is God's own self-revelation, given through the vehicle of inspiration. Because it is God's own word, it is absolutely authoritative and sufficient for every need, a thorough furnisher unto all good works (2 Tim. 3:15-17).

Developing a Biblical Philosophy of Ministry

"Therefore," Paul says, *"I charge you, Timothy, in the sight of God and the Lord Jesus Christ…Preach the word."* That terse command, *"preach the word,"* constitutes the mandate of pastoral ministry.

In these three single-syllable words, the Christian pastor discovers the task to which his Lord has called and commissioned him. Every pastoral function is contained in the crucible of this command. *"Preach the word"* is the umbrella under which all true gospel ministry abides, the context in which all true ministerial function must be interpreted. This charge is the compass by which the Christian pastor navigates the direction his ministry will take, the blueprint by which he builds the church, the pattern by which he measures every message, the grid through which he interprets every church activity, and the scale by which he measures what is and what is not legitimate in his calling. *"Preach the word"* is the pastor's job description.

The Pastoral Epistles in general, and the letter of 2 *Timothy* in particular, provide the New Testament church with a God-ordained philosophy of ministry. The importance of adopting and maintaining a Biblical philosophy of ministry cannot be overstated. Paul knew that Timothy's discouragement was largely due to the fact that he had lost sight of his goal. He had lost focus and Biblical perspective. He needed to recapture, consequently, a clearly defined goal in ministry.

How can a pastor *"make full proof of his ministry"* if he can no longer see the goal of ministry (2 Tim. 4:5c; cf. Col. 4:17)? Without a sense of purpose, i.e. without an understanding of the overarching goal and objective of the pastorate, a pastor will minister reactively instead of proactively. Without purpose, the pastor tends to spending all of his time and energy "playing catch up" or "putting out brush fires."

What is a "philosophy of ministry?" It is a set of principles that determines how he will function in his ministry. A Biblical philosophy of ministry gives direction, enabling the pastor to define what is and what is not essential, freeing him from "the tyranny of the urgent." In the same way that a poor or inadequate job description is the primary cause of substandard job performance in the corporate world, a poorly defined goal of ministry is responsible for much current weakness in the church.

In 1 Corinthians 2:1-5, Paul demonstrates from his own experience how a clearly defined goal governs and controls his decisions. Though Paul had the intellectual capacity and verbal, rhetorical skills to fascinate his Corinthian audience, he consciously and deliberately avoided the temptation. In fact, he decisively *determined* to avoid *"excellency of speech...enticing words of man's wisdom"* and the sophistry that was so popular in that day, in order to preach the simple message of Christ crucified in the power of the Holy Spirit. Why did he choose to avoid the rhetorical forms of the day in favor of a thoroughly biblical and Christ-centered message? Because sophistry was inconsistent with the overarching purpose of his ministry.

What was that purpose? Paul's ultimate purpose in ministry was to glorify God by exposing Christ, so that his hearers would put their faith in God's power, not man's wisdom. If Paul was concerned to be popular among the Corinthians — if that was goal — he would have undoubtedly followed a very different path, perhaps engaging them is some philosophical dissertation that would have left them breathless and awestruck at his skill. He knew, however, that to properly represent Christ, he had to deliberately and decisively obscure his personal credentials and abilities. His sense of purpose, consequently, determined his method of preaching.

The fact that Paul had a clearly defined goal for ministry is evident in verses like 2 Timothy 4:6-7 and Acts 20:33. How could he say *"I have finished my course"* or *"I count not my life dear unto myself that I might finish my course with joy"* if he didn't know specifically what course he was to travel? Obviously, he couldn't. "If a captain does not know for what port he is heading, then no wind is the right wind."

To properly assess the goal of pastoral ministry, one must first understand the goal of the church. Because pastors are servants of the church, given to her by God for her spiritual benefit, goals that smack of personal ambition are always inappropriate. The purpose of pastoral ministry is inseparably tied to the edification of the church. Preachers exist to assist the church fulfill her calling; hence, the pastor has no right to build a personal empire or to pursue personal notoriety. Individualism, self-promotion, and personal gain are foreign to the very nature of Biblical ministry.

What is, then, the purpose of the church? The church is a repository of divine truth (Jno. 17:14; 2 Tim. 3:15). Her task is to faithfully keep the trust God has given her by dispensing and disseminating truth with accuracy and integrity (Titus 2:1). Secondly, the church is a home away from home for God's children (Heb. 3:6). It is the context God has established for loving fellowship and mutual ministry (Eph. 3:15-19; 4:12-16).

Thirdly, the church is a training center where God's people are equipped with the knowledge of how to exercise their spiritual gifts (Eph. 4:11-12). Finally, the church is God's light in a dark world (Mt. 5:13-16; Phi. 2:15). Her task is both conservative (i.e. protecting God's truth and caring for one another) and contemporary (i.e. equipping the saints and deploying them into the real world of ministry, and calling sinners to repentance).

The gospel ministry exists to facilitate the achievement of these goals. In the light of these overarching objectives, what is the purpose of pastoral ministry? Are questions like "What do people want?" or "How can we get people interested?" appropriate goals? Should we attempt to make the church more "user-friendly" or "seeker-sensitive"? As the mega-church phenomenon reveals, over-concern with what the world thinks of the church inevitably produces theological and ethical compromise.

A *man of God* must never ask "What kind of ministry do I want?" for God has already outlined the parameters of gospel ministry in the word. His goal must be a thoroughly Biblical ministry, because he is under obligation to God to preach the word.

Colossians 1:28-29 spells out the purpose and function of the gospel ministry: *"Whom we preach, warning every man, and teaching every man in all wisdom; that we may present every man perfect in Christ Jesus: whereunto I also labor, striving according to his working, which worketh in me mightily."* Paul knew his goal and *labored* to the point of exhaustion (*striving*) in order to attain it. What was that goal? To *"present every man perfect* (complete and mature) *in Christ."*

How did he go about maturing the saints? By *preaching* Christ. What did preaching Christ involve? *Warning* and *teaching* the people *in all wisdom.* How could he accomplish such a difficult task? Through the strength of the Holy Spirit who was *working in him mightily.*

In simple terms, Paul defined his ministry in terms of *preaching the word.* Even the Lord Jesus Christ "preached the word" (Mr. 1:38; Mr. 2:2; Lk. 4:17; Lk. 24:27,32). If the Savior *"expounded the Scriptures,"* dare we his servants do less?

Second Timothy is written to encourage Timothy (and every subsequent gospel minister) to pursue an unashamed, unapologetic, unflinching, and unceasing proclamation of the word of God as the primary mandate on his life, regardless of opposition from the world or from within the church, for the glory of God and the good of men. It reminds us that God's word is what people really need. It is a reminder desperately needed by the church at this late date in human history.

1
Paul's Swan Song

Paul, an apostle of Jesus Christ by the will of God, according to the promise of life which is in Christ Jesus, to Timothy, my dearly beloved son: Grace, mercy, and peace, from God the Father and Christ Jesus our Lord. (2 Timothy 1:1-2)

Unlike *1ˢᵗ Timothy* and *Titus* which were written within the same time-frame, *2ⁿᵈ Timothy* was penned some years later while Paul was imprisoned at Rome. It is likely the last letter Paul wrote, penned shortly before his martyrdom in A.D. 64.

Though Paul was under house arrest in Rome at the close of the book of *Acts*, it is likely that he was released and permitted to continue his ministerial labors for a brief period before being rearrested under a more serious charge (cf. 2 Tim. 2:9). The case for two Roman imprisonments is as follows:

(1) In 2 Timothy 4:16-17, he reflects on his *"first answer,"* i.e. defense, probably a reference to the trial he awaited before Caesar. Though he had expressed a certain tenuousness about the outcome of that trial in the *Philippian* letter (Phi. 1:19-25), it seems evident that he was *"delivered out of the mouth of the lion"* (2 Tim. 4:17).

(2) John Mark was not present during Paul's Mamertine imprisonment (cf. 2 Tim. 4:11), though he was present when Paul, under house arrest, wrote to the Colossians (cf. Col. 4:10). Timothy himself was also with the

apostle during his first imprisonment (Col. 1:1), but obviously is not present here.

(3) *Philippians,* which was written during the first Roman imprisonment, expresses a tone of uncertainty regarding his future. *Second Timothy,* however, conveys a very definitive sense that the end is near.

Also, unlike 1 *Timothy* and *Titus,* this letter is quite personal. The other two pastoral epistles are predominately ecclesiastical in emphasis — outlining the principles and procedures of church function. In contrast, 2 *Timothy* is primarily a letter of personal encouragement to Timothy himself. There is less instruction and more exhortation (or encouragement) in 2 *Timothy* than there is in the other two pastoral epistles.

It is probable that Timothy was at Ephesus when Paul sent this second epistle to him. It is further apparent that Timothy was feeling a bit discouraged and afraid. The nature of Paul's exhortations indicates that Timothy was struggling to cope with the pressure of persecution: *"God has not given us the spirit of fear...Be not thou therefore ashamed of the testimony of our Lord, nor of me his prisoner...be strong in the grace that is in Christ Jesus...endure hardness as a good soldier of Jesus Christ...watch thou in all things, endure afflictions..."* etc.

Perhaps he was afraid that he would soon have to face the same kind of trouble that had touched Paul's life. Whatever the direct cause of Timothy's sinking spell, Paul is evidently interested to encourage his young protégé in the ministry.

Isn't it significant that Paul uses his final letter to speak a word of consolation to a struggling colleague? Like his Savior before him (cf. John 14-16), Paul is not preoccupied with his own impending death, but with his brother's needs. Indeed, he asks Timothy to come to see him before winter, a request that superficially sounds quite selfish. On further thought, however, the request is likely intended to let Timothy know how much he is loved and needed by the dying apostle.

Paul's language throughout the letter is unusually tender and sympathetic. He addresses Timothy as his *"dearly beloved son"* (1:2; cf. 2:1). He concludes the letter with an especially tender twist to his characteristic benediction: *"The Lord Jesus Christ be with thy spirit"* (4:22). The reference to Timothy's *spirit* indicates Paul's awareness of the young preacher's "soul struggles," a very kind way of saying "Timothy, I care."

Paul's tactic throughout the letter is to use as an example his own experience with and mindset toward trials to encourage Timothy to persevere (cf. 1:12, 15; 2:9-13; 3:10-14; 4:5-8, 16-18). Paul hopes that his strong-minded resolve to endure coupled with his expression of confidence in the Lord and the example of how God had taken care of him would encourage Timothy to endure afflictions in steadfast faith.

Just as a son would value such an encouraging farewell letter from a loving father, Timothy must have drawn tremendous strength from Paul's words. Whether Timothy ever saw him in person again or not is unclear. That Timothy is with him in the presence of Jesus Christ now, however, cannot be doubted.

2
Stir Up the Gift of God

I thank God, whom I serve from my forefathers with pure conscience, that without ceasing I have remembrance of thee in my prayers night and day; greatly desiring to see thee, being mindful of thy tears, that I may be filled with joy; when I call to remembrance the unfeigned faith that is in thee, which dwelt first in thy grandmother Lois, and thy mother Eunice; and I am persuaded that in thee also. Wherefore I put thee in remembrance that thou stir up the gift of God, which is in thee by the putting on of my hands. (2 Timothy 1:3-6)

The first section of *2 Timothy* — 1:3 through 2:13 — consists of various exhortations to faithfulness. Paul wants Timothy to exhibit courageous leadership as a minister of the gospel of Jesus Christ. Instead of giving in to the temptation to faint in discouragement, he wants Timothy to improve and cultivate the spiritual gift that God had given him. He encourages his young protégé in three ways.

By Expressing Personal Affection for Him

Paul encourages Timothy by expressing his personal affection for him: "*I thank God, whom I serve from my forefathers with pure conscience, that without ceasing I have remembrance of thee in my prayers night and day; greatly desiring to see thee, being mindful of thy tears, that I may be filled with joy*" (1:3-4).

Three particular comments here convey Paul's love to Timothy. First, Paul informs him, "I'm praying for you, Timothy." Such prayer was not merely sporadic, but *"without ceasing...night and day."* To be remembered before a throne of grace on such a consistent basis is a token of genuine, brotherly love. A sense of duty may incite someone to pray for another once or twice, but only love can compel the kind of intense intercession Paul practiced on Timothy's behalf.

Secondly, Paul says, "I want to see you so *that I may be filled with joy"* (cf. v. 4). It would be one thing for Paul to ask to see Timothy so that he might impart some needed instruction or knowledge to Timothy. But it is another thing for him to say, "Timothy, I want to see you, not for your benefit, but for mine." The very suggestion that he might be a blessing to one he no doubt considered his spiritual senior must have been a great encouragement to Timothy. Only loved ones speak to each other in terms of endearment like these.

Thirdly, he reveals his sympathy for Timothy's struggles: *"...being mindful of thy tears."* Perhaps Paul refers to the young preacher's sorrow expressed the last time they parted from each other. Or possibly he has heard that Timothy is feeling emotionally fragile and fatigued these days. Whatever the particular reference to Timothy's fears may be, Paul is evidently saying, "I am aware of your heartache and it touches me deeply." Only love can provoke such tender feelings of sympathy for another.

By Reflecting on His Rich Heritage

Next, Paul encourages Timothy by reflecting on his rich heritage: *"When I call to remembrance the unfeigned faith that is in thee, which dwelt first in thy grandmother Lois, and thy mother Eunice; and I am persuaded that in thee also"* (v.5).

Unfeigned faith is faith without pretense. Timothy's grandmother and mother were true believers (cf. Acts 16:1). Paul expresses great confidence in the sincerity of their faith. These pious Christian women had left an indelible impression on Paul, and he now reflects fondly on their authentic commitment and devotion to Christ.

Further, Paul affirms his confidence in the sincerity of Timothy's faith. He is saying, "Timothy, you have a rich heritage. Both your grandmother and your mother were godly women, and I perceive the same kind of genuine devotion to the Lord in you that I witnessed in them." One can readily see how this reminder of his rich heritage and affirmation of confidence in Timothy's own relationship to the Lord would encourage the young preacher.

By Reminding of His God-Given Responsibilities

Finally, Paul reminds Timothy of his God-given responsibilities: *"Wherefore I put thee in remembrance that thou stir up the gift of God, which is in thee by the putting on of my hands"* (1:6).

In lieu of Paul's personal affection for him and his own Christian heritage, Timothy is now exhorted to industrious faithfulness. *"Stir up the gift of God which is in thee"* implies an obligation on his part. Though this gift is not identified in specific terms, it seems clear that Paul refers to the "gift of preaching," a gift that God endows upon every man he calls into the ministry. He proceeds to indicate that this gift was recognized at Timothy's ordination to the gospel ministry (i.e. *"by the putting on of my hands"*; cf. 1 Tim. 4:14).

When God gives a man a preaching gift, it is intended for the benefit of others, not the man himself. He is, then, a steward—one entrusted with the property of another. He is obligated, therefore, to faithfully manage his stewardship (cf. 1 Cor. 4:2; Rom. 1:14). Paul says to Timothy, "God has given you a special gift, brother. Many of us publicly acknowledged it at your ordination. Therefore, I encourage you to exercise that gift."

The Greek word translated *stir up* literally means "to kindle or revive a fire; to cause to burn; to inflame." Because it is possible for a minister's gift to grow stale and stagnant, he must be diligent to stoke the fire by regular study, reading, meditation, and personal prayer. Without such deliberate effort to keep the embers of zeal burning brightly, a gospel minister (and every believer, for that matter) will soon grow cold and useless in the service of Jesus Christ.

The prophet once bemoaned the fact that none in his day would bestir himself *"to take hold"* of the Lord (cf. Is. 64:7). Paul does not want Timothy to allow discouragement to lead him into spiritual indolence and apathy. May every recipient of God's special gift of gospel ministry rouse himself to energetic service to Christ.

3
Ashamed of the Gospel

For God hath not given us the spirit of fear; but of power, and of love, and of a sound mind. Be not thou therefore ashamed of the testimony of our Lord, nor of me his prisoner: but be thou partaker of the afflictions of the gospel according to the power of God. (2 Timothy 1:7-8)

Timothy's trials at Ephesus were significant. The temptation to soften the gospel because of the threat of persecution was great. The twin emotions of fear and embarrassment—fear concerning potential rejection because of the gospel and embarrassment over the fact that the gospel was increasingly less and less popular and more and more disdained by the world—controlled his thinking. It seemed that he was in danger of becoming ashamed of the gospel.

That temptation to timidity and embarrassment is something with which most believers struggle when they first discover the world's disapproving frown. I'll never forget my first encounter with someone who stridently opposed the Christian gospel. Because I was reared in a Christian home and a small community with traditional, Biblical values, it was quite a shock to me to discover that my university professor was actually antagonistic to the word of God. I had had teachers who were basically neutral, but this particular man was actually antagonistic toward the Biblical worldview. I struggled with the same emotions as Timothy when I sensed that many in the class were sympathetic to his ideas. I felt intimidated, reluctant to speak up, and afraid of becoming an object of ridicule.

Christians exhibit that they are ashamed of the gospel when they try to accommodate the spirit and methods of the world. The popular movement in Christianity toward more "user-friendly" churches, providing entertainment, and jettisoning traditional for contemporary worship styles may each signal a fundamental embarrassment with the church as Jesus Christ established it.

Because the doctrines of human depravity, God's sovereignty in salvation, blood redemption, and the eternal punishment of the wicked offend modern sensibilities, many Christians feel compelled to soften their stance on these issues. Because of the simplicity of the church as Christ set it up, many Primitive Baptists feel a tinge of embarrassment when others question their approach to church life. Because the Biblical emphasis on the supernatural like special creation, the virgin birth, and the bodily resurrection of Christ is so contrary to the naturalistic and skeptical mentality that prevails in our culture, Christian people often feel a bit intimidated by the world. It doesn't take many situations in which a university professor claims that anyone who believes the Bible is ignorant and superstitious to begin to feel that you as a believer are the odd man out.

It is to such people that Paul's poignant words are directed: "*God has not given us the spirit of fear...be not thou therefore ashamed of the testimony of our Lord...*" If the temptation to be ashamed of the gospel was not real, and if Timothy was not struggling with a bit of embarrassment, Paul would have no reason to write, "Don't be ashamed" (cf. Rom. 1:16).

Paul does not want Timothy to allow his emotional struggles to silence his Christian testimony. He urges him to fight back against his own inclinations and inhibitions. He wants him to be courageous and unflinching in the face of opposition. So, he reminds him that *the spirit of fear* (i.e. cowardice, timidity) does not come from God.

How many times did Jesus encourage his disciples to *fear not*? Over 115 times in the Bible, the Holy Spirit reminds God's children to *be not afraid* or *fear not*. In Matthew 10:28, Jesus said, *"Fear not them which can kill the body, but after that they have no more that they can do."* The worst thing that man could ever do to one of God's children is to take away natural life. Man cannot touch the soul. Therefore, we should not fear what man may do unto us.

A resolute trust in God is the antidote to fear (cf. Ps. 56:3). If we know that he is with us (cf. Heb. 13:5; Is. 41:10) and that he loves us with perfect love (cf. 1 Jno. 4:18), then there is no reason to give fear an entrance into our hearts.

Instead of the spirit of fear, God has given us the spirit *of power* (courage). He told Joshua to *"be strong and of a good courage, for the Lord thy God is with thee whithersoever thou goest"* (Jos. 1:9). Paul's own confidence in God made him unflinching in the face of opposition. Such a spirit of holy boldness marked the early saints and reminded people of the spirit of holy boldness that Jesus had exhibited during his own personal ministry (Acts 4:13).

Further, God gives his children the spirit *of love*. He sheds abroad His own love in their hearts by the Holy Ghost which is given unto them (Rom. 5:5), enabling them to look with pity even upon their persecutors (cf. Acts 7:60).

Finally, He gives them a *sound mind*. He enables them to think about life and the world in a healthy, not delusional, way. Their understanding of human depravity enables them to make sense of persecution. Their hope of glory by and by helps them to cope with the present disappointments in this world.

Because God has equipped his people with the resources to enable them to be faithful, they must never be ashamed of the gospel, or of the Lord's people. Instead, they must deem it an honor to partake in the afflictions of the gospel of Jesus Christ our Lord.

Jesus! and shall it ever be
A mortal man ashamed of Thee?
Ashamed of Thee, whom angels praise,
Whose glories shine through endless days?

Ashamed of Jesus? Sooner far
Let evening blush to own a star.
He sheds the beams of light divine
O'er this benighted soul of mine.

Ashamed of Jesus? Just as soon
Let midnight be ashamed of noon.
'Tis midnight with my soul till He,
Bright Morning Star, bids darkness flee.

Ashamed of Jesus, that dear Friend
On whom my hopes of heaven depend?
No; when I blush, be this my shame,
That I no more revere His name.

Ashamed of Jesus? Yes, I may
When I've no guilt to wash away,
No tear to wipe, no joy to crave,
No fears to quell, no soul to save.

Till then — nor is the boasting vain —
Till then I boast a Savior slain.
And oh, may this my portion be,
That Christ is not ashamed of me!

- Joseph Grigg (1722-1768)

4

Partaking of Gospel Afflictions

Be not thou therefore ashamed of the testimony of our Lord, nor of me his prisoner: but be thou partaker of the afflictions of the gospel according to the power of God; who hath saved us, and called us with an holy calling, not according to our works, but according to his own purpose and grace, which was given us in Christ Jesus before the world began, but is now made manifest by the appearing of our Savior Jesus Christ, who hath abolished death, and hath brought life and immortality to light through the gospel: whereunto I am appointed a preacher, and an apostle, and a teacher of the Gentiles. For the which cause I also suffer these things: nevertheless I am not ashamed: for I know whom I have believed, and am persuaded that he is able to keep that which I have committed unto him against that day. (2 Timothy 1:8-12)

Instead of being ashamed of the gospel, Timothy is urged to *partake* (Gr. *koinonia* meaning "to share in common") of the afflictions of the gospel. To equip him with the necessary courage and constraint to meet such a challenge, Paul offers Timothy three helps: 1) An Encouraging Word; 2) A Motivating Truth; 3) A Living Example.

An Encouraging Word

If Timothy is to partake of the afflictions of the gospel, how will he be able to bear such a burden? Paul answers by the phrase *"...according to the power of God."* Timothy can bear gospel afflictions because God's power has been pledged to him.

Power. What an encouraging word! The Greek word *dunamis* refers to inherent ability. It is the word used when Scripture describes the miracles and signs wrought by Christ and the apostles. It is also the word used to speak of the resurrection of Jesus Christ from the dead (cf. Rom. 1:4). Paul is saying that the very same Divine ability exhibited in the mighty works of God and the resurrection of Christ is at Timothy's disposal to enable him to bear the afflictions of the gospel.

With dynamic, resurrection power on his side, Timothy could endure whatever trials he might face. He could do all things through Christ who strengthened him (cf. Phi. 4:13). So can we. It is no wonder that Paul prayed for the saints at Ephesus that they might know *"the exceeding greatness of his power to usward who believe according to the working of his mighty power when he raised [Christ] from the dead"* (Eph. 1:19).

A Motivating Truth

Next, Paul cites a two-fold motivation for partaking of gospel afflictions. First, the gift of salvation should compel Timothy and every believer to gladly bear whatever afflictions a confession of Christ and His truth might bring: *"Who hath saved us and called us with a holy calling; not according to our works, but according to his own purpose and grace, which was given us in Christ Jesus before the world began"* (v. 9).

The God we serve loved His people and purposed their redemption *before the world began*. He further effectually *calls* them to himself by His free and sovereign grace in regeneration. It is a blessing bestowed upon them regardless of any personal merit, for all have sinned and come short of the glory of God. This work of God, planned before time began and applied to the individual in time, is an act of *salvation*, or rescue from danger. Because of God's covenant provisions and application of such through Christ to each object of His eternal love, they need never fear the danger of Divine wrath or eternal separation from the Lord.

Far from encouraging an attitude of slothfulness, this truth stimulates gratitude and motivates the believer to a life of faith and obedience. Even though such a life involves afflictions, the believer deems it an honor to suffer for Jesus' sake.

Secondly, the blessings and benefits we derive from the gospel itself should motivate believers to partake in the afflictions that arise by virtue of associating ourselves with it: *"But is now made manifest by the appearing of our Savior Jesus Christ, who hath abolished death, and hath brought life and immortality to light through the gospel"* (v. 8).

Notice the use of the past tense in this passage: God *"hath saved"* us, *"hath abolished death,"* and *"hath brought life and immortality to light through the gospel."* Such language speaks of the accomplishment of Christ on the cross. If the wages of sin is death and Christ abolished death, then obviously He abolished sin (cf. Rom. 6:23). That is an objective fact.

And that fact is revealed in the gospel. Note that the gospel is not the means of eternal life or immortality. Rather, Christ himself is the means of eternal life. The gospel, however, shines the light on the fact of salvation. Its role is to manifest, reveal, and make known the great benefits that the Savior has procured for us.

Without the light of the gospel, man can only conjecture about ultimate issues. On his deathbed, Socrates said, "I hope to go hence to good men, but of that I am not very confident; nor doth it become any wise man to be positive that so it will be. I must now die, and you shall live; but which of us is in the better state, the living or the dead? God only knows." There is no comfort in speculation.

The gospel not only answers such speculation on the immortality of the soul, it also reveals the resurrection of the body, a truth that the wise men of the ages had no concept of whatsoever. Oh, what light the gospel shines upon every subject!

Is it any wonder that Paul would cite the glorious benefits of the gospel as an incentive to participate in the afflictions of the gospel? No doubt, he intends to say that the blessings associated with the gospel message far outweigh whatever conflicts we as believers are called upon to endure on its behalf.

5
Be Faithful

For the which cause I also suffer these things: nevertheless I am not ashamed: for I know whom I have believed, and am persuaded that he is able to keep that which I have committed unto him against that day. Hold fast the form of sound words, which thou hast heard of me, in faith and love which is in Christ Jesus. That good thing which was committed unto thee keep by the Holy Ghost which dwelleth in us. This thou knowest, that all they which are in Asia be turned away from me; of whom are Phygellus and Hermogenes. The Lord give mercy unto the house of Onesiphorus; for he oft refreshed me, and was not ashamed of my chain: but, when he was in Rome, he sought me out very diligently, and found me. The Lord grant unto him that he may find mercy of the Lord in that day: and in how many things he ministered unto me at Ephesus, thou knowest very well. (2 Timothy 1:12-18)*

Paul wants Timothy to be willing to suffer for the gospel, not to succumb to the temptation to be ashamed of the gospel. In order to achieve that objective, he encourages him with a reminder of Divine empowerment (v. 8b), and reminds him of God's saving grace as a powerful incentive to faithfulness (vs. 9-10). Now, he cites himself as a living example of unashamed fidelity to the Savior, even in the face of persecution: *"For the which cause I also suffer these things: nevertheless I am not ashamed: for I know whom I have believed and am persuaded that he is able to keep that which I have committed unto him against that day"* (v. 12).

This autobiographical snapshot is intended to influence Timothy to be faithful in his ministry and Christian confession. Paul is not characteristically self-focused. When he does refer to himself and his experience, it is always with a view to offering others an example or object lesson of what it means to respond Christianly to a given situation. It is a tactful way of saying, "Timothy, this is my perspective on suffering for the sake of the gospel, and it should be yours too. I am not ashamed, and neither should you be ashamed of the gospel."

Why was Paul unashamed of Christ and his gospel even though it had brought him such difficulty? Because he knew that the God in whom he trusted was able to protect and preserve him. Such a familiarity with God's character lends itself to this firm persuasion that the Bible calls "faith."

Faith in God, in other words, is the secret of faithfulness to God. Paul approached his life and ministry with a conscious commitment to resist the urge to protect himself, and to rather abandon himself to the safekeeping of Christ. He was content to leave his reputation, his physical comfort, his personal safety, and his daily provision to the One whom he knew to be both trustworthy and able to provide his needs.

The strong tone of confidence Paul expressed must have resonated in Timothy's heart. "Indeed," he thought, "I have lost sight of the Lord. If Paul can endure the pressures of serving Christ —pressures that are greater than my own—then I surely can and should too." Strength and resolve under the pressure of affliction is a powerful example to our brethren of the Lord's capacity to sustain His faithful servants.

The three verbs in verse 12—*believed, persuaded, committed*—reveal the secret of Paul's resilience. His entire life might be summarized in these three terms (cf. Acts 27:25; Rom. 8:38; Acts 20:24). Whatever risk is involved in turning oneself over, totally and completely, to the Lord Jesus Christ is minimized when one can say with Paul, "I know *whom* I have believed."

Having cited his own personal experience, Paul is now ready to urge Timothy to faithfulness: *"Hold fast the form of sound words, which thou hast heard of me, in faith and love which is in Christ Jesus. That good thing which was committed unto thee keep by the Holy Ghost which dwelleth in us"* (vs. 13-14). Timothy is to adhere to the "sketch" or "outline" that he had heard from Paul—the *"form of sound words."* These *sound* or wholesome words (see 1 Tim. 6:3) are called such because they are conducive to the healthy state of the church. His steadfast commitment to these basic truths is to be marked by the twin graces of *"faith and love"*—faith toward God and love toward others.

Paul makes reference to Timothy's stewardship of the truth of Christ in the clause *"that good thing which was committed to thee"* (cf. 1 Tim. 6:20). The doctrine of Christ is indeed a *"good thing"*—the word *good* referring to that which is aesthetically beautiful, expressing harmony, balance, and proportion. Therefore, Timothy is to *keep* (or guard) it. He must never be careless in his attitude toward the truth of the gospel, but vigilant and protective of such a sacred trust. And how may he achieve such a level of faithful stewardship? Paul answers, *"by the Holy Ghost which dwelleth in us."*

In verses 15-18, Paul reverts once more to his own experience, citing two further examples—one negative and the other positive—for Timothy's benefit. The first is an example of infidelity: *"This thou knowest, that all they which are in Asia be turned away from me; of whom are Phygellus and Hermogenes"* (v. 15). By implication, Paul employs this case, one which was familiar to Timothy, to gently warn him not to defect like they did from the path of obedience. Such defections in the ministry bring great sadness to the hearts of those who, like Paul, love the Lord and his gospel above everything else.

Then he cites the positive example of someone who had demonstrated an unashamed and unflinching fidelity to Christ and his servant Paul: *"The Lord give mercy to the house of Onesiphorus; for he oft refreshed me and was not ashamed of my chain. But when he was in Rome, he sought me out very diligently, and found me. The Lord grant unto him that he may find mercy of the Lord in that day: and in how many things he ministered unto me at Ephesus, thou knowest very well"* (vs. 16-18).

Obviously, Paul wants to urge Timothy to follow the example of Onesiphorus in laboring indefatigably and unashamedly in the service of Christ, even though it may involve personal sacrifice. Though Paul was indeed a lonely man in prison, Onesiphorus had encouraged him in the Lord. He had proven himself faithful at a time when others had buckled beneath the load. Perhaps the Holy Spirit used this example to buoy Timothy's flagging faith so that he too might prove to be a faithful servant of Christ and His people.

6
True Apostolic Succession

Thou therefore my son, be strong in the grace that is in Christ Jesus. And the things that thou hast heard of me among many witnesses, the same commit thou unto faithful men who shall be able to teach others also. (2 Timothy 2:1-2)

In chapter two, Paul continues his effort to encourage Timothy and spur him to action. He does so by way of two admonitions (vs. 1-2) and three word-pictures that serve to illustrate the nature of the gospel ministry (vs. 3-6). Let's consider the admonitions of verses one and two.

Be Strong

The imperative *"be strong"* suggests the need for courage and steadfastness. In modern vernacular, Paul might have imbibed the young preacher to "get tough," for the expressions mean the same thing. Neither the gospel ministry nor the Christian life is a picnic. Both involve the need for courage, perseverance, and tough-mindedness.

How might Timothy comply with this imperative to be strong? The answer resides in the expression *"in the grace that is in Christ Jesus."* He will find the source of his strength in the grace of Christ, not in himself. Just as the Ephesian saints were to *"be strong in the Lord and the power of His might"* (cf. Eph. 6:10), so Timothy is to rely on the grace, or the unmerited gifts and resources, that only the Lord Jesus Christ can impart.

Commit to Faithful Men

Why must Timothy *be strong*? Because he will play a crucial role in the future of the church of God. It is his responsibility to keep the relay of apostolic truth going. Verse two describes a principle that we might call "true apostolic succession."

The idea of "apostolic succession" is a staple of Roman Catholic theology and the basis of its claim to authority. Catholics insist, and rightly so, that apostolicity is a mark of the true church. Further, Catholicism claims that the Roman pontiffs are the successors of the apostles, occupying the official position of, the apostle Peter.[1]

The claim is that when Peter died in Rome, he ended his pontificate, and that the Bishops of Rome who came after him occupied his authoritative, apostolic office. Catholicism builds an historical case for papal succession to the present day, insisting that each new pontiff serves in the apostolic office.

Though the details differ, the Baptists have likewise claimed a line of historical succession to the early church. While Catholicism argues for their link to the true church on the basis of the continuation of the apostolic office, some Baptists[2] argue on the grounds of an unbroken line of baptisms.

I reject Catholicism's claim for apostolic succession by virtue of the Biblical principle that we have no more apostles in the church today. The New Testament teaches that the apostolic office was only temporary (cf. Eph. 2:20; Rev. 2:2; Heb. 2:3-4; Eph. 3:3). Paul claims to be the last of the apostles for he was the last one to *see* the risen Christ (cf. 1 Cor. 15:7-9). There is no man living today who could possibly meet the three tests of apostolicity (i.e. apostles were recipients of direct revelation, eyewitnesses of the risen Christ, and endowed with capacity to do signs and wonders).

I am also skeptical of the evidence by which some Baptists trace their lineage to the primitive church by an unbroken line of

1   Catholic Encyclopaedia.
2   As in B. H. Carroll's "Trail of Blood"

baptisms. Though I have encountered several interesting arguments for this position, the evidence for historical succession always seems a bit forced or coerced.

One might wonder, then, is there such a thing as "apostolic succession"? The answer is "yes." There is a true church that manifests the criteria of apostolicity in this world. Its "succession," however, is not necessarily *historical,* but *theological.*

In other words, the real test of a church's apostolic authenticity is not determined by whether or not it can establish a historical connection to the apostles. Instead, it is determined by asking the question, "Does this church proclaim the apostolic gospel and function according to the apostolic pattern?"

Notice the four generations included in verse two: (1) Paul taught (2) Timothy the truth; Timothy, in turn, was to pass that truth on to (3) "faithful men," who were then to disseminate it to (4) "others also." This is true apostolic succession.

On a practical note, we might ask ourselves if we share Paul's passion for the communication of the apostolic gospel to others. Are we interested in the future of the true gospel? Do we have this long-term, transgenerational perspective for the kingdom of God?

Unlike Hezekiah, David was not merely concerned about "peace in his days" (cf. Is. 39:8). He was also concerned about the generations to come (cf. Ps. 102:18; 145:4). So was the prophet Joel (cf. Joel 1:3). If we are truly committed to the gospel of the Lord Jesus Christ, we must also adopt this long-term, far-reaching mentality concerning the cause of God and truth. May we start with our own families (cf. Deut. 6:5ff), seeking to inculcate the truth of God's word to our children, and never fail to faithfully run our leg in this perpetual relay of truth.

> *Give ear, O my people, to my law: incline your ears to the words of my mouth.*
>
> *I will open my mouth in a parable: I will utter dark sayings of old:*

Which we have heard and known, and our fathers have told us.

We will not hide them from their children, shewing to the generation to come the praises of the LORD, and his strength, and his wonderful works that he hath done.

For he established a testimony in Jacob, and appointed a law in Israel, which he commanded our fathers, that they should make them known to their children:

That the generation to come might know them, even the children which should be born; who should arise and declare them to their children:

That they might set their hope in God, and not forget the works of God, but keep his commandments:

And might not be as their fathers, a stubborn and rebellious generation; a generation that set not their heart aright, and whose spirit was not steadfast with God.

- Psalm 78:1-8

7

The Nature of the Gospel Ministry

Thou therefore endure hardness, as a good soldier of Jesus Christ. No man that warreth entangleth himself with the affairs of this life; that he may please him who hath chosen him to be a soldier. And if a man also strive for masteries, yet is he not crowned, except he strive lawfully. The husbandman that laboreth must be first partaker of the fruits. Consider what I say; and the Lord give thee understanding in all things. (2 Timothy 2:3-7)

In verses 3-7, Paul employs three vivid metaphors to emphasize the nature of the ministry to which Timothy had been called. First, he compares the gospel ministry to the life of a soldier; next, to the performance of an athlete. Finally, he illustrates the nature of the ministry by comparing it to the activity of a farmer. Let's consider these three images.

A Soldier

The first parallel between the ministry and the life of a soldier is that it is a life of hardship; therefore, endurance is critical (v. 3). A soldier does not expect to carry out his duties in an atmosphere of luxury and personal comfort. Instead, he understands that sleeping on the hard ground with nothing but the stars as his canopy, eating rations from a can, and living in daily jeopardy of his life is part and parcel of his commission.

Even so, the gospel ministry is fraught with hardship. The language Jesus employed to describe John the Baptist in Matthew 11:8 suggests that much. The minister must not harbor any preconceived notions concerning the kind of treatment he will receive from people. He must not be overly sensitive, or soft and wimpy about the rigorous time demands, energy required, or significant emotional challenges associated with his calling.

It is not an easy thing to consider that one's calling may require him to relocate every so often, especially if he has a family that has put down roots in a certain place. Neither is it comfortable to be "on call" 24/7, or to try to live up to the expectations of others. Criticism "goes with the territory" and rare is the minister who does not feel the sting of its barbs. Hardness is indigenous to the gospel ministry, just as it is to the life of a soldier.

Preachers like soldiers, therefore, must make up their minds in advance that they will persevere, i.e. keep on keeping on. A long-term mentality—"I'm in it for the long haul—"is basic and fundamental to the minister's approach to his God-given tasks.

Further, like a soldier, a preacher must not become too enamored with *"the affairs of this life"* (v. 4). Warriors keep their priorities in order. Nothing takes precedence over the battle he has been enlisted to fight. Though America boasts a para-military of "weekend warriors," the Roman army of Paul's day knew nothing of the kind. Soldiers were "full-time" servants of the king. Even so, gospel ministers must not so entangle themselves in the world that they are only "part-time" servants of Christ.

An Athlete

Next, Paul employs the image of an athlete to describe the nature of the gospel ministry: *"And if a man strive for the masteries, yet is he not crowned, except he strive lawfully"* (v. 5).

A runner competing for the gold medal in the Olympic games must run according to the rules, else he will be disqualified. Even so, the gospel minister is not at liberty to function in this office according to his own preferences. If he once adopts the attitude of the maverick and presumes to offer "strange fire" (cf. Lev. 10:1-7), he has overstepped his bounds and may very well be disqualified.

Paul knew that even after he had preached to others, he himself could become a "castaway" (cf. 1 Cor. 9:27). Every minister "worth his salt," as the saying goes, knows the same thing. He realizes that if he does not carry out his responsibilities according to the principles laid down in God's word, he risks removal from the game and perhaps, even expulsion from the team. The end does not justify the means in the service of Christ. How sad it is to expend great effort and energy to finish the race, only to be disqualified because of a bad attitude, unethical tactics, or some moral of theological lapse in one's life! And no one, regardless of past usefulness, is exempt from such a possibility: *"He that doeth wrong shall receive for the wrong which he hath done: and there is no respect of persons"* (Col. 3:25).

A Farmer

Finally, the ministry is similar to farming: *"The husbandman [farmer] that laboreth must be first partaker of the fruits"* (v. 6). Paul cites a generally accepted principle in agriculture, namely, that the man who plants and cultivates the crop is the first to taste the harvest.

Even so, the preacher who proclaims the word must first internalize and incarnate that word in his own life. He must never merely function in a mechanical way. Instead, he should preach from his own experience. The things he teaches others must be things he understands and practices himself. Taking sermons from the internet or a "pastor's annual" may very well violate this principle of personally digesting the message one shares with others.

When ministry of the word is coupled with personal testimony — i.e. when a preacher preaches from the overflow of his own experience of a genuine devotion to Christ and authentic discipleship — the sermon will be a real message from God instead of a weekly homily or lecture.

Paul adds the exhortation, *"Consider what I say and the Lord give you understanding in all things"* (v. 7). Timothy needed this reminder. He was facing a time of hardship in his ministry. He needed to be encouraged to endure, to remain committed, to play by the rules, and to minister from his heart.

8

Reasons to Persevere

Remember that Jesus Christ of the seed of David was raised from the dead according to my gospel: wherein I suffer trouble, as an evil doer, even unto bonds; but the word of God is not bound. Therefore I endure all things for the elect's sakes, that they may also obtain the salvation which is in Christ Jesus with eternal glory. It is a faithful saying: For if we be dead with him, we shall also live with him: If we suffer, we shall also reign with him: if we deny him, he also will deny us: if we believe not, yet he abideth faithful: he cannot deny himself. (2 Timothy 2:8-13)

After describing the nature of the gospel ministry in such vivid metaphors, Paul returns to the language of exhortation in verses 8-13. He wants Timothy to be faithful, to keep-on-keeping-on, to endure, to persevere. To that end, he gives him several reasons to "keep to the path" in these verses.

The Resurrection of Jesus Christ (v. 8)

Paul first incites Timothy to remember that Jesus Christ is alive: *"Remember that Jesus Christ of the seed of David was raised again from the dead according to my gospel."* I know of no incentive to faithfulness more powerful and compelling than this.

The reference to David's lineage, i.e. *"...of the seed of David,"* is Paul's way of emphasizing the human nature of Jesus (cf. Mt. 1:1). Here, as well as in Romans 1:3-4, Paul employs this expression to remind his readers that the genuine humanness of Jesus is as central to the gospel he preached as his deity. It is a title that sets the Christ of faith in his historical context. That the Second Divine Person assumed a real and genuine human nature in the incarnation as the fulfillment of the Davidic covenant (cf. 2 Sam. 7: Is. 11:1; Jer. 23:5; Eze. 34:23) is a key emphasis of the apostolic gospel. *Remembering* the fact of his incarnation and real humanity is a safeguard to troublesome Christological heresies like Arianism and Apollinarianism, emphases of the Jehovah's Witness cult and other non-Christian religions.

But Paul's *gospel* not only affirms the fact of the incarnation, but also the fact of the resurrection. Paul preached that the man Christ Jesus who came to die for the sins of God's elect *was raised again from the dead*. David's royal seed, and consequently, his kingly dynasty, continues.

To say that "Jesus lives" does not mean that He lives on merely by virtue of His ongoing influence or in terms of His legacy. Sometimes adoring fans claim that "Elvis lives," by which statement they mean that he lives on through his music and in the memories of his fans. But Jesus does not merely live in the memories of His followers, or through the vehicle of His church. He actually and personally lives.

How Christ's servants need to *"remember that Jesus Christ"* is alive! The resurrection of Christ means that He has already solved our biggest problem; therefore, no other problem we will ever encounter is a match for him. Because He lives, I can face every tomorrow. What an incentive to persevere!

The Power of God's Word (v. 9)

Paul's mention of the gospel that he preached reminds him, once more, of the afflictions he was suffering for the gospel's sake: *"Wherein I suffer trouble as an evildoer, even unto bonds..."* Again, he returns to the issue at hand, i.e. Timothy's fear of persecution. And he admits that trouble does indeed follow allegiance to the gospel.

But, then, he adds another reason to persevere: *"...but the word of God is not bound."*

Though God's servant was restrained by fetters and chains, God's gospel was not. In fact, the gospel seemed to grow as rapidly as compound interest as a result of Paul's imprisonment (cf. Phi. 1:12-13). As Paul reflected on his first incarceration and remembered how the Philippian jailor was converted, leading to the baptism of his entire family, and how even members of Caesar's household (probably soldiers in the Praetorian Guard) were won to the faith as they rotated six-hour shifts of being chained to the Baptist preacher (cf. Phi. 4:22), his confidence in the Lord was vivified: *"...the word of God is not bound."* No wonder he tended to think of himself as *"an ambassador in bonds"* (cf. Eph. 6:20)! In spite of his circumstances, Paul lived to preach the good news of Christ crucified.

Would not such a reflection encourage Timothy to persevere? If the capacity of Christ's gospel to influence lives was no greater than the preacher's physical ability and circumstances—i.e. if the power of the gospel was limited by human limitations—then there would be little incentive to be faithful when the way is hard. But seeing that the gospel is not limited by physical obstacles, there is every reason to be faithful to proclaim it.

A Salvation for the Elect (v. 10)

Thirdly, Paul indicates by communicating his own example of total commitment to the gospel of Christ that Timothy should be willing to endure suffering for the sake of God's elect: *"Therefore I endure all things for the elect's sakes, that they may also obtain the salvation which is in Christ Jesus with eternal glory."*

Paul wants Timothy to put the welfare of God's people above his own. The driving passion of Paul's heart was that God's children might find the salvation that comes through the gospel (cf. Rom. 10:1-3). The word *also* suggests the thought of "in addition to." His point is clear. There is a salvation in Christ Jesus that has to do with *"eternal glory."* All of God's elect will enjoy this salvation. But in addition to that, there is another salvation in Christ that comes by means of the gospel. It is a salvation from error, worldly entrapments, a sense of hopelessness, despair, and futility. Paul's sufferings have nothing whatsoever to do with the eternal salvation of God's elect. But they have much to do with their gospel salvation.

Because the word of God is not bound, and because God's children need the liberation, joy, and peace that comes through the gospel, Paul was willing to endure personal hardship to that end. What greater example of "neighbor love" exists than his sacrificial example? Timothy, he might have said, don't give up, for many more of God's elect need the gospel salvation that you now enjoy.

A Faithful Saying (vs. 11-13)

Finally, Paul reminds Timothy of an axiomatic truth as an incentive to stick-to-it: *"It is a faithful saying: For if we be dead with him, we shall also live with him; if we suffer, we shall also reign with him: if we deny him, he will also deny us: If we believe not, yet he abideth faithful: he cannot deny himself."* Of course, an axiom is an evident truth—a well established, generally accepted fact. Christian people everywhere, says Paul, concur with the great doctrine of spiritual union with Christ. And because God in his marvelous grace has brought us into a relational oneness with Christ, the best is yet to come. The saints are preserved in grace, and though this life involves suffering and adversity, glory is coming for all those Jesus Christ represented in his death, burial and resurrection.

But an eternal security premised on Divine faithfulness does not guarantee a life of temporal blessedness in the interim. Gospel blessings and the assurance of salvation may be forfeited in this world if the child of God lives in disobedience to the Father.

Simply put, this axiomatic statement might be summarized as follows: "Timothy, remember that you cannot lose your eternal salvation. Even unbelief is covered by His blood. But you may experience the withdrawal of His daily fellowship if you fail to be faithful to Him."

Is the loss of Christ's manifest presence and smiling favor a significant loss in the life of the child of God? Absolutely! It means that though the child of grace will live in glory at last, yet he may forfeit every blessing worth having this side of eternal bliss. He may lose his sanity, his family, his assurance, his joy, his home in the church, and so much more. This sobering "reality check" is yet another reason to persevere, to faithfully endure in the life of Christian discipleship and gospel profession.

9

An Approved Workman

Of these things put them in remembrance, charging them before the Lord that they strive not about words to no profit, but to the subverting of the hearers. Study to shew thyself approved unto God, a workman that needeth not to be ashamed, rightly dividing the word of truth. But shun profane and vain babblings: for they will increase unto more ungodliness. And their word will eat as doth a canker: of whom is Hymenaeus and Philetus; who concerning the truth have erred, saying that the resurrection is past already; and overthrow the faith of some. Nevertheless the foundation of God standeth sure, having this seal, The Lord knoweth them that are his. And, Let every one that nameth the name of Christ depart from iniquity. (2 Timothy 2:14-19)

In verses 14-19, Paul discusses four concepts that are key to Christian ministry: *the primacy of truth, the peril of error, the preeminence of grace,* and *the priority of holiness.* An understanding of these four principles will help Timothy to be proactive, not reactive, in his ministry.

Truth (vs. 14-16)

A fourth metaphor in this chapter describing the nature of the gospel ministry is now employed. The minister is *a workman.* The word *study* includes the idea of diligence. Like any kind of worker or laborer whose work will be inspected, the minister must not be lazy, but diligent in his labors, so that he will have no cause to be ashamed when his work is inspected: "*Study to show thyself approved unto God, a workman that needeth not to be ashamed...*"

His goal is to be an *approved*, not an *ashamed* worker (cf. 2:4; Gal. 1:10; 1 Ths. 2:4). Hence, his preoccupation must be with "*the word of truth,*" not "*profane and vain babblings,*" an expression that suggests the thought of disputing about verbal trifles (vs. 14, 16). He knows that a war of words does not profit but rather subverts (overthrows) the hearers (v. 14b). Commenting on this verse, Warren Wiersbe writes, "I fear that some 'sharing times' do more harm than good as well-meaning people exchange their 'spiritual ignorance'." Since social media has given a teaching platform to every non-credentialed bible "scholar" and the equally opinionated bible "experts" who critique their thoughts, we have a real-world example of Paul's warning in these verses.

Instead, the minister is to be a student of the word, mining from its depths treasures both old and new (cf. Mt. 13:52). Paul wants Timothy to be neither ashamed before men (cf. 1:8) nor to have occasion to be ashamed before God when his labors are judged (cf. 2:15).

In order to be an approved worker, the minister must not only shun laziness and godless chatter, but he must also avoid biblical carelessness. A trustworthy worker takes special care of the tools of his trade; likewise, the unashamed gospel workman takes special care to handle the word of God accurately.

Instead of biblical carelessness, he is to "*rightly divide the word of truth.*" The phrase literally means "to cut straight" and suggests the thought of accuracy in Biblical interpretation. Just as a farmer plows a straight row, and a seamstress cuts a straight line, so the studious workman in the word of truth is careful to teach each aspect of God's word so that it fits harmoniously together to make a coherent whole.

Vincent says of this phrase:

"The thought is that the minister of the gospel is to present the truth rightly, not abridging it, not handling it as a charlatan (2 Cor. 2:17), not making it a matter of wordy strife (2 Tim. 2:14), but treating it honestly and fully, in a straight forward way."[1]

Biblical truth is primary in Christian ministry; therefore, the gospel minister must work to discover the sense of the text, never allowing himself to be mentally sluggish in such an important task.

The old stereotype of ministry as a sedentary life marked by soft hands and big bellies could not be more foreign to the biblical model. Paul wants Timothy to work hard, to stretch his mental muscles, to burn the midnight oil, to put strenuous effort into biblical discovery, accurate interpretation, and pulpit excellence.

Error (vs. 17-18)

Paul proceeds in verses 17-18 to discuss the peril of error. An approved workman knows the danger of false doctrine. First, it *"will increase unto more ungodliness"* (v. 16b). This expression indicates that there is a connection between ideas and ethics — between what a person believes and how a person behaves. Erroneous thinking inevitably leads to erroneous living. Ideas have real-life consequences.

Second, error will acts as a *canker*, i.e. gangrene, spreading, infecting, and destroying the rest of the body. False teaching is not merely a static annoyance that the church can afford to overlook, but a dynamic mutation that will soon metastasize to invade and destroy the entire body of believers unless it is exposed and removed.

As an illustration of the destructive nature of theological error, Paul cites the case of Hymanaeus and Philetus, *"who concerning the truth have erred, saying that the resurrection is past already"* (v. 18). Perhaps these two men were teaching that the resurrection

---

1   Marvin R. Vincent, *The Word Studies in the New Testament (Vol. 4)*

occurred when many people who slept in the graves awoke after the resurrection of Jesus (cf. Mt. 27:53). Or possibly they were teaching that the resurrection was only a "spiritual resurrection," occurring at the point a person is born again. Whatever the particular logic of their argument, this much is evident—they were taking a future event and applying it to the past. They were not *"rightly dividing the word of truth."*

Was it a material deviation from the truth? Paul indicates that it was. In fact, Hymanaeus and Philetus gained a following. Their error had the effect of *"overthrowing the faith of some."* Perhaps a desire to be novel and sensational motivated this departure from the apostolic doctrine of the bodily resurrection at the last day. Whatever the motive, this error grew like an infectious disease within the church.

Grace (v. 19a)

Does the fact that the faith of these poor souls was overthrown mean that they were either not truly regenerated or that they lost their eternal salvation? Not at all; Paul says, *"Nevertheless..."*, i.e. in spite of the fact that they were led astray into error, *"...the foundation of God standeth sure having this seal, The Lord knoweth them that are his."*

A confused mind does not equate to apostasy from a state of grace, for *"the foundation of God standeth sure having this seal, The Lord knoweth them that are his."* This is one of the greatest eternal security verses in the Bible, teaching that even man's unbelief (or overthrown faith) does not negate God's covenant faithfulness.

Paul exhorts Timothy to be concerned about the peril of error, but, at the same time, to rest in the preserving power of Divine grace. Truth is vitally important and error is extremely perilous, but neither determines the eternal destiny of God's elect. Instead, truth and error have everything to do with true worship and faithful service to God in this life.

Holiness (v. 19b)

Finally, Paul reminds Timothy that the doctrine of grace is not a license to sin: *"And let every one who nameth the name of Christ depart from iniquity."* Eternal preservation is not an excuse or justification for sinful living.

Instead, this truth, when properly understood, promotes holiness of life. It is error that leads to ungodliness (v. 16). The truth of salvation by grace is the greatest incentive to godliness a person will ever know. Let every professing Christian, therefore, depart from iniquity.

By recalling these five key terms and teaching them proactively to the church, Timothy may be an approved and unashamed workman in the service of the great God of heaven.

10
Vessels of Honor

But in a great house there are not only vessels of gold and of silver, but also of wood and of earth; and some to honor, and some to dishonor. If a man therefore purge himself from these, he shall be a vessel unto honor, sanctified, and meet for the master's use, and prepared unto every good work. Flee also youthful lusts: but follow righteousness, faith, charity, peace, with them that call on the Lord out of a pure heart. (2 Timothy 2:20-22)

The preacher is not only compared to a soldier, an athlete, a farmer, and a workman, he is also now compared to *a vessel.* But what kind of vessel will he be — honorable or dishonorable?

After talking about the sure foundation on which our eternal security rests, Paul proceeds to discuss the practical aspect of this truth: *"But in a great house there are not only vessels of gold and of silver, but also of wood and earth; and some to honor and some to dishonor."* Though we rejoice in the good news of eternal security, we must not become lazy or slothful in our service to the Lord. The *foundation* of this *great house* is solid, for it depends solely upon God for its strength. But the utensils that are used in the ordinary course of daily life within the house may be either *vessels of honor* or *of dishonor*, depending upon whether or not a person is committed to Christ and his service.

Paul employs an illustration with which we can identify. In any house, one may find both very expensive vessels like china, crystal, and gold or silver utensils, and very crude vessels, like garbage cans, grease buckets, and bed pans. Even so, in the family of God, there are vessels of honor, i.e. people whose lives are useful and holy, and vessels of dishonor, i.e. people who are living below the level of their privileges in Christ. The *vessels* in this passage stand for people (cf. Acts 9:15).

Paul wants Timothy to *"purge himself from these,"* that is, not to be contaminated by the dishonorable vessels by becoming too involved with this world. Every believer must make a conscious effort to protect himself from the corrupting influences of worldly-minded men (cf. Ps. 1:1; 1 Cor. 15:33; Jas. 1:27b), to be thoroughly committed to the Lord Jesus Christ, and to rise above the kind of mediocrity that characterizes the lives of so many people. The name Timothy means "God-honoring"; hence, Paul essentially exhorts him here to live up to his name.

In a word, Paul wants Timothy to strive for excellence in ministry —to be the best servant of Christ that he could possibly be—to be available. If he rises above the *status quo*, Timothy will be an honorable vessel to the Lord, one that the Master will deem to be valuable (*"sanctified"*) and *fit* for use in His service.

"Sanctified and meet for the Master's use..." *Sanctified* means "separated for a holy purpose." Just as a householder keeps his most precious china in special cabinet, bringing it forth for use on very special occasions, so the Lord Jesus takes those who have committed themselves to Him and employs them to do His special bidding. The obscure preacher named Ananias must have been such a devoted and pious servant, for Christ employed him for the special task of proclaiming the gospel to Paul (Acts 9). I have always been just a bit surprised that the Lord did not choose Peter, John or one of the other apostles for that task, but an ordinary minister who is mentioned neither before nor after this episode. Ananias was a vessel fit for the Master's use, and the Master used him at this important moment in Christian history.

Paul and Barnabas, likewise, were honorable vessels, fit for the Master's use, as Acts 13:2 indicates. God used them in a very special evangelistic effort as the gospel spread into Asia Minor. There is no greater honor than to be deemed fit for holy service by the Master.

Human vessels of honor must not only be available, they must also be clean: "*Flee also youthful lusts: but follow after righteousness, faith, charity, peace, with them that call on the Lord out of a pure heart.*" The old preacher put it succinctly: "God's people like good food, but they like it on a clean platter."

It is likely that lust, like pride, is a problem for virtually everyone, but particularly so for the young. Timothy must be ready, therefore, to run away from temptation of this stripe. Like Joseph who fled from the wife of Potiphar, Timothy must make a conscious and deliberate effort to get away from lust. Only then can he "*possess his vessel in sanctification and honor*" (1 Ths. 4:4).

Then after making an effort to flee sexual immorality, Timothy must *follow after* (lit. pursue) a nobler goal than personal gratification. His life ambition must focus on *righteousness*, i.e. obedience to God's word, *faith*, i.e. trust in God's name, *charity*, i.e. love for God's people, and *peace*, i.e. inner quietness from God's presence.

If he takes this high road, will he be alone in life? No, for there are others who seek the same goal: "*...with them that call on the Lord out of a pure heart.*" They, too, want to be honorable vessels in the service of Christ. They share this godly ambition — this holy unction to live truly Christian lives.

Do we regularly think of ourselves as vessels in the Lord's house? What kind of vessel are you — honorable or dishonorable?

11
Dealing with Contentious People

But foolish and unlearned questions avoid, knowing that they do gender strifes. And the servant of the Lord must not strive; but be gentle unto all men, apt to teach, patient, in meekness instructing those that oppose themselves; if God peradventure will give them repentance to the acknowledging of the truth; and that they may recover themselves out of the snare of the devil, who are taken captive by him at his will. (2 Timothy 2:23-26)

Paul concludes this chapter on the nature of the gospel ministry with an exhortation concerning the spirit and attitude in which that ministry should be conducted. After warning Timothy once again about the dangers of being preoccupied with trifling questions, he says: *"And the servant of the Lord must not strive; but be gentle unto all men, apt to teach, patient, in meekness instructing those that oppose themselves; if God peradventure will give them repentance to the acknowledging of the truth; and that they may recover themselves out of the snare of the devil, who are taken captive by him at his will."*

How important is this passage for every minister, for rare is the man who will not need to engage with religious detractors at some point in his ministry! Paul wants Timothy to know that the manner in which he interacts with critics and opponents is crucial.

To introduce this final exhortation, Paul employs one more metaphor concerning the nature of gospel ministry. He has already compared a minister to a soldier, athlete, farmer, workman, and vessel. Now he reminds Timothy that a minister is a *bondslave*.

A minister is a *"servant (Gr. doulos) of the Lord."* A *doulos*, or bondservant, was one bound completely to a master so that he/she had no freedom apart from the master's will. Unlike a mere employee whose loyalty to an employer is determined by contract, a *doulos*, or slave, was not his own but the sole possession of his master.

By keeping this subservient position in mind—namely, that I am the property of another—the gospel minister will be equipped to maintain perspective when the work of ministry seems especially challenging. One of the most significant of these ministerial challenges is the exacting task of dealing with difficult people.

Like every minister, Timothy had ample occasion in Ephesus to deal with people who are fond of contention. So Paul warns him against the danger of adopting the same kind of fighting spirit.

The word *strive* speaks of "a quarrelsome spirit." It is translated "to fight" in James 4:2 and suggests the thought of someone who is contentious. Gospel ministers must not allow themselves to become argumentative. They must never allow a pugnacious spirit to manifest itself in discussion of scripture. The goal is not to embarrass an opponent or even to win an argument. It is to protect the little lambs from deception and if possible, to convert the detractor. Yes, the minister should never shrink from defending the truth of God when necessary, but he must always do so with candor and kindness.

In place of this quarrelsome spirit, the minister is to be *"gentle unto all men."* Just as Paul dealt gently with the Thessalonian believers (cf. 1 Ths. 2:7), every preacher should exhibit genuine love and tenderness toward those whom he serves, even those who are disputatious.

Further, instead of adopting the spirit of the contentious individual, the minister must be *"apt to teach"* and *"patient."* The Greek word translated *patient*, meaning "patient under personal injury," occurs only here in the New Testament. It suggests the idea of lacking resentment even when suffering mistreatment.

The expression *apt to teach* is explained now in verse 25: "*In meekness instructing those that oppose themselves...*" The real problem with contentious persons, says Paul, is that they are ignorant of the truth and need to be instructed. The minister's approach to such cases must be to calmly show them what the truth is. And if they are reluctant to embrace it, he must continue to try to convince them of their error. If he can but remember that such persons have been ensnared by the devil, it will make him compassionate to their plight.

Yes, there may be a time when the quarrelsome individual so persists in such an ungodly attitude that attempts to instruct him may only exacerbate the tension. At such a time, the Biblical counsel to leave a person to himself is plain: "*Make no friendship with an angry man and with a furious man thou shalt not go, lest thou learn his ways and get a snare to thy soul*" (cf. Pro. 22:24). But until then, the servant of the Lord must be patient, meek, and persistent in his attempts to instruct such a one.

Verses 25b-26 paint the plight of the contentious person in very graphic terms. Two practical lessons might be deduced from these verses.

First, people tend to be their own worst enemies: "*...instructing those that oppose themselves.*" Walt Kelly's famous comic strip character Pogo Possum put it poignantly: "We have met the enemy and he is us." There is nothing more self-destructive than a spirit of bitterness and animosity. It actually harms the person who harbors it, more than the person at whom the anger is directed (cf. Mt. 18:34).

Secondly, the potential success of any attempt to rescue the contentious party is a two-sided coin. Success depends first on God's grace: "*...if God peradventure will give them repentance to the acknowledging of the truth.*" The word *peradventure* suggests that this may or may not happen. There is hope that God will intervene and tender the hard heart of his disobedient child, but ultimately, restoration depends on Him. Sometimes people reach a point that nothing but Divine intervention can rescue them from the road they are traveling.

Success also depends on the person himself/herself: *"And that they may recover themselves out of the snare of the devil."* In the final analysis, this individual must swallow his/her pride and admit that he has strayed from the Lord and his word. Responsibility for such a person's recovery is not on the minister or the church, but the individual himself.

This poignant passage sets the tone for all Christian ministers who must deal with problems and problem people within the church. In the midst of being a good soldier and workman in God's vineyard, it is incumbent on every pastor/teacher to remember this very relevant counsel concerning the proper spirit in which gospel ministry is to be conducted.

12
Dangerous Days Ahead

This know also, that in the last days perilous times shall come. For men shall be lovers of their own selves, covetous, boasters, proud, blasphemers, disobedient to parents, unthankful, unholy, without natural affection, trucebreakers, false accusers, incontinent, fierce, despisers of those that are good, traitors, heady, highminded, lovers of pleasures more than lovers of God; having a form of godliness, but denying the power thereof: from such turn away. For of this sort are they which creep into houses, and lead captive silly women laden with sins, led away with divers lusts, ever learning, and never able to come to the knowledge of the truth. Now as Jannes and Jambres withstood Moses, so do these also resist the truth: men of corrupt minds, reprobate concerning the faith. But they shall proceed no further: for their folly shall be manifest unto all men, as theirs also was. (2 Timothy 3:1-9)

Scripture does not speak optimistically about this world and its condition over time. Though secular thinkers predict that the world will progressively develop until it achieves utopia, the Holy Spirit indicates that it will systematically decline and decay until it finally destroys itself.

It is important for the believer to think accurately at this point. *"This know also,"* says Paul, *"that in the last days perilous times shall come."* Nothing fosters a spirit of disillusionment quite like unrealistic expectations. And nothing prepares the believer to persevere quite like a healthy dose of reality.

The reality is that prior to the Second Coming of Christ, the world will become an increasingly dangerous place to live. *Perilous* means "dangerous; hard to bear." And the perils facing believers in the last days will be primarily moral, not physical, dangers.

Paul's list of eighteen vices characterizing the last days have always existed in some measure. But they will be more intensive as the end of time nears. Let's analyze them a bit more closely.

What People Will Love

The Greek root *phileo* is found three times in verses 2-4: (1) "*...lovers of their own selves*" is *philautoi*; (2) "*...covetous,*" meaning "money lovers," is *philargyroi*; (3) "*...lovers of pleasure*" is *philendonoi.* As the end approaches, people will be self-lovers, money-lovers, and pleasure-lovers. Narcissism, Materialism, and Hedonism will be the dominant ethos. And of course, these loves will predominate over love for God. To this agrees the prophecy of the last days in Matthew 24:12: "*And because iniquity shall abound, the love of many shall wax cold.*"

Man's basic responsibility is to "*love God with all his heart, soul, mind, and strength*" (Mt. 22:37). But in the last days he will turn away from God and turn to Self, Silver, and Sex as his religion. It is shocking to see how contemporary this passage is to our own day.

How People Will Treat Others

Secondly, the list includes a description of how people will treat others in the last days. "*...Boasters, proud,*" and "*blasphemers*" describe attitudes in which a person feels superior to someone else, attitudes that inevitably lead to treating others with contempt.

Blasphemers literally means verbally abusive. Further, there will be a serious breakdown of respect for authority, as the clause "*...disobedient to parents*" indicates. That will spill over to a loss of reverence for God, expressing itself as being *unthankful* for the goodness of God, and *unholy*, a term that describes a person who experiences no fellowship with God but lives a merely secular existence.

There will also be a loss of family affection, as the Greek *astorgoi*, *"without natural affection,"* indicates, and a loss of general compassion to others, for *aspondoi* (*"trucebreakers"*) means unforgiving and irreconcilable.

Slander (*"false accusers"*) will be commonplace, and men will be *incontinent* (without self-control), *fierce* (brutal and savage), and *"despisers of those who are good"* (cf. Pro. 29:10).

Treachery (*traitors*, the word used for Judas Iscariot in Lk. 6:16), rashness and recklessness (*heady* meaning "falling headlong"), and conceitedness (*highminded*) will mark interpersonal relationships in the last days.

What religion men possess will merely be external and formal (v. 5), so Timothy is urged to have nothing to do with such hypocrites.

Examples

In verses 6-9, Paul gives examples of the tactics employed by these kinds of people. They *"creep into houses,"* he says, and *"lead captive silly women laden with sins."* The word *creep* means literally "worm one's way into." It suggests the thought of dishonesty and subterfuge.

Silly women means "weak-willed women" and refers to those who are easily swayed by evil desires. It is not a slur against females as a gender, but a description of a certain class of people who are very impressionable. The adjective could just as easily be applied to males, for some of them are weak-willed and easily influenced as well. Such persons become easy prey to false teachers. Though they want to pose as educated people, they are fundamentally ignorant of the truth and, consequently, unwise (v. 7).

Verses 6-9 are predicated on the principle that the Christian home is strategically important to the spiritual health of the church and the moral stability of the wider community. Satan knows that if he can breakdown the family, he can weaken the church and destroy society; consequently, he makes the home a prime target of his infernal assault against the kingdom of God.

How do these *creepers* (v. 6) who peddle the secular value system outlined in verses 2-5 infiltrate and undermine the Christian home with their threats to Biblical morality? By what means are they able to sway the family matriarch (v. 6b) — and through her, the husband and the children — to compromise the kingdom ethics of the gospel of Christ?

Clearly, the passage indicates that moral apostasy in a culture is the product of unbiblical ideas. Notice the references to Christian "truth" in verses 6-8: "*Ever learning, and never able to come to the knowledge of the truth...so do these also resist the truth: men of corrupt minds, reprobate concerning the faith* [lit. the body of revealed truth]." Paul says that these peddlers of secular values operate from a completely different worldview than those who believe in Jesus Christ. Ideas have consequences, and the consequence of moral danger that believers will face in the last days derives from the intellectual threat of a reprobate way of thinking about life and the world.

Then how, again, does this diabolical effort to undermine the Christian ethic make its way into the homes of those who believe in Christ? The *creepers* worm their way into the home chiefly by means of popular media, like television, the internet, and print media.

The technological revolution of the 20th century, both in the West and throughout the world, poses a real threat to the priority of thinking Christianly, and thereby, to Christian ethics. If believers — whether women or men — are *silly*, that is, foolish, undiscerning, and unwilling to resist, they will be led into captivity by the fallen world system around them. A love of "Vanity Fair," as Bunyan described this fallen world system, will prove disastrous to the believer that seeks to be faithful to the Lord and his word. Indeed, the last days are perilous. The threats facing the Christian home and the gospel testimony of the Church are very real and very serious.

Next, Paul, cites the two Egyptian magicians who *withstood* Moses and Aaron. Their names were *Jannes and Jambres,* meaning "the rebel" and "the opponent." Paul likens the false teachers at Ephesus to these two men. Jannes and Jambres were *men of corrupt minds, resisting the truth* of God.

Paul is confident, however, that these purveyors of false ideas will not be ultimately successful: "*But they shall proceed no further: for their folly shall be manifest unto all men, as their's* [that is, Pharoah's magicians' folly] *also was*" (v. 9). The apostle does not reveal just how far God may suffer falsehood to proceed, but underscores the important fact that He will eventually expose it for what it is.

There is great comfort in the knowledge that truth will at last prevail over error. Certainly it will ultimately prevail when the Lord Jesus returns the second time and treads beneath his feet everything that is contrary to righteousness (cf. 1 Cor. 15:25; Rev. 21:27). Further, truth may prevail in more local instances, as the case of Jannes and Jambres indicates. These two magicians were able to duplicate the wonders of Moses only up to a point. But when Moses' serpent swallowed theirs, it was evident to all that the dark arts were no match for the power of Jehovah (cf. Ex. 8:18-19).

We, too, may be confident that error will finally be exposed for what it is. Christ and His word are more powerful than Satan and his infernal lies. The "little book," though apparently insignificant by popular standards, is yet held aloft by a colossal angel (cf. Rev. 10:1ff), in spite of every attempt to dismiss it and defeat it. The glory of man with all of its impressive fanfare and intimidating might is temporary and passing at best, fading like the flower of the field, but the word of God shall stand forever (cf. Is. 40:6). Such confidence in God's prevailing truth was Luther's impetus to write:

And though this world with devils filled
Should threaten to undo us;
We will not fear, for God hath willed
His truth to triumph through us.
The Prince of Darkness grim,
We tremble not for him,
His rage we can endure,
For, lo, his doom is sure,
One little word shall fell him.

Though the perilous *last days*—that is, the period just prior to the Redeemer's return—was yet future, it is evident that Timothy was already facing some of these cultural pressures in his day. At this late date in history some two thousand years after Timothy, we are presented with an even greater concentration of these moral dangers. May we be vigilant, therefore, to the challenges facing us and be faithful to our Lord Jesus Christ and his truth.

13
More Cultural Dangers

But thou hast fully known my doctrine, manner of life, purpose, faith, longsuffering, charity, patience, persecutions, afflictions, which came unto me at Antioch, at Iconium, at Lystra; what persecutions I endured: but out of them all the Lord delivered me. Yea, and all that will live godly in Christ Jesus shall suffer persecution. But evil men and seducers shall wax worse and worse, deceiving, and being deceived. (2 Timothy 3:10-13)

In verses 10-13, Paul continues his description of the perilous times that will characterize civilization as the return of Christ nears. And again, he takes a page from his own experience as an object lesson for Timothy (and all believers) to follow when facing the perils of an increasingly godless society.

Paul, An Exception to the "Creepers" (vs. 10)

In contrast to those in popular culture who peddled false doctrine, Paul reminds Timothy that the tactics and character of his ministry were very different. He did not subtly *creep into houses*, attempting to circumvent the family's structure of authority by preying on the most vulnerable. There was nothing in Paul's strategy for the spread of the gospel that smacked of secrecy and subterfuge.

Instead, he practiced an open, conspicuous, and public life and labor, even though it came at great personal cost: "*But thou hast fully known my doctrine, manner of life, purpose, faith, longsuffering, charity, patience…"* (v. 10).

Like the Lord Jesus Christ before him, Paul conducted his ministry in the light of public scrutiny. He was not afraid that someone may ask him hard questions. In fact, he invited investigation and urged people to *"search the Scriptures to see if"* the things he preached were true (cf. Acts 17:11). He did not handle the word of God deceitfully, like so many of the religious fakes and phonies of his day (cf. 2 Cor. 2:17). He had no ulterior motives and no hidden agendas. He did not employ *"flattering words…nor a cloak of covetousness…nor of men"* did he seek glory (1 Ths. 2:5-6a). So open, above-board, and transparent was his conduct and teaching that he could subject himself without hesitation to the Thessalonians, saying, *"Ye are witnesses, and God also, how holily and justly and unblamably we behaved ourselves among you that believe"* (1 Ths. 2:10).

Paul, in other words, was not a demagogue, using his position of influence for a personal agenda. Instead, integrity of motive, message and methodology marked his ministry. He was comfortable to expose every part of his personal conduct in gospel ministry to public gaze.

Unlike the *creepers*, his *doctrine*, i.e. the content of his teaching, was evident. He had no esoteric convictions that he was unwilling to publicly espouse. There was no "fine print" that ordinary people who listened to his sermons might miss. Readers of his epistles need not "read between the lines" to discern Paul's meaning. Timothy, and others familiar with the apostle, *fully knew his doctrine*.

Neither was there inconsistency between Paul's teaching on Christian ethics and his personal lifestyle. His *manner of life*, i.e. conduct, behavior, was open to scrutiny. He did not preach sacrifice while living in opulence. He did not insist upon a high work ethic among professing Christians while practicing personal laziness.

Paul was not afraid that investigation into his private world would undermine his public testimony.

Neither was there concern that his true motives might be exposed as inauthentic upon further scrutiny: *"Thou hast fully known my... purpose,"* i.e. motivation. Of course, the peddlers of false doctrine were renowned demagogues. It was not uncommon to discover after the fact that these "shade-tree theologians" had bad hearts, using their influence for personal ends, whether the personal privilege took the form of profit, pleasure, position, or power. Paul, on the contrary, could not be charged with any lesser motivation than a passion for the cause of Christ and the glory of His worthy name. The preponderance of evidence beginning with all that he had sacrificed for the gospel was a compelling argument for the integrity of his motives.

Further, his exemplary virtues distinguished the apostle from the *creepers. Faith* [lit. fidelity], *longsuffering, charity,* and *patience* stand in stark contrast to the trickery, deception, and exploitative tactics of these worldly teachers. Paul exuded trustworthiness and integrity in handling God's word (*"thou hast...known my faith"*), self-restraint and forbearance toward detractors (*"...longsuffering"*), sacrificial love and benevolence for the ignorant (*"...charity"*), and perseverance under trial (*"...patience"*).[1]

The moral character of a preacher of Christ's gospel is just as important as the message he proclaims. That may not necessarily be the case in regard to certain professions in the secular world. A physician may still be a good doctor even though he is overweight or in poor physical health. A farmer may still raise a good crop even though he cannot get along with his neighbors. A scientist may still excel in the laboratory in spite of his poor temperament. But a preacher of the gospel whose life does not reflect the ethical standards of that gospel undercuts the very message he urges upon

---

1   The Greek term *hupomone,* translated "patience" speaks of endurance in adversity, and is distinguished from *makrothumia,* translated "longsuffering," which speaks of forbearance toward people.

his hearers. Paul insists that one of the primary components of his successful ministry to the Thessalonians was the absence of duplicity between his personal example and his public testimony: *"For our gospel came not unto you in word only, but in power, and in the Holy Ghost, and in much assurance; **as ye know what manner of men we were among you for your sake**"* (1 Ths. 1:5). The ministry is a character profession—the message that a man of God preaches will never rise above the level of his personal godliness.

Physical Dangers (vs. 11-13)

Even further, Paul's sterling character as a minister of the gospel differed from the *creepers* in terms of his willingness to suffer personal loss and privation for the cause of Christ: *"Thou hast fully known my...persecutions, afflictions, which came unto me at Antioch, at Iconium, at Lystra; what persecutions I endured: but out of them all the Lord delivered me"* (v. 11). A demagogue is unwilling to incur personal inconvenience to promote his views. The apostle Paul, however, was frequently the target of *persecution* (recrimination suffered as a result of his views) and the subject of *affliction* (other privations associated with gospel ministry). He was no stranger to trouble in his ministry.

He mentions Timothy's familiarity of the difficulty he faced on three separate occasions: at *Antioch, Iconium,* and *Lystra.* Each of these cities was in the region known as Galatia. The first is a reference to Paul's trouble at Antioch of Pisidia, the account of which is recorded in Acts 13:14-52. Here Paul met with significant verbal opposition from the unbelieving Jews, who publicly *"contradicted and blasphemed"* (v. 45) his preaching. When the outside pressure from these Judaizers reached a fevered pitch, Paul moved on to Iconium (v. 50).

Next, he mentions the trouble with which he met at Iconium. The account to which he has reference is recorded in Acts 14:1-7. Here the unbelieving Jews *"stirred up the Gentiles, and made their minds evil affected against the brethren"* (v. 2). Yet, in spite of these saboteurs, Paul continued to boldly preach the gospel until finally, the division in the city between those who agreed with Paul and those who sided with the unbelieving Jews became physical (vs. 3-5). Upon the realization that he was about to be caught in the middle of a riot, Paul moved on to Lystra.

Here, in Lystra, the opposition to Paul and his gospel became full-blown persecution. Acts 14:8-20 records the narrative of Paul's trouble in Lystra, the hometown of young Timothy. Not long after arriving in Lystra and healing a paralyzed man, the same unbelieving Jews that had undercut Paul's labors in Antioch and Iconium showed up and convinced the citizenry to stone Paul (v. 19). After the stoning, they dragged what appeared to be his dead body out of the city, leaving Paul's brethren to mourn the passing of this faithful servant. In spite of the blunt-force trauma, however, Paul stood up and made a beeline back through the city gates and began preaching again. One can only imagine the profound effect of both the fact that he was alive and that he had the temerity to resume his gospel preaching after suffering such persecution had on the citizens of Lystra.

What persecutions he endured! *"But out of them all the Lord delivered"* him. These physical dangers were only a precursor to the kind of beatings, stonings and imprisonments that Paul would suffer in his tenure as a servant of the Lord Jesus Christ (cf. 2 Cor. 11:23-28). And not only Paul. Danger is in store for every true Christian: *"Yea, and all that will live godly in Christ Jesus shall suffer persecution"* (v. 12).

It is not a safe thing to be a Christian in this ungodly world. Not only does the believer face the moral dangers specified in verses 2-5, and the intellectual dangers implied in verses 6-9, but also the physical dangers outlined in verses 10-13. Like Paul, those who would be true to the Lord in a fallen world risk public recrimination. Persecution, in one of its many forms, is every true Christian's lot.

Jesus himself taught the same: *"And ye shall be hated of all men for my name's sake"* (Mt. 10:22); *"Then shall they deliver you up to be afflicted, and shall kill you: and ye shall be hated of all nations for my name's sake"* (Mt. 24:9); *"The servant is not greater than his lord. If they have persecuted me, they will also persecute you..."* (Jno. 15:20); *"They shall put you out of the synagogue: yea, the time cometh, that whosoever killeth you will think that he doeth God service"* (Jno. 16:2). So many of Christ's true disciples have suffered personal pain and loss from this unbelieving world throughout the two millennia since those words were spoken, some even to the blood of martyrdom.

Such public animosity toward Christ and his gospel church will only increase as the last days speed toward a close: *"But evil men and seducers shall wax worse and worse, deceiving and being deceived"* (v. 13). Evil men, who persecute those who are good, and seducers, who creep into houses to draw the unsuspecting away from the way of righteousness, will step up the intensity of their opposition to Christ as the end of this world nears. Their primary tactic will be to stir a cloud of confusion so that as many as possible will lose focus on the truth of God. Some of these men will participate in this campaign of deception willingly, for they are "deceivers" themselves, like their father, the devil (cf. Jno. 8:44). Others will participate unwittingly, for they will "be deceived," thinking that they are doing God's will.

I wish I could promise God's children that this world will get better and better, but I cannot. That is simply not true. Instead, the enemies of righteousness will intensify in the last days.

Is there no hope for survival then? Yes, indeed. The same Lord that delivered Paul out of all his persecutions will deliver those who, like Paul, are faithful disciples of Jesus Christ. He may deliver them *in* the fiery trial, like He delivered the three Hebrews (cf. Dan. 3), or He may deliver them *through* the trial, like He did Paul. One thing is certain. He will ultimately deliver them *from* every persecution, even if that persecution results in the loss of physical life. Death is the believer's ultimate release from trouble (cf. Rev. 7:14) and though men may kill the body, they cannot kill the soul (cf. Mt. 10:28). What comfort there is in knowing that *"many are the afflictions of the righteous: but the Lord delivereth him out of them all"* (Ps. 34:19)!

14
Surviving the Last Days

But continue thou in the things which thou hast learned and hast been assured of, knowing of whom thou hast learned them; and that from a child thou hast known the Holy Scriptures, which are able to make thee wise unto salvation through faith which is in Christ Jesus. All Scripture is given by inspiration of God, and is profitable for doctrine, for reproof, for correction, for instruction in righteousness: that the man of God may be perfect, thoroughly furnished unto all good works. (2 Timothy 3:14-17)

How is *the man of God* (v. 17) to survive days of moral and spiritual apostasy, such as Paul outlines in 2 Timothy 3? By what means may he resist compromise with the spirit of the age and the deception peddled by *evil men and seducers* (v. 13)? To what resource may he turn to prevent the kind of discouragement that invariably follows on the heels of public opposition to godliness (cf. v. 12)? In verses 14-17, the apostle highlights the single most powerful Christian resource for living faithfully and productively in the last days—the word of God.

The same *Holy Scriptures* that Timothy was taught as a child, given to God's people by Divine inspiration and profitable in Timothy's personal experience heretofore, would continue to adequately furnish, or equip, him for the journey forward. Likewise, everyone who wants to be "God's man" will find the Scriptures sufficient as both a survival manual and survival resource for faithful discipleship in days of spiritual and moral declension.

Timothy, the Christian

It is important to notice a general observation about the passage. The passage does not speak so much about Timothy as a gospel minister as it does about Timothy as a Christian. Paul will talk about Timothy as a preacher in the next chapter. Chapter 3, on the contrary, speaks in more general terms. These principles apply to every believer, not just those who have been called to serve in the official capacity of public, gospel ministry.

The perils of the last days will not only affect ministers, but Christian people in general. And the solution to surviving the last days as faithful disciples of the Lord Jesus Christ is the same for every believer, both the pulpit and the pew.

How crucial it is for preachers to aspire to be genuine Christians, above everything else! The easiest thing in the world is for preachers to start thinking of themselves in a different class than rank-and-file believers, to take their identity from what they do rather than their relationship to Jesus Christ. But shepherds are sheep too. And the goal of the Christian life is not simply to deliver nice sermons, but to be like Jesus in every part of life. It is not great talent that God blesses, so much as great Christian character. The highest ambition any person may entertain in life is to be a genuine Christ-follower. Nothing is more important.

The Centrality of God's Word

This means, then, that if Timothy (and every believer, for that matter) wants to survive the last days, he must live a biblically-saturated life. The Christian who immerses himself/herself in the word of God will discover the wisdom, motivation, and resources necessary to be faithful to God in days of apostasy. God's word is central, not peripheral, to spiritual stability.

Notice the repeated reference to the word of God in 2 Timothy 3:14-17. This passage describes Timothy's life-long relationship to the Bible. It is as if Paul is reminding him, "Timothy, God's word has been your companion from the very beginning of your life. You've embraced it in your own experience and proved it to be true, over and over again. Now, when you face the challenges of moral, intellectual and spiritual danger, don't abandon it, for this blessed book will completely equip you with every needed resource for living a faithful Christian life."

It is simply impossible to be a stable and productive Christian without systematic exposure to the Holy Scriptures. The fruitful believer, according to Psalm 1:2-3, is someone who continually ruminates on God's word: *"Blessed is the man...[whose] delight is in the law of the Lord; and in his law doeth he meditate day and night. And he shall be like a tree planted by the rivers of water, that bringeth forth his fruit in his season; his leaf also shall not wither; and whatsoever he doeth shall prosper."* This familiar passage inseparably ties spiritual growth and prosperity to regular Bible intake.

How will Timothy keep God's word uppermost in his mind? A life in which Scripture is central requires discipline: *"...exercise thyself unto godliness"* (1 Tim. 4:7). As we noticed in the study of this verse, *exercise* derives from the Greek *gumnasio*, the origin of our English word "gymnasium." It suggests the thought of disciplined training, just as an athlete training for competition would follow a disciplined program at the gym. Such discipline, of course, requires conscious and deliberate effort. It doesn't happen automatically.

Structured effort in three particular areas, then, is essential to regular Bible intake. Timothy (and every Christian) must regularly practice the disciplines of *reading* (1 Tim. 4:13a), *studying* (2 Tim. 2:15a), and *meditating upon* (1 Tim. 4:15a) God's word. Reading informs and renews the mind with God's truth. Studying confirms and deepens personal conviction of the truth. Meditation, i.e. musing and ruminating on the Scripture, distills and crystallizes the application of God's word to the circumstances of life.

Confidence in God's Word

Holy Scripture, then, is the single resource necessary for spiritual survival in the last days. I recently read an article about prepping for disaster. The author asked the question, "If you could choose just one item to take with you in the event of a terror attack, economic collapse, electrical shutdown, natural disaster, or some other kind of emergency, what item would you consider the most crucial?" One person indicated that he would take a knife; another, a firestarter; another, a tarp; and still another, some rope or cordage. The author then proceeded to argue that people survived off-grid long before these items were available. They made knives from sharpened rock, started fire via friction, made cordage from vines, and constructed shelter from mud, straw, branches and leaves. Instead, he insisted, the single survival resource more necessary than every other is knowledge. "Knowledge," he wrote, "will get you through any situation, and it doesn't weigh anything."

That is precisely Paul's point in 2 Timothy 3:14-17. Nothing is more basic and fundamental to Christian faithfulness in the face of the relentless assault of secular values than the knowledge of God as it is revealed in Holy Scripture. Paul wants Timothy, and every believer (for that matter), to have complete confidence in the integrity and sufficiency of the Bible.

By reminding Timothy that he had known the Scriptures from childhood (v. 15), Paul is not simply engaging in a bit of nostalgia. This reminder implies that Timothy's rich, biblical heritage had served him well thus far in life. Biblical truth had shaped his worldview, encouraged him in life's trials, and instructed him at every crossroads of decision. "Timothy," he says, "if God's word has adequately equipped you for life thus far, it will be enough to motivate and guide you to the very end."

Therefore, Paul urges, the need of the hour is not a new program or tactic, but a continuation in the tried and true path that has served you so well to this point: "*But continue thou in the things that thou hast learned and hast been assured of, knowing of whom thou hast learned them*" (v. 14). *Continue*, of course, means "to keep going in the same direction." There is no need to reinvent the wheel, Paul urges. Just because the times are changing does not mean that the message, the mode, or the methods are obsolete.

How many professing Christians today need this reminder! They have long since lost confidence in the word of God to meet the needs of human beings; consequently, they think that the church must adapt its message and remodel its entire approach to ministry just to appeal to the popular palate. The teaching and preaching of God's word, they argue, is no longer plausible. "Modern people simply are not interested in preaching," church growth experts tell us. "They want dramatic presentations, slick video productions, brief motivational chats they can relate to, and high-tech, participatory praise experiences." And by all means, don't be preachy. Remove the pulpit and replace it with a bar stool; get rid of every hint of liturgical form and create a relaxed, casual atmosphere; abandon hymnals and bibles for a big screen projector; and most important of all, replace the singing of stuffy, theological hymns with cutting-edge, contemporary praise music.

But Paul counsels Timothy that the one thing needful when the world has lost its mind is a redoubling of focus on the word of God: "*Continue in the things thou hast learned...*" Though "experts" reject the centrality of the Bible on pragmatic grounds, it still pleases God "*by the foolishness of preaching to save them that believe*" (cf. 1 Cor. 1:21). In fact, there is no substitute for the word of God in the life of the church, whether corporately or individually, and only those who are confident in its power will spiritually survive the perilous last days.

Three Reasons for Biblical Confidence

Then Paul highlights three particular reasons that Timothy (and every believer) has to be confident in his Bible. He may be confident in *the inspiration, the authority,* and *the sufficiency of scripture.* Let's take a closer look at each of these various emphases.

First, Timothy may be confident that **scripture is Divinely inspired**: *"All scripture is given by inspiration of God..."* (3:16a). *Theopneustos,* the Greek word translated by the phrase *inspiration of God* means "God-breathed." The idea is that when we read Scripture written, we are reading the very word that God spoke.

In primitive cultures where writing was less refined, a spoken word was considered more reliable than a written word. Even in America as recently as fifty to one-hundred years ago, a man's word was (as the saying goes) his bond. So trustworthy was a person's word that business transactions were commonly made on the basis of a mere verbal agreement and handshake. No written contract was necessary. Of course, that is not the case any longer. Today, people insist on having a promise in writing, for the day when a person could be trusted to keep his word is long past.

Add to this understanding the familiar relationship of breathing with speaking. If you hold your hand in front of your mouth while talking, you will feel puffs of breath on your hand. Paul's point, therefore, is that *scripture* (lit. sacred writings) is the very spoken testimony of God. He wants us to know that if we could hear God speak today, He wouldn't say anything more or less than what He has already said and what has been written down in the Bible.

So Scripture, according to 2 Timothy 3:16, is the very word of God. It is *theopneustos*—i.e. God-breathed. Though we are reading the words of Moses in the Pentateuch, David in the Psalms, Daniel in the prophecy that bears his name, or John in his Gospel, these men were writing the very words that God would have them to write, for the human authors were superintended by the Holy Spirit. And though Moses, David, Daniel, Peter, Paul, John and the rest of the Bible writers were fallible men, inspiration means that God kept them from error in everything they wrote.

Second Peter 1:20-21 expresses this basic and fundamental "first principle" concerning the Divine inspiration of the Bible: "*Knowing this first, that no prophecy of the scripture is of any private interpretation. For the prophecy came not in old time by the will of man: but holy men of God spake as they were moved by the Holy Ghost.*" This verse means that the words the Bible writers penned were not merely their own, personal opinions. Instead, they were *moved*, or "carried along," by the Holy Spirit. Inspiration is the technical theological term to speak of the process by which God guided fallible men in the composition of scripture so that the words they wrote were providentially preserved from error. Inspiration — the supernatural origin of scripture — then, assumes Biblical inerrancy.

Of course, the *scripture* under consideration in 2 Timothy 3:16 is a reference primarily to the Old Testament, for the New Testament was a work in process at the time Paul wrote. Just as Jesus referred to Old Testament "scripture" when he urged the Pharisees to "*Search the scriptures...for they are they that testify of me*" (Jno. 5:39), so Paul affirms here that the Old Testament is the very word of God. But in the same way the Bible writers of the Old Testament were superintended by the Holy Spirit so that they wrote the very words that God intended for them to write, so Peter, and Paul, and John and the other writers of the New Testament were also supernaturally carried along by the Holy Ghost as Divine revelation was composed. *All* scripture — whether the history, prophecy, poetry, wisdom literature, Gospels or epistles — is given by Divine inspiration.

It is interesting to connect the reference to inspired *scripture* in verse 16 to the reference in verse 15 concerning the *holy scriptures* Timothy was taught. Evidently, Paul considered the Bible used by Timothy's mother and grandmother to be Divinely inspired scripture. This fact confounds the argument of the higher critics who claim that only the original autographs were inspired, for it is highly improbable that Timothy's matriarchal mentors were in possession of original autographs of the Old Testament. By equating the copies of the autographs that were employed in Timothy's early education with Divine inspiration, Paul implies his conviction for not only the original inspiration of scripture but also the ongoing, providential preservation of God's word.

Because of such subtle arguments made by these higher critics and self-proclaimed scholars, many modern Christians who affirm the doctrine of Divine inspiration have found it necessary to safeguard their belief in the inspiration of God's word by adding the adjectives *verbal* and *plenary*. It is not uncommon to hear a believer today express an orthodoxy bibliology by saying, "I believe in the verbal, plenary inspiration of the Bible."

What do these adjectives mean? *Verbal* expresses the idea that the very words of the Bible are inspired. Modern skeptics may claim that they believe the Bible is inspired, but what they mean is that the Bible contains the word of God along with many statements, claims, and ideas that are erroneous, inaccurate, and embellished. They believe the Bible is a mixture of truth and error, of God's message and man's opinions. They may be comfortable to affirm that the Bible is the *word* of God, while denying that it is at the same time the very *words* of God.

Verbal inspiration, on the contrary, affirms that the very words of the Bible are God's words, supernatural in origin and supernaturally protected from corruption: "*The words of the Lord are pure words, as silver tried in a furnace of earth purified seven times; Thou shalt keep them, O Lord; Thou shalt preserve them, from this generation for ever*" (Ps. 12:6-7).

Plenary means "complete, entire, comprehensive," and suggests the idea that every word of the Bible is inspired. There are no uninspired words in the Bible: "*All* scripture is given by inspiration of God..."

So, *verbal, plenary inspiration* means that the very words of, as well as every word in, the Bible is the supernatural revelation of God. Or, to put it simply, the Bible is the word of God.

That means, necessarily, that the Bible is infallible. Because the God who authored holy scripture cannot err (cf. Deut. 32:4), the Bible cannot err (cf. Jno. 10:35b). The contemporary debate over the inerrancy of Scripture among professing Christians is simply one more evidence that the enemy of our souls is still at work to sabotage the kingdom of God. Just as the old serpent attacked the integrity of God's revelation to man in Eden, so liberal theology continues to challenge Biblical inerrancy today.

Why, you wonder, is inerrancy such a hotly contested issue? The answer is that inerrancy assumes inspiration. Attacking Biblical inerrancy, therefore, is really an assault on Biblical inspiration. If liberal scholars are successful in the quest to prove that Scripture is an amalgam of truth and error, history and legend, fact and fiction, they have dealt a massive blow against confidence in the fundamental conviction that the Bible is the word of God.

This brings us to the second important reminder. Timothy may be confident in **the authority of Scripture**. Because the Bible is God's very own word, it speaks with absolute and ultimate authority on every issue of faith and life.

Inspiration assumes authority. Commenting on 2 Timothy 3:16, John Calvin says,

> In order to uphold the authority of the Scripture, [Paul] declares that it is divinely inspired; for, if it be so, it is beyond all controversy that men ought to receive it with reverence. This is a principle that distinguishes our religion from all others, that we know that God hath spoken to us, and are fully convinced that the prophets did not speak at their own suggestion, but that, being organs of the Holy Spirit, they only uttered what they had been commissioned from heaven to declare.[1]

---

1   John Calvin, *Calvin's Commentaries, Volume XXI*, pp. 248-249.

When the prophets prefaced their respective prophecies with the familiar formula *"Thus saith the Lord,"* they indicated that the message they were about to deliver carried Divine authority. That same Divine authority pervades every syllable of both Testaments so that when we read what Scripture says we are reading what God has spoken.

The Lord Jesus affirmed Biblical authority in John 17:17: *"Sanctify them through thy truth: **thy word is truth**."* Many people in our post-modern world, however, do not believe there is any such thing as absolute truth. Instead, they regard themselves as the final authority. They are relativists, operating from the premise, "You determine your truth and I'll determine my truth." But there is no such thing as "your truth" and "my truth." There is only *"the* truth."

How long could any part of a civilized society survive if it abandoned the idea of absolute truth? Could a heart surgeon maintain his license to practice medicine if he believes the heart, according to "his truth," is really the appendix? Could jurisprudence long survive if antithetical testimony from witnesses in a trial is considered equally plausible? Would traffic on city streets continue to flow freely if one person believes that a red light means "go" while another interprets it to mean "stop"? Could economic institutions endure if people jettison mathematics? Does 2+2 still equal 4, or could it possibly equal 5, or 11, or 63?

Even the arts cannot legitimately embrace the premise that all is relative. The Christian apologist Ravi Zacharias tells a story of visiting an Ivy League university campus. Prior to his speaking engagement that evening, a school administrator gave him a tour of the campus, showcasing a number of the abstract sculptures. Over and again, the university official commented on the way these various sculptures captured the essence of the school's relativistic philosophy of education. Finally, Zacharias replied, "If these impressive works of art are intended to teach that there are no absolutes, I have just one question: Why are they all sitting on the ground?"

Where, then, may a person go to find absolute truth in these confusing and dangerous days? Is there a standard by which reality and ethics may be measured? Indeed, there is. God's word, the Bible, is truth.

Everything it says is true. Every precept, every promise, every prophecy is true. It is true in its historical record, in its chronological facts and figures, in its theological claims, in its anthropological assessments, in its scientific statements, and in its philosophical counsel. It is true in its information, its guidance, its logic, its predictions, and its warnings. It tells us the truth about God, about man, about heaven, about hell, about life, about death, about society, about the past, about the future, and about everything else that pertains to life and godliness. The Bible speaks with ultimate authority because the Bible is God's very own word. This brings us to the final important observation.

Thirdly, Timothy may be confident not only in the inspiration and the authority of Scripture, but also in *the sufficiency of Scripture*. Second Timothy 3:16 affirms that the Bible is *"profitable for doctrine, for reproof, for correction, and for instruction in righteousness."* The Bible is not merely intended to satisfy our curiosity, or to provide fodder for conversation. It is given to help us, to do us good. It is profitable. And it will profit a person academically, ethically, socially, domestically, economically, psychologically, and spiritually. No other proposed source document can make such a comprehensive claim.

Do you need knowledge? God's word is *profitable for doctrine*. Here is sufficient information concerning the character of God, the nature of man, the origin of the universe, the meaning of life, the standards of morality, the way of redemption, the purpose of suffering, and much more. The Bible will teach you why the world is in the shape that it is, how to live in peace and harmony with

God and men, how to worship, how to live and how to die. But most importantly, the Bible is *"able to make you wise unto salvation through faith which is in Christ Jesus"* (2 Tim. 3:15b).

Notice that 2 Timothy 3:15 does not say that the Bible is the instrument of eternal salvation. It says that it is the means of *wisdom* concerning eternal salvation. To those who believe in the Lord Jesus Christ, the Bible is a sufficient resource of information regarding the greatest of all gifts—the gift of eternal life through Jesus Christ our Lord.

God's sufficient word is also *profitable for reproof*—that is, for convincing a person of his errors. It does so by revealing who God is and showing man just how far short he comes in comparing to the Holy One. The Bible aims to comfort the afflicted, but before it can do so, it must first afflict the comfortable by revealing that sin is the root cause of his affliction. To the individual who knows that something is wrong in his heart, in his marriage, in his life, and in his world, but doesn't know how to unravel the complex web of problems or where to look for answers; to the person who seeks to discover the source of the problem so that it can be addressed and resolved, God's word will reveal the need and accurately diagnose the malady.

Furthermore, the Bible is *profitable for correction*. Not only does it diagnose the disease, but it reveals the remedy. It shows a person what is wrong, and then counsels that same person on how to get right again. Unlike the specialized society in which we live, the child of God does not have to go to one expert to discover the need and another to remedy it. The word of God is itself sufficient to both reveal the source and to apply the solution.

Finally, Scripture is *profitable for instruction in righteousness*. It provides the rule for a holy life and conduct. *Instruction in righteousness* means disciplined training in righteous living. After educating, exposing, and righting the believer's life, the Bible regulates his future thinking, attitudes and behavior. In other words, Holy Scripture is profitable for revealing truth, exposing where we've gone wrong, showing how to get right again, and then telling us how to stay right.

Of course, it will not profit the unregenerate or the unbeliever. Only *the man of God* — a description specific to those who have been born again — may benefit from it (cf. v. 17). The benefit he derives from this word, however, is exhaustive: "...*that the man of God may be perfect, throughly furnished unto all good works.*" Through and through, God's holy word adequately equips God's child for spiritual life and labor. No room in the believer's life of discipleship has been left unfurnished by God's word. All things that pertain to life and godliness have already been given to him in the Bible (cf. 2 Pet. 1:3).

Timothy may have confidence that the word of God he was taught as a youth, and which he presently possesses, is a Divinely inspired, authoritative, and all-sufficient survival resource for living in the last days. As the brazen godlessness and evil of our world intensifies, may we find God's word to be both a sanctuary and an arsenal for the living of these days.

> *Far below the storm of doubt upon the world is beating,*
> *Sons of men in battle long the enemy withstand;*
> *Safe am I, within the castle of God's word retreating,*
> *Nothing there can reach me, 'tis Beulah Land.*
>
> - C. Austin Miles (1868-1946)

15
The Shepherd's Charge

I charge thee therefore before God, and the Lord Jesus Christ, who shall judge the quick and the dead at his appearing and his kingdom; preach the word; be instant in season, out of season; reprove, rebuke, exhort with all longsuffering and doctrine. For the time will come when they will not endure sound doctrine; but after their own lusts shall they heap to themselves teachers, having itching ears; and they shall turn away their ears from the truth, and shall be turned unto fables. But watch thou in all things, endure afflictions, do the work of an evangelist, make full proof of thy ministry. (2 Timothy 4:1-5)

Paul concludes his "Swan Song" epistle with a final charge to Timothy, the pastor of the church at Ephesus: *I charge thee therefore before God, and the Lord Jesus Christ...*

Pastoral ministry is the act of shepherding the flock of God. In fact, the masculine noun "pastor" is derived from the Greek word (*poimen*) for "shepherd." The *poimen* cares for God's sheep by providing for their spiritual nourishment, protecting them from predators, and overseeing their spiritual welfare.

The shepherd's role is at the same time one of service (i.e. he exists to supply the needs of the flock) and leadership (i.e. he exercises oversight of the flock as one who must answer to the Great Shepherd for their condition). The pastorate is the personal, or the people, side of ministry involving actual day in and day out interaction, at a grass roots level, with real people who live in a real world.

Preach the word. This is the essence of the pastor's responsibility. The shepherd's primary calling is to feed the sheep (cf. Jno. 21:15ff; Acts 20:28; Jer. 3:15; Ecc. 12:9-11; 1 Pet. 5:1-3). What, then, is he to feed them? He is to feed them *"the word of God."* The need of the hour is not clever preaching or beautiful sermons, but the powerful, anointed preaching of the tested and timeless word of God.

This conviction for preaching the word is essential to effective pastoral ministry. God's charge to every minister is *"Stand in the court of the Lord's house, and speak unto all the cities of Judah which come to worship in the Lord's house, all the words that I command thee to speak unto them; diminish not a word"* (Jer. 26:2). Because *"God has spoken, who can but prophesy"* (cf. Amos 3:8b). If He had not spoken, we would not dare to speak; but He has spoken, once and for all, and, therefore, *"woe is unto [us] if [we] preach not the gospel."* Like Micaiah who said *"As the Lord liveth, even what my God saith, **that** will I speak"* (2 Chr. 18:13), today's pastors must commit themselves afresh to a thoroughly Biblical ministry, if they will be faithful to their charge.

Timothy needed a renewed conviction of the authority and power of God's word. We do also. Every salesman must believe in his product, and every soldier must have total confidence in his weapon. Likewise, every pastor must believe that he holds in his hands the very word of God, an adequate resource for every need. The proverbial "line in the sand" in the Christian community today, is between those who really believe in the authority and sufficiency of Scripture, and those who do not.

Where there is no conviction for the Bible's authority, there will be no commitment to a totally Biblical ministry. In 1880, Henry Ward Beecher began to promote a needs-based philosophy of ministry. Instead of starting with God, convinced that God's word is always profitable (2 Tim. 3:16), he started with man by finding a need and then preaching to it. His most famous disciple, Harry Emerson Fosdick, took the baton and continued the race for "relevant" preaching. In the 1920's, Fosdick wrote, "The sermon is uninteresting because it has no connection with the real interests of the people...The sermon must tackle a real problem." Following his cue, others have done much to popularize the idea that preachers must treat people as consumers and give them what they want.

But to whom must preaching be relevant? To people? Well, certainly not in the first place. In the first place, preaching must be true to God. All true preaching begins with the conviction that much needs to be said about the things that people don't want to hear, like sin, repentance, the holiness of God, and the certainty of judgment. What people need most is the word of God. Anything less is a placebo.

In Jeremiah's day, the prophets had jettisoned the word of God for their own ideas. His diatribe against an unconverted ministry in Jeremiah 23:9-40 is painfully contemporary. The prophets of his day were speaking a *"vision of their own heart, and not out of the mouth of the Lord"* (v. 16), avoiding negative themes that people did not want to hear (vs. 17-22).

God said, *"they think to cause my people to forget my name by the dreams that they tell"* (v. 27). The failure to preach the word inevitably leads to forgetting God for a more man-centered and subjective message. Biblical preaching must not start with experience, but theology (cf. 2 Pet. 1:19). It is not primarily a matter of telling people what is on one's heart, but of declaring what is on God's mind.

Preach the word, Paul says. The shepherd is charged to preach the word, not his feelings, impressions, theories, dreams, or visions; not cliches, platitudes, daily headlines, social theory, political platforms, popular trends, or personal opinions. The Bible is the pastor's "teacher's manual" and the church's "textbook;" no curriculum of study is more important; no subject is more useful; no message is more relevant.

"But," someone objects, "the word of God is not popular. It's just not very loving or compassionate to preach what the Bible has to say about certain subjects." But how compassionate would it be for a physician to hide from a patient with a terminal illness the true nature of his disease, thus denying him the only medicine that would affect a cure? Who is more compassionate, the neighbor who allows his friend to perish while the house burns around him because he doesn't want to disturb his sleep, or the man who screams "Fire!" and risks life and limb to rescue his sleeping friend? The most compassionate thing a pastor can do for God's people is to give them the truth of God's word, even if it makes them temporarily uncomfortably. A conviction that we have in our possession the one resource that people need the most is basic and fundamental to authentic pastoral ministry. Therefore, Paul charges Timothy, *preach the word.*

What specifically is involved in the charge to *preach the word*? How should Timothy go about the task of preaching the word? Paul specifies two primary ingredients necessary to the preaching task.

Preaching the word involves **preparation:** *"Be instant in season, out of season"* (2 Tim. 4:2b). The imperative *"be instant in season, out of season"* means be prepared at all times. *Instant* carries the idea of "standing by on ready," both when it is convenient (*in season*), and when it is evidently inconvenient (*out of season*). Timothy was to anticipate occasions when preaching the word of God would be awkward and unpopular, and commit himself in advance to faithful and diligent Biblical proclamation. Don't allow fear to distract you, says Paul. Be prepared for every eventuality.

This command to be ready at every opportunity also speaks of the need for diligent and ongoing study and prayer in the life of the shepherd. Ezra *"prepared his heart to seek the law of the Lord, and to teach in Israel statutes and judgments, and to do it"* (Ezra 7:10). The effectiveness and power of a pulpit ministry will be in direct proportion to the pastor's personal holiness. If he *"restrains prayer before God"* (Job 15:4) and neglects to feed his own soul through diligent study of the word, his words will ring hollow in the hearts of his hearers.

Alexander Whyte called laziness the "unpardonable sin of the ministry." Pastors must discipline their lives so that they don't fritter their days away in idleness. Although God can use sermons that are "without form and void," yet such borders on the miraculous and to rely on that possibility while neglecting one's study may very well be a form of tempting the Lord. "Timothy," Paul says, "be prepared; devote diligent attention to study and personal devotion so that whenever the occasion is presented, you will be able to preach God's word."

Secondly, preaching the word involves **both a negative and a positive dimension** - *"…reprove, rebuke, exhort with all longsuffering and doctrine"* (2 Tim. 4:2c). Paul wants Timothy to correct those whose thinking is awry (*reprove*), *rebuke* those who are living comfortably in sin, and to encourage those who are burdened and cast down (*exhort*).

This two-sided emphasis of both confrontation and comfort is critical to shepherding God's flock. A shepherd whose only concern is to comfort and console his flock, but cares nothing about correcting the lambs that perpetually wander away or confronting the old ram or dominant ewe that bullies the weaker members of the fold, is only emphasizing one dimension of preaching the word. Likewise, the shepherd who is only concerned to reprove and rebuke, but who does not also encourage and console, is equally lopsided in his emphasis.

I suspect people have never really liked admonition. Especially today, there is a potent distaste for anything that is perceived as negative. There is an unspoken law that preaching should never be negative. But how can a pastor preach the cross, with its inherent element of offense to man's pride (cf. Gal. 5:11), without sounding negative? How can a man preach about sin, self-control, and judgment to come, like Paul did before Felix and Drusilla (cf. Acts 24), without being confrontational?

When Paul faced the potentially intimidating task of preaching before the notable Felix and Drusilla, he did not soften or accommodate his message in order to win their favor. He did not *tickle the ears* of these dignitaries. He did not say, "It's certainly a privilege to speak to such important people."

Granted, neither did he disrespect them or give the impression of contempt for them. He merely "*preached the word*" to them, sparing no quarter and pulling no punches.   He preached about "*righteousness, temperance, and judgment to come.*" Not the kind of message calculated to win a popularity contest, is it?

A faithful shepherd of God's flock must approach pulpit ministry with a quiet confidence that "all scripture...is profitable" (cf. 3:16), whether or not people want to hear about certain subjects. Fidelity to the Great Shepherd under whose commission we serve requires the commitment to teach the whole counsel of God (cf. Acts 20:27), not just the parts we like the best.

True Biblical preaching will inevitably expose areas in the lives of our hearers that are inconsistent with the will of God, bringing them to the crisis of decision. It will call sin "sin," not sickness, and challenge people to repent. It will reveal wordly ideas that have made inroads into the thought patterns of the people and call upon them to renew their minds with God's truth. Correction and confrontation are intrinsic to the faithful exposition of God's word.

Reprove indicates that preaching involves the element of **persuasion.** The word means "to convince, to correct by persuasion." It suggests that preaching should be primarily persuasive, not entertaining. Preaching that does not aim to persuade the hearers to change is not genuine Biblical preaching.

Paul was persuasive (cf. 2 Cor. 5:11; Acts 13:43; Acts 18:4, 13; Acts 19:8, 26; Acts 26:28; Acts 28:23). Why was he so compelling and persuasive? Because he was himself persuaded of the facts of the gospel (cf. 2 Tim. 1:12; Rom. 8:38). If a minister is not persuaded himself, he will have little success in persuading his hearers.

It is possible for the shepherd to become so concerned to expose sin, however, that he fails to comfort and encourage God's people. Sheep not only need to be challenged; they also need to be fed.

Many of the people who attend upon a respective ministry come to worship each Lord's Day with heavy, pressing burdens upon them. The cares of daily life and the soul struggles they experience take a toll upon their spiritual stamina. Many of them feel defeated, discouraged, and hopeless. They need *exhortation* (lit. encouragement). Words of faith and hope, fitly spoken, serve to renew their strength so that they can mount up with eagle's wings and press onward.

God's people need regular and fresh views of their Savior, lest they become weary and faint in their minds. Because sheep are easily tired and fatigued, shepherds must labor to maintain an indefatigable spirit themselves, so that they can lift the drooping hands and confirm the wobbly knees of the sheep who come to drink at the pastor's weekly fountain.

Both the negative (*reproof* and *rebuke*) and the positive (*encouragement*) dimensions of preaching, Paul suggests, are to be discharged "*in much longsuffering and doctrine.*" Because sheep are slow learners by nature, they frequently make the same mistakes and fall into the same snares, time and again. Shepherding may be, consequently, a very frustrating task. Patience, therefore, is of the essence.

Shepherding God's flock is a long-term, not a short-term, endeavor. Spiritual growth will not occur overnight. It may, in fact, take many years for any significant improvement to be seen in a local congregation. The same lessons must be taught over and over again.

Great patience, however, does not imply passivity and inaction. In the spirit of patience, Timothy was to commit himself to consistent and careful instruction (i.e. *doctrine*).

This attitude of patient teaching is essential to pastoral ministry. Second Timothy 2:24 says that *"the servant of the Lord must not strive, but be gentle unto all men, apt to teach, patient, in meekness instructing those that oppose themselves..."* The patient and consistent teaching of God's word, over the long term, convincing, correcting, and comforting is the mandate of pastoral ministry.

The Gravity of this Charge (2 Tim. 4:1)

The language of verse 1 is carefully calculated to remind Timothy of the gravity of the solemn task to which he had been called. *"I charge you,"* Paul says, *"in the sight of God and the Lord Jesus Christ who shall judge the quick and the dead at his appearing and his kingdom..."* The pastor who lives with a consciousness of God's holy presence and Christ's exalted authority as Judge and King will necessarily take his charge seriously.

To be charged *"in the sight of God"* implies a seriousness comparable to the taking of an oath or a vow. The very fact that Paul invokes God's presence in his charge to Timothy indicates that he considered the pastorate to be among life's most serious and solemn commitments. "Remember," he says to Timothy, "that God is watching." The command to *preach the word*, therefore, is not a mere personal preference. It is a Divine commission given to Timothy in the sight of God, the Judge of all men. Because of the awesome nature of the shepherd's charge, a casual, cavalier approach to ministry is always inappropriate. Gospel ministry is a serious, awe-inspiring responsibility.

An awareness of the solemn charge he has been given will inevitably produce a spirit of urgency, passion, fire, and zeal in the heart of God's servant. Though he will not abuse his hearers by disrespect or disinterest in their capacities, he will ultimately be compelled by the knowledge that he must answer to God for how he has used the holy word committed to his trust (cf. 2 Tim. 2:15). Such a mindset will help the pastor to preach, therefore, for an audience of One, not for the accolades of men. Donald Coggan has written,

> The Christian preacher has a boundary set for him. When he enters the pulpit, he is not an entirely free man. There is a very real sense in which it may be said of him that the Almighty has set him his bounds that he shall not pass. He is not at liberty to invent or choose his message: it has been committed to him, and it is for him to declare, expound, and commend it to his hearers...It is a great thing to come under the magnificent tyranny of the Gospel.

Again, this does not mean that ministers are justified to disregard the people to whom they preach. A true shepherd loves his sheep and desires their happiness. The mind of a scholar without the compassion of the shepherd will do little to promote the health of the flock.

Ideally, the pastor should labor not only to be *"acceptable to God"* but also *"approved before men"* (Rom. 14:18). Paul labored to *"approve* [lit. to recommend himself to his hearer's conscience – cf. 2 Cor. 4:2 & 5:11] *himself as the minister of God"* by manifesting a Christian attitude and deportment, modeling by an exemplary life the very gospel that he preached (cf. 2 Cor. 6:4-10).

Granted, it is imperative that ministers develop the spiritual maturity to be able to say with Paul, *"It is a small thing with me that I should be judged of you or of man's judgment"* (1 Cor. 4:3), yet a true pastor, because he loves the people to whom he ministers, will not be needlessly offensive or unkind. He delights to see a contented flock and desires to be a *"helper of their joy"* not a lord over their faith (2 Cor. 1:24).

Neither will he be satisfied to present God's word in a dull, uninteresting manner, but will cultivate the use of illustrations and other helps, for these, like windows which add light to a house, enhance the listener's ability to apply the truth to life. Love, however, does not mean that he forbears to tell them the truth, or that he seeks to please his hearers by giving them the kind of sermon they want to hear instead of giving them God's word..

Why Preach the Word? (2 Tim. 4:3-4)

Why should a pastor-teacher commit himself to a thoroughly Biblical ministry? As already noted, because he is under orders from God. But there are many other reasons as well.

According to Ephesians 4:11-16, every function of the local church depends upon the clear, consistent, and accurate ministry of the word. Have you ever wondered why the pulpit is in the center of the building? Not because the preacher is the focal point of church life, but because the word of God is central to the life of the church.

God's word is the scepter by which Christ rules the church and the food by which he nourishes it. It is the hammer by which he breaks the proud heart and the fire by which he inflames the cold and complacent heart. It is the goad by which he stabs awake the slumbering conscience and the nail by which he firmly fixes and establishes the wandering mind. It is the light by which he illumines the path so the little lamb does not stumble into danger.

The preaching of God's word is essential because it is the only way to maintain a God-centered emphasis in church life. Without the objectivity of God's revelation, Christian faith slides precariously into subjectivity.

The shepherd should preach the word, moreover, because it is his only authority. First Peter 4:11 says, "If any man speak, let him speak as the oracles [i.e. mouthpiece] of God." The only way he can be God's mouthpiece is by speaking God's words from the Bible. When he speaks God's word, God speaks, through that word, to his people: "Today, if you will hear his voice, harden not your heart..." (Heb. 3:15).

Did you notice the word *therefore* in 2 Timothy 4:1: "*I charge thee therefore...preach the word*"? The word references Paul's theme in chapter 3, particularly the subject of Biblical inspiration in verses 15-17. Because perilous times are ahead, he says, and God's authoritative word is the key survival resource for faithful discipleship in a day of apostasy, *therefore* Timothy, the word must be faithfully and consistently preached.

Again, he should preach the word because it is the only real power he has. The power of one's ministry is not the pastor's personality or charisma, but the word of God. No man has the capacity to transform his hearers, but God has promised to use his word to sanctify and change them (cf. Jno. 17:17; 2 Cor. 3:18).

Finally, he should preach the word because it is the means by which God's kingdom is extended and Satan's diminished (cf. Acts 26:18). If we desire the growth and expansion of the kingdom of God, the preaching of God's word is central, not peripheral.

The immediate reason Paul gives to Timothy concerning the importance of preaching the word is recorded in verses 3 and 4. "Timothy," Paul says, "preach the word, because *the time will come when they will not endure sound doctrine.*" The days will come, Paul predicts, when people will not put up with sound doctrine, but, motivated by personal preference, will surround themselves with teachers whose primary concern will be to tell them what they want to hear.

In other words, people will bring a philosophy of consumerism from the marketplace into the church, and, in response to their demand, many preachers will adopt a "supply and demand" model of pulpit ministry.

This sounds strangely familiar to the philosophy and marketing emphasis of the church-growth movement, doesn't it? A willingness to say what the listeners want to hear in the name of growing the church inevitably leads to a religion characterized by speculation, not Divine authority ("*...they shall be turned unto fables*"

– v. 4), and a *"famine of hearing the words of the Lord"* (Amos 8:11). A commitment to preach the word in times like these, even though there is no apparent demand for it, is indispensable. Paul wants Timothy to give the people what they need, not what they want — to deal with them as worshipers, not consumers — to be more concerned with faithfulness than popularity or success.

Paul's prophecy speaks with unparalleled relevance to the modern situation. What is *sound doctrine*? It is obviously something more than mere "teaching." Though the idea of "teaching" is inherent in the concept of "doctrine," yet doctrine involves more than education.

The resistance Paul anticipates in the church is not a resistance to "teaching." In fact, Paul implies, the very opposite is true. People will *"heap to themselves teachers,"* that is, they will surround themselves with a multitude of instructors that suit their particular tastes. John Stott says, "They do not first listen and decide whether or not what they heard is true; they first decide what they want to hear and then select teachers who will oblige by towing their line."

The plethora of teachers on today's Christian landscape makes the fulfillment of this prophecy uncomfortably relevant. Today, a person can virtually "pick and choose" his/her favorite teachers from a smorgasbord of religious media, based on each teacher's particular emphasis, charisma, or popularity. Though it is not wrong to appreciate different spiritual leaders for their peculiar talents or to learn from more than one preacher, the danger Paul pinpoints refers to a way of thinking.

The time will come, he warns, when Christians will adopt a consumer mentality toward the gospel, practicing a form of selective hearing, instead of viewing the teacher as a means to the end of following the Lord Jesus Christ. No, the aversion he anticipates is not an aversion to "teaching" *per se*, but an aversion to the theological exposition of God's word.

Far from making the preaching of God's word irrelevant, the modern allergy to doctrinal preaching and Biblical exposition makes it all the more necessary. Though many preachers, Paul anticipates, will cater to popular preferences, Timothy was to be ready for this challenge and commit himself ahead of time to resist the urge to be swept away by the demands of his audience.

Challenges to Preaching the Word (2 Timothy 4:3-4)

Because the pew will always be a reflection of the pulpit (Hos. 4:9), a pastor's commitment to God's word will eventually transfer to the people he serves. Part of the pastor's responsibility, therefore, is to cultivate within the flock a respect and love for the word of God by his own commitment to the centrality of Scripture.

The way he handles the word will inevitably communicate to them either an attitude of reverence or of disrespect, submission or skepticism, conviction concerning its sufficiency or its inadequacy. He must, with patience and persistence, teach them, both verbally and by example, how to listen to God's word. In a day when there are so many distractions, this is no small challenge.

Already, I've made reference to the problem of selective hearing that Paul anticipates (vs. 3-4). But this challenge to doctrinal exposition in the pulpit is not peculiar to our day. Jeremiah wrote, *"A wonderful and horrible thing is committed in the land; the prophets prophesy falsely, and the priests bear rule by their means* [i.e. on their own authority]; *and my people love to have it so: and what will ye do in the end thereof?"* (Jer. 5:30-31).

Notice that the spiritual malaise of God's people was initiated by the ministry's lack of commitment to God's word. Motivated, perhaps, by a desire for popularity, they stepped outside the parameters of their God-given authority and began to speak a vision out of their own heart and the people loved to have it so; consequently, they received their reward—popularity among the people.

Again, God's people must be taught to approach God's word, not
with itching ears, but with hungry hearts. The hungry heart, as
Nehemiah 8 demonstrates, *requests* God's word (cf. Neh. 8:1).
Hungry hearers come expectantly and eagerly, seeking a taste of
that "bread of life" to satisfy their famished souls.

They also *respect* God's word. When Ezra opened the book of the
Law, the people stood up (cf. Neh. 8:5), in a spontaneous gesture of
reverence. They listened attentively (cf. Neh. 8:3) and worshipfully
(cf. Neh. 8:6). They were so riveted to the voice of God in Scripture,
hearing it as God's personal message to them (cf. 1 Ths. 2:13; 2 Cor.
5:20), that they stood for at least five hours listening to it read,
explained, and applied to their lives (cf. Neh. 8:8). Thirdly, hungry
hearts *respond* to God's word (cf. Neh. 8:9-18), in contrition for their
sins, joy for God's grace, and obedience to God's commandments.

The pastor must teach the flock of God he serves about the danger
of losing the benefit of God's word because of a lack of
understanding (cf. Mt. 13:19), a failure to consider the cost of
discipleship (cf. Mt. 13:20-21), and the distractions of ordinary life
(cf. Mt. 13:22), consistently reminding them that a fruitful and
productive Christian life is inseparably tied to the way one receives
the word of God (cf. Mt. 13:23).

He must plead with them to "*receive with meekness the engrafted
word which is able to save [their] souls*" (Jas. 1:21) and to avoid "the
rebel sigh" that resists and resents God's truth and despises his
chastening. And he must encourage them to come to public
worship with the attitude of Cornelius, saying, "*We are all here
present before God, to hear all things that are commanded thee of God*"
(Acts 10:33).

Perhaps one of the greatest challenges to the preaching of God's
word today is technology. Every pastor must contend with the
numbing effect television and social media has on a person's ability
to hear God's word proclaimed. In all candor, the challenge of
grabbing the attention of people who have been entertained in

technicolor all week is one of the most difficult tasks the preacher faces.

The world in which we minister is, in many ways, different from previous generations. The typographic culture of the past is gone in favor of a photographic culture. In his book *Amusing Ourselves to Death*, Neil Postman tells the story of the Lincoln-Douglas debate in Peoria, Illinois in 1854. The people stood for seven hours, listening to (and comprehending!) very complex, systematic arguments, without the aid of pictures or images. Today, we can't even concentrate on a half-hour television program without a break every few minutes for a "happy meal" commercial.

In the light of the way that television and the internet has desensitized modern aural abilities and attention spans, some believe that the systematic preaching and teaching of God's word is out-of-date. But there is nothing more dramatic and exciting than a sense of God. Consider Isaiah's response when he saw the thrice-holy Sovereign in Isaiah 6. Was he politely bored with God? On the contrary, the prophet was terrified. It was a life-shattering, soul-shaking experience. What about Job's reaction to a sight of God's power and majesty in Job 38-41? Did he yawn through the Divine display? Not at all. Instead, he replied, *"I have heard of thee by the hearing of the ear but now mine eye seeth thee; wherefore, I abhor myself, and repent in dust and ashes"* (Job 42:5).

And what about the effect an encounter with the risen Christ had on the disciples? Did they react to the reality of Jesus' resurrection by continuing to huddle in fear of the Jews and despair of the future? No, they turned the world upside down in holy boldness and evangelistic fervor. Indeed, the church can effectively compete for public attention with this techno-saturated world, not by adopting the world's tactics but by faithfully proclaiming a God-centered, Christ-exalting, thoroughly biblical message. Helping God's people to rediscover the word of God, therefore, must begin with a rediscovery of God's word—in all of its beauty, authority, and sufficiency—by the shepherd himself.

The church and its ministry also has one further resource that the world doesn't have. We have the power of the Holy Spirit. This supernatural resource is more powerful than the power of technology: *"Even the Spirit of truth; whom the world cannot receive, because it seeth him not, neither knoweth him: but ye know him; for he dwelleth with you, and shall be in you"* (Jno. 14:17). And the word that we preach is *"the sword of the Spirit"* (Eph. 6:17), a powerful weapon in the fight of faith.   With such a powerful Helper at his side, the Christian pastor can resist the temptation to accommodate the culture and recommit himself to the faithful preaching and teaching of the word of God. So, Timothy, *preach the word.*

How to Fulfill this Charge (2 Timothy 4:5)

In the light of the antagonistic environment in which he seeks to shepherd God's sheep, how is Timothy to fulfill his charge? How can he be faithful to his commission when so many factors are working together to divert him from his task? Paul lists two important attitudes and one important activity to which Timothy must give attention if he would *"make full proof of his ministry."*

First, he must maintain *an attitude of sound-mindedness: "But watch thou in all things"* (v. 5a). The command to *watch* means to be sober and sound-minded. The Greek word, *nepho*, refers to "a state of mind free from the excessive influence of passion, lust, or emotion." Paul is saying, "Timothy, keep your head. Don't lose your senses."

Preachers need passionate hearts, but they also need cool heads. The *sophron* root, a synonym to *nepho*, is frequently translated "temperate," "sober," or "self-controlled" in the New Testament. "Timothy," Paul says, "stay in control of your own thinking. Don't lose your theological equilibrium. Don't allow the climate of your day distract you from your charge. Don't allow the pressures of pastoral ministry and the apparent lack of success in preaching the word make you discouraged, disillusioned, and defeated. Don't allow the apparent success of those who preach to the popular palate tempt you to abandon your task or lose your spiritual focus. Don't be diverted from your charge. Be calm. Be alert. Stay awake. Keep a sound-mind."

Of course, Timothy's natural timidity and sensitivity made him prone to the irrationality of discouragement anyway. Furthermore, a religious climate characterized by consumerism merely compounded his natural weakness. Paul's reminder was, therefore, especially pertinent. To those who minister in an environment that closely parallels Timothy's, Paul's admonition to guard our thinking against discouragement is equally timely.

Secondly, he must maintain a *willingness to suffer hardship: "... endure afflictions" (v. 5b)*. Timothy was not naturally tough or tenacious. In fact, like many of God's servants, he was somewhat sensitive and easily discouraged. Pastoral ministry, however, with its inherent tendency toward conflict, coupled with the way that God's word cuts cross-grain against man's fallen nature, is a context that invites suffering and persecution. Perseverance, consequently, is imperative. Not only do pastors need the compassion and gentleness of a nursing mother (cf. 1 Ths. 2:7), they also need the tenacity of a bulldog.

Though the minister of the word expects opposition and criticism when he first begins his ministry, seldom does he realize the power that these problems and disappointments possess to influence his thinking over the long run. Rare is the man who has been in pastoral ministry for more than a decade whose heart is completely free from a temptation to cynicism and bitterness. The pressures of ministry are significant; the frustrations and disappointments are many; the progress, if any, is slow; the compensation, marginal; the struggle, intense; the fear of failure, strong; the pain of rejection is almost more than any man can handle.

How can a sensitive servant-hearted leader like Timothy keep the edge on his spirit in the face of such pressure? It is much easier to give in to the impulse to complain and retaliate in anger—to vent his frustration and to let others know how much he has sacrificed. The subtle danger of ministry is that the moment bitterness takes root in the heart—the very moment the shepherd allows himself the privilege of relishing past hurts and tallying the score of ministerial sacrifice—he forfeits his influence over the hearts of God's sheep. An angry preacher cannot preach and an angry shepherd cannot pastor.

The devil is extremely crafty. If anger doesn't get the best of a pastor, despair will. When he sees the ugliness of pastoral anger, many pastors are so repulsed by the state of their own heart that they repent in dust and ashes. The next disappointment, however, or the next rejection, tempts them to another sin. Gun-shy of falling into bitterness again, he now says "Well, what's the use? It's never going to be any different for me. I'm just trying too hard. I need to lighten up and pour my energy into other pursuits." How many ministers have allowed the pain to accrue over the years until they have all but given up hope of a fruitful and effective ministry? The spirit of self-forgetfulness and holy zeal with which they began their labors has been replaced by the self-pity and apathy of despair. It was just too hard.

Every gospel minister, but especially those who are temperamentally akin to Timothy, is a potential casualty in this fight of faith. Satan's assault is relentless. It never lets up. Paul's admonition, consequently, is especially relevant to every gospel minister: *Endure afflictions.* "Timothy," Paul says, "be willing to suffer for Jesus Christ. Be ready to bear the scorn and reproach that faithful preaching of the word inevitably brings. Like a soldier on the battlefield, make up your mind that you are going to fulfill your mission, regardless of the rigors and hardships it brings" (cf. 2 Tim. 2:3).

Finally, Paul directs Timothy to an important action. To *make full proof of his ministry* when the challenges facing him are so great, Timothy must **be evangelistic:** *"...do the work of an evangelist"* (v. 5c). The first two imperatives refer to attitudes that would enable Timothy to be faithful to his charge. The command *"do the work of an evangelist"* is a pastoral activity.

"Timothy," Paul says, "even though you are a pastor and your primary responsibility is to edify the flock by the consistent preaching and teaching of God's word, don't forget that your field of labor is more broad than the local congregation at Ephesus. In fact, the field is the world; therefore, don't become so ingrown and concerned about self-perpetuation that you forget the most basic commission to the church – the commission to make disciples of all nations (cf. Mt. 28:18-20). Don't lose focus on the big picture. You are pastor of Ephesus Church, but you are also an ambassador of King Jesus; therefore, reach out to others in evangelistic ministry. Edify the flock over which the Holy Spirit has made you overseer, and then, herald the good news of salvation by the sovereign grace of God in Jesus Christ our Lord to others in every place that the Lord may open a door of opportunity. I know that your gifts are not primarily evangelistic, but do the work of an evangelist nonetheless."

The pastorate is primarily conservative. It aims to protect and guard the truth, as a faithful steward would protect a sacred trust. Its goal is conservation of the flock from the predators of false teaching and sin. Evangelism, however, is primarily progressive. It aims to promote the kingdom of God by proclaiming the gospel (cf. Acts 26:18). It seeks to make converts and to call God's children who are living in the world to repentance.

The church is not only a conservative (cf. 1 Tim. 3:15), but also an evangelistic institution. The aggressive character of the kingdom of God is vividly expressed in such verses as Isaiah 9:7 (*"...of the increase of His government and peace there shall be no end..."*), Daniel

2:44 *("...it shall break in pieces and consume all these kingdoms...")*, and Matthew 13:33 *("The kingdom of heaven is like leaven...hid in three measures of meal, till the whole was leavened")*.

This last reference speaks of yeast. God's kingdom is like yeast, says Jesus. What is more aggressive than yeast? It doesn't stop until it has penetrated and permeated the entire loaf. An emphasis on the conservative dimension of the church without attention to the progressive dimension of the church as Jesus established it, produces an attitude that is concerned merely with self-perpetuation and survival, and that is a recipe for disaster.

"Do the work of an evangelist" is also a command to Timothy, in the course of preaching the word to the Ephesian flock, not to neglect "evangelistic preaching." Pastoral preaching tends to be instructive. It aims to edify, or to build up and strengthen, the believer. Evangelistic preaching, on the contrary, tends to be persuasive. It aims to challenge and to motivate people to repent.

If the church at Ephesus was functioning as it should, the members would be bringing new people to public worship on a regular basis. Initially, these people would need conversion, not edification. Thus, the preaching of evangelistic messages from God's word would periodically be necessary.

Furthermore, because evangelism is essentially a matter of highlighting the contrast between Christ and the world (i.e. *"What shall it profit a man if he gain the whole world and lose his own soul..."*; *"Strait is the gate...that leads unto life...broad is the way...that leads to destruction"*; *"A man's life consisteth not in the abundance of the things that he possesseth..."*; *"Silver and gold have we none...but in the name of Jesus of Nazareth, rise and walk..."*; etc.), every existing believer needs to hear evangelistic preaching from time to time. Even the mature Christian needs ongoing conversion and repentance; none are exempt from the influx of worldliness. Timothy, *"do the work of an evangelist."*

By following these commands, Timothy would resist the temptation to compromise his commitment, and would be able to discharge his commission, making full proof of his ministry. Like Timothy, every pastor/teacher ministers in a pagan and unfriendly environment. Like him, every preacher labors under heavy burdens and foreboding threats. And like Timothy, many ministers struggle with their own weaknesses and fears. Again, like Timothy, the servant of Christ has been given a grave and serious charge. Paul's words to Pastor Timothy, happily, are his words to every pastor/teacher in subsequent ages.

When the pressures of the pastorate begin to take a toll on the pastor's enthusiasm; when he starts to lose focus; when he feels himself becoming increasingly disheartened, what should he do? Second Timothy 4:1-5 answers, "Remember your charge: Preach the word. Preach the word. Preach the word. Preach the word." Everything depends upon God using his word as it is faithfully and accurately proclaimed by a godly shepherd week by week and year by year. Only in this way will we be able to say, like the dying Paul, "*I have finished my course; I have fought a good fight; I have kept the faith.*" And only thus will he hear from the Heavenly Shepherd one day, "*Well done, thou good and faithful servant.*"

16

The Dying Apostle's Epilogue

For I am now ready to be offered, and the time of my departure is at hand. I have fought a good fight, I have finished my course, I have kept the faith: henceforth there is laid up for me a crown of righteousness, which the Lord, the righteous judge, shall give me at that day: and not to me only, but unto all them also that love his appearing. (2 Timothy 4:6-8)

W hen a man knows he is to be hanged...it concentrates his mind wonderfully." This comment by the 18th century British lexicographer and wit Samuel Johnson, England's parallel to America's Mark Twain, is at the same time a unique (and perhaps inappropriate) form of gallows humor and astute observation on life and death.

Johnson allegedly made this comment in reference to William Dodd, an Anglican clergyman. The story goes that Dodd had been convicted in a loan scam and sentenced to death by hanging. He borrowed money under pretense of assisting a student who was the son of the 4th Earl of Chesterfield. But Dr. Dodd never gave the young gentleman the money. Instead, he pocketed the money and when he failed to repay the loan, Dodd was taken to court, convicted, and sentenced to death.

Many citizens felt that the punishment was too severe for the crime. The celebrated Johnson concurred. So Johnson decided to rescue Dodd from the hangman's noose by composing a plea for clemency to the court. For some reason, however, Johnson signed the letter in Dodd's name, as if Dr. Dodd was the author.

The eloquent and well-intentioned plea was denied and the clergyman was hanged as scheduled. Later, after the letter was published and made available to the public, one of Johnson's associates, suspecting him to be the actual author, expressed his suspicions to Johnson, hoping to secure a confession that Samuel Johnson was the true author: "I do not think he wrote it; it seems too well-written." Johnson replied matter-of-factly, "Depend on it, sir; when a man knows he is to be hanged in a fortnight, it concentrates his mind wonderfully."

It is true, isn't it? A dying man's last words are characteristically focused and meaningful. Superficial ramblings about the stock market, or some project at work, or the weather forecast are not typical death-bed topics of thought and conversation. In the few breaths remaining, a dying man tends to think about the most important of themes in a final attempt to sum-up a life lived.

Consider, for example, the dying words of several eminent Christians throughout history:

- *"Beautiful!"* - Elizabeth Barrett Browning, 18th Century British poet, when her husband asked her how she felt.
- *"I am still in the land of the dying, but I shall soon be in the land of the living."* - John Newton, Anglican clergyman and author of the beloved hymn "Amazing Grace."
- *"Let us cross the river to the other side and rest beneath the shade of the trees."* - General Thomas "Stonewall" Jackson
- *"There is only one book."* - Sir Walter Raleigh, when his son-in-law asked him which book he should read.
- *"My affections are so much in heaven that I can leave you all without a regret; yet I do not love you less, but God more."* - William Wilberforce, 19th Century member of British Parliament and Abolitionist of the Slave Trade.
- *"I have the hope which inspired the dying malefactor. And now my work is done; I have nothing to do but go to the grave and thence to my Father."* - Lady Selina, Countess of Huntingdon

- *"Called...held...kept...I can go home on that"* - Frances Ridley Havergal, hymnwriter, after a friend read Isaiah 42:6 in her hearing (*"I the Lord have called thee in righteousness, and will hold thine hand, and will keep thee."*)

- *"I am glad to hear it; but, O brother Payne! the long-wished-for day is come at last, in which I shall see that glory in another manner than I have ever done, or was capable of doing in this world."* - John Owen, on August 24, 1683, to William Payne (a colleague in ministry) when Payne reported to the dying preacher that his book *Meditations on the Glory of Christ* had gone to press that day.

- *"I go to a rest prepared; my sun has arisen and...is now about to set — no, it is about to rise to the zenith of immortal glory...Oh, thought divine! I shall soon be in a world where time, age, pain and sorrow are unknown. My body fails, my spirit expands. How willingly would I live to preach Christ! But I die to be with Him, which is far better."* - George Whitefield, 18th Century British evangelist, at the conclusion of his final sermon at Exeter, Massachusetts on September 29, 1770.

- *"Oh, how sweet to die!"* - Elder S. A. Payne, Primitive Baptist pastor in Texas, who died at the tender age of 33.

The Biblical examples offer even further proof of the principle that a believer's last words are frequently especially substantive and weighty. Consider, for instance, the last words of King David: *"These be the last words of David...Although my house be not so with God, yet he hath made with me an everlasting covenant, ordered in all things and sure: and this is all my salvation, and all my desire; although he maketh it not to grow"* (2 Sam. 23:5). David's death-bed confession affirms that the ground of his assurance of salvation is the everlasting covenant of grace.

Add to this the example of Stephen, the first Christian martyr. As the mob hurled stones at his body and gnashed upon him with teeth of hateful vitriol, like a rabid dog snarling at a child, Stephen said, *"Behold, I see the heavens opened, and the Son of man standing on the right hand of God."* Then, he prayed, *"Lord Jesus, receive my spirit...Lay not this sin to their charge,"* and then he fell asleep (Acts

7:54-60). This epilogue of Stephen's life indicates both the powerful testimony that a gracious spirit may have upon a watching world, and the encouraging truth that the risen Christ never leaves his children in their time of crisis.

Without doubt, the most significant last words every spoken fell from the lips of the Savior on the cross: *"He said, It is finished: and he bowed his head, and gave up the ghost"* (Jno. 19:30). Matthew 27:50 says that Jesus spoke these words *"with a loud voice."* Never has a more triumphant epilogue echoed throughout the world. No peroration in history has infused such hope and enthusiasm to a broken world as this. Never has a summation of a single life been more accurate. The truth expressed in the Savior's last words (and literally, last *word*, for *"It is finished"* is a single word in the Greek — *tetelestai)*, has been the consolation of sensible sinners for the past two thousand years.

Indeed, the prospect of imminent death concentrates the mind wonderfully. And Paul's mind, displayed in 2 Timothy 4:6-8, is especially concentrated and focused. As he anticipates the end of his earthly life and pilgrimage, his last words are especially reflective, courageous, and hopeful. Notice his triumphant, three-directional perspective as he approaches the end of his earthly journey.

He Looks Downward with Courage

"For I am now ready to be offered, and the time of my departure is at hand" (4:6). Paul looks downward into the grave with faith and courage. "Timothy," he says, "I'm dying; but I want you to know that I am not afraid. I am ready to depart and to be with the Lord, for it is far better."

Such language is foreign to the way people naturally think. The world's perspective on death is either an attitude of dreadful fear, on the one hand, or morbid preoccupation, on the other: *"...and deliver them who through fear of death were all their lifetime subject to bondage"* (Heb. 2:15); *"He that sinneth against me wrongeth his own soul: all that hate me love death"* (Pro. 8:36). One person cannot bear to think about it at all, and another sees it as the solution to every inconvenience in life. This unbelieving world sees death either as a great tragedy or necessary inconvenience. Paul's Christian perspective, however, fits into neither of these categories.

Instead, the aged apostle sees his death as an extension of his life of devotion to Christ in a final act of worship. *Offered* means "poured out as a libation, or drink offering." I am ready, Paul says, to have my life poured out, like David poured out the water from Bethlehem's well unto the Lord, in Christian martyrdom.

Of course, this was how Paul had lived his entire Christian life. He had poured himself out as an oblation in service to Jesus Christ, suffering the loss of worldly esteem, material possessions, personal comfort, and secular success, on the altar of Christian life and ministry (cf. Phi. 3:7ff). He did not consider his life as something to be cautiously guarded, like one might protect a priceless treasure, but was willing to *spend and be spen*t for the cause of Christ (cf. Acts 20:24; 2 Cor. 12:15).

Paul modeled a life of total surrender and ongoing sacrifice that is the essence of gospel discipleship. He offered his entire being on the altar of Christian service as a *living sacrifice* (cf. Rom. 12:1). Now, he applies that same perspective to the event of his demise, intending to die as he had lived, as an act of devotion and worship to Christ.

When the believer understands that his life is not his own, but that he has been bought with a price (cf. 1 Cor. 6:19-20), he may face life and death in the same triumphant faith and courage. The Christian is under no illusion that he will be spared from suffering or pain. His expectations for the future are very realistic. In the world, he knows, trouble is inevitable; but in Christ, he knows as well, peace is available and victory, possible (cf. Jno. 16:33). Neither life nor death, therefore, can *move* him (cf. Acts 20:24a).

The English minister Richard Baxter (1615-1691) captures this sentiment in a poem that was likely written for the benefit of his saintly wife as she lay on her death bed:

Lord, it belongs not to my care
Whether I die or live;
To love and serve Thee is my share,
And this Thy grace must give.

If life be long, I will be glad,
That I may long obey;
If short, yet why should I be sad
To welcome endless day?

Christ leads me through no darker rooms
Than He went through before;
He that unto God's kingdom comes
Must enter by this door.

Come, Lord, when grace hath made me meet
Thy blessed face to see;
For if Thy work on earth be sweet
What will Thy glory be!

Then I shall end my sad complaints
And weary sinful days,
And join with the triumphant saints
That sing my Savior's praise.

My knowledge of that life is small,
The eye of faith is dim;
But 'tis enough that Christ knows all,
And I shall be with Him.

The poem is based on Philippians 1:21: *"For to me to live is Christ, and to die is gain."* Here Paul defines life in terms of fellowship with Jesus Christ, and death as the passageway into even more of that fellowship which was his chief delight here.

The second word Paul employs to describe his perspective on death and the grave is *departure*: "*...and the time of my departure is at hand.*" The Christian perspective of death is not marked by finality and cessation of existence, as the atheist believes; neither does it involve a reincarnation and return to earthly existence for a do-over, as the Hindu and Buddhist believes; nor is it a matter of transition to a middle-world of long-term suspense, as the papal doctrine of purgatory suggest; rather, it is marked by *continuation* of conscious existence in the presence of God. Paul considered his death to be a *departure* (cf. Phi. 1:23).

The Greek word translated *departure* is *analusis*, from which we get the English word "analysis." To analyze something, of course, is to dissect and parse it, like an attorney breaking down evidence in a case to its minutest detail or a physician diagnosing an illness by considering each separate symptom. Paul's time of analysis — when his body would be separated from his soul was near.

The use of this term to describe what happens at death indicates that the child of God does not altogether perish when he dies. Rather, the soul, parsed from the body, departs and arrives at once in the presence of the Lord (cf. 2 Cor. 5:8). Just as an airplane does not cease to exist when it departs from one airport, but soon arrives at another, so the very moment the eyes of the body close in the darkness of earthly pain and death, the eyes of the soul awaken in realms of heavenly light and bliss. To be absent from the body is to be present[1] with the Lord.

The etymology of the word *analusis* also includes the idea of partitioning, or *resolution*. An auditor analyzes and partitions the results of his investigation in order to arrive at a resolution, or conclusion. In saying "*the time of my resolution has come*," Paul anticipates that moment when all of the tension and injustice and heartache of his life would be resolved in a single, triumphant conclusion in the presence of God.

---

1   The word in 2 Cor. 5:8 means, literally, "at home."

For the believer, then, death is not the ultimate tragedy. Paul is not afraid to die, even though he knows that he will die as a Christian martyr.[2] Obviously, neither does he have some kind of morbid death-wish. One doesn't have to read very far in his epistles to see that Paul did not see this life as a misery to be escaped, but a rich gift to be enjoyed (cf. 1 Tim. 6:17), a high prize to be attained (cf. Phi. 3:14), and a privileged stewardship to be discharged (cf. Acts 20:24). No, Paul did not despise his earthly life and existence, but lived with a passion and enthusiasm and purpose for the glory of Jesus Christ. *"For to me to live is Christ."*

He knew, however, that reality was not limited to the earthly realm and that life in an ultimate sense would continue for him after death. So, he is not panic-stricken but calm and courageous as he looks downward to the dust from whence he came.

He Looks Backward with Contentment

"I have fought a good fight, I have finished my course, I have kept the faith" (4:7). Secondly, Paul's last words include a backward look at life that breathes a spirit of calm contentment.

So many have occasion for regret as they come to the end of life in this world. Unresolved conflicts, broken promises, wasted time, missed opportunities—these sad tales are all too commonplace among the dying. But the dying apostle's words bespeak a quietness and satisfaction that is uncommon among men. What a powerful testimony of faith is here! Though Paul's adverse circumstances and impending death might have occasioned harsh critique from the secular, unbelieving world—though some might say, "What a waste of talent his life has been! He could have been a leading figure in Judaism, a wealthy and politically powerful celebrity had he not counted everything loss for Christ"—yet he is

---

2   It is likely the libation imagery Paul employs suggests the thought that his life-blood would be poured out as a martyr for the name of Christ.

not ashamed. He has no regret. *I have fought a good fight, I have finished my course, I have kept the faith!*

Note the three-fold metaphor employed to describe his life. First, Paul compares himself to a **soldier**: "*I have fought a good fight.*" The life of Christian discipleship is a spiritual war. Military imagery pervades the Pauline epistles as once and again the apostle reminds believers that they live and serve Christ in a fallen world under the sway of a formidable foe. The Christian campaign against this triple threat of the world, the flesh, and the devil, however, is not a futile effort, but a *good fight*—a holy war.

Not all warfare is sinful. There is such a thing as a "just war." There is "*a time of war*," as well as "*a time of* peace" (cf. Ecc. 3:8). And the effort to promote the glory of God and protect the integrity of truth is a battle worth fighting in this ungodly world. Paul reflects on his life without regret saying, "The conflict between truth and error, light and darkness, good and evil in which my life has been invested is a noble cause, and I am privileged to have played a role in advancing the kingdom of God."

Next, Paul changes metaphors to the **marathon runner**: "*I have finished my course.*" The Christian life is not only a battle; it is also a race. And what kind of race is it? The race of Christian discipleship is not a sprint but a long-distance marathon; therefore, patience is of the essence. The same apostle emphasizes the importance of consistency and endurance over the long-haul when writing to the Hebrews, "*Let us run with patience the race that is set before us*" (Heb. 12:1b).

For most people, the goal in a marathon is not to finish ahead of everyone else, but simply to finish. If I were to enter such a race, I would define "victory" in terms of simply finishing the race, not defeating all the other runners. In the same manner, victory in the Christian life is a matter of running all the way through the finish line.

How many begin well, but falter when they "hit the wall"? When the lungs begin to burn and the feet and legs grow numb, the easiest thing in the world is to drop out of the race. But Paul had not yielded to the temptation to quit. Now, as he nears the end of his earthly life and pilgrimage, he feels the joy and satisfaction of finishing the race that Christ had marked out for him to run (cf. Acts 20:24).

Thirdly, Paul employs the metaphor of the *steward*, or *manager*: "*I have kept the faith.*" A steward is someone who has been given responsibility for managing the affairs of another, like a manager who has been given authority to conduct business in the interest of the owner.

To Paul and every gospel minister, Christ has given a stewardship of his truth. *The faith* refers to the body of revealed truth, i.e. the Christian *evangel*. What a precious treasure it is! As Paul now reflects on his personal history as an apostle of Jesus Christ, his conscience is placid and clear regarding the sacred trust that had been committed to his care: "*I have kept the faith.*" He had not compromised the gospel in the interest of personal popularity. He had not departed from the simplicity that is in Christ in the name of pleasing men. The purity and integrity of the doctrine had not been sacrificed on the altar of cultural relevance and acceptance. He had been steadfast and unmovable in preaching all the counsel of God in the face of opposition, ridicule, and more severe forms of persecution. In a word, Paul had been faithful.

"*It is required in stewards that a man be found faithful*" (1 Cor. 4:2). The number one criteria for those commissioned as guardians of the gospel trust is fidelity to the Owner of this treasure of truth. The Christian motto, like the United States Marine Corps, must always be *Semper Fidelis*, Always Faithful. Paul dies with a clear conscience that he had not shirked the sacred task that had been assigned to him.

He Looks Forward with Confidence (4:8)

"Henceforth there is laid up for me a crown of righteousness, which the Lord, the righteous judge, shall give me at that day: and not to me only, but unto all them also that love his appearing." Finally, Paul confidently anticipates the happy prospect that awaits him in glory.

Do not miss the connective *henceforth*. It means "from this point forward." The apostle has analyzed the present and reflected on the past. Now, he looks forward to the future with an attitude of hope and Christian optimism that is based solely on God's sovereign grace in Christ.

It is important to note that Paul does not say *therefore*, but *henceforth*. I suspect that eight out of ten people, at least, interpret verse 8 as if the crown referenced will be given to Paul as a reward for his faithful Christian life and ministry. But he does not say "I have fought the good fight...finished the race...and kept the faith; therefore, a crown awaits me." There is no *therefore* in the text. The crown is not a response to the life he had lived. Paul does not say "for that reason," or "consequently," or "as a result." He simply declares that *henceforth*, or "from this point forward," or "subsequently," or "in the future," a crown awaits him. This point is important, for Paul does not anticipate heavenly glory as a reward due to his own works.

The crown that will be given to Paul is a reward that Christ by his merit procured for Paul, not a reward Paul earned for himself. It is *a crown of righteousness*, that is, an imputed righteousness credited to Paul as a result of Christ's perfect obedience, not his own.

Interestingly, the Greek word for crown is not *diadema* (like a king's crown) but *stephanos*, the victor's crown. When a champion in the Greek games was crowned by the judge of competition, he did not receive a gold medal around his neck, but a garland wreath. Paul looks forward to that moment when *"the Lord, the righteous Judge,"* would give him a crown of victory, for Paul and all who are God's elect have been *"given the victory through Jesus Christ the Lord"* (cf. 1 Cor. 15:57). They are indeed champions over sin, death, hell and the devil seeing that they are *"more than conquerors through him that loved"* them (cf. Rom. 8:37). When his race of faith is completed, Paul looks forward to the medal ceremony, a reward that would be granted to him on the basis of grace and grace alone.

When will this crowning ceremony take place? Paul answers *"...at that day."* That the *day* referenced is the day of Christ's return is supported by 1 Peter 5:4: *"And when the chief Shepherd shall appear, ye shall receive a crown of glory that fadeth not away."*

That Paul does not anticipate a reward for his life of faithful service is further evident by the fact that he is not the only one who will receive such an honor: *"...and not to me only, but unto all them also that love his appearing."* The victor's crown will be given to every heaven-born soul, for Jesus Christ procured righteousness on behalf of all who were given to him in covenant by the Father: *"In the Lord shall all the seed of Israel be justified, and shall glory"* (Is. 45:25); *"Who shall lay anything to the charge of God's elect? It is God that justifieth"* (Rom. 8:33); *"Then shall the righteous shine forth as the sun in the kingdom of their Father"* (Mt. 13:43).

Although each of those chosen by the Father, redeemed by the Son, and called by the Holy Spirit will share in the glory of heavenly bliss, special assurance is given in the text to believers who joyfully anticipate the second coming of Christ, that is, *that love his appearing.* The point is simply this: *If you love his appearing now, that is evidence you will also participate in the victory celebration.*

It is the same thought expressed in Hebrews 9:28: *"But unto them that look for him shall he appear the second time, without sin unto salvation."* In contrast to the unbelieving world that either denies or dreads the Redeemer's return (cf. 2 Pet. 3:3; Rev. 7:7b; Rev. 6:16), the Christian should live every moment desiring that momentous day: "*Looking for that blessed hope and the glorious appearing of the great God and our Savior Jesus Christ; who gave himself for us that he might redeem us from all iniquity, and purify unto himself a peculiar people, zealous of good works*" (Titus 2:13-14). All who share in this blessed hope may face death in confidence, like Paul, as they anticipate the victory celebration awaiting them in heavenly glory.

17
Come Before Winter

Do thy diligence to come shortly unto me: for Demas hath forsaken me, having loved this present world, and is departed unto Thessalonica; Crescens to Galatia, Titus unto Dalmatia. Only Luke is with me. Take Mark, and bring him with thee: for he is profitable to me for the ministry. And Tychicus have I sent to Ephesus. The cloke that I left at Troas with Carpus, when thou comest, bring with thee, and the books, but especially the parchments. Alexander the coppersmith did me much evil: the Lord reward him according to his works: of whom be thou ware also; for he hath greatly withstood our words. At my first answer no man stood with me, but all men forsook me: I pray God that it may not be laid to their charge. Notwithstanding the Lord stood with me, and strengthened me; that by me the preaching might be fully known, and that all the Gentiles might hear: and I was delivered out of the mouth of the lion. And the Lord shall deliver me from every evil work, and will preserve me unto his heavenly kingdom: to whom be glory for ever and ever. Amen. Salute Prisca and Aquila, and the household of Onesiphorus. Erastus abode at Corinth: but Trophimus have I left at Miletum sick. Do thy diligence to come before winter. Eubulus greeteth thee, and Pudens, and Linus, and Claudia, and all the brethren. The Lord Jesus Christ be with thy spirit. Grace be with you. Amen. (2 Timothy 4:9-22)

The apostle concludes this especially personal letter to his young son in the faith with an earnest request for Timothy to *come before winter*. Timothy was in Ephesus, 800 miles from Rome, but Paul asks him to make a diligent effort to come soon.

Paul's request implies two important thoughts. First, Paul wants Timothy to know that if he delays, he may never see Paul again in this world. Timothy's proposed journey to Rome would necessarily involve some sea travel, and shipping lanes were characteristically closed during the winter simply because of the dangers (cf. Acts 27:9-14). Paul suspects he may not live until spring; therefore, he urges Timothy to "do thy diligence to come shortly unto me."

What an important principle to remember! The door of opportunity will not always be open; therefore, the believer must *"redeem the time, because the days are evil"* (Eph. 5:16). The Lord Jesus himself modeled this principle of living with urgency, avoiding procrastination, a making the most of the opportunity: *"I must work the works of him that sent me, while it is day: the night cometh when no man can work"* (Jno. 9:4). Whether we talk about the winter of mature years (cf. Ecc. 12:1ff), the winter of persecution (cf. Jno. 9:4), or the winter of trial and affliction such as the isolated apostle now faces in the Mamertine prison, every believer will encounter circumstances in his/her life in which opportunities are limited. Before winter arrives, therefore, the Christian must be diligent to do what he can for the glory of God.

Secondly, Paul intends to reinforce the encouraging thought with which he began the letter regarding his opinion of Timothy's usefulness in ministry: *"Greatly desiring to see thee...that I may be filled with joy"* (1:4). He wants Timothy to know that he looks at him as a peer—as someone from whom he might obtain spiritual and personal benefit. What a refreshingly humble spirit the eminent apostle demonstrates!

As the final winter of Paul's life approaches, the incarcerated apostle models for Timothy (and us) the kind of healthy-minded perspective that we have come to expect from him. From his example, we may learn five helpful bits of counsel concerning preparation for those wintertime seasons of our life.

First, *remember the precious resource of godly friends*. In this passage, Paul highlights three loyal friends from whom he drew tremendous strength. In verses 9 and 21, he urges Timothy to make an effort to come to him. He treasured Timothy's fellowship and longed to reminisce about their history together. In verse 11, he also mentions Luke, the beloved physician, who was with him. What a blessing to have Dr. Luke's faithful care in his infirmity. Then, in verse 17, he mentions the best friend of all: "*The Lord stood with me and strengthened me.*" When every creature-help failed him, the Lord Jesus Christ was there to sustain and support him.

What comfort is to be found in the blessing of godly friends! Spurgeon once said, "Friendship is one of the sweetest joys of life. Many might have failed beneath the bitterness of their trial had they not found a friend." One of my favorite sketches shows Winnie the Pooh and Piglet walking hand-in-hand down the road with the caption, "Never forget who was there for you when no one else was." Indeed, the kind fellowship of a friend in the loneliness of trial and affliction is a particular mercy from God.

Preachers, especially, need the benefit of close friendship with other ministers. But it is not typically an easy thing for a man, and especially a gospel minister, to admit the need of friends. Males like to project the image popularized in the well-known Simon and Garfunkel song:

> *I've built walls*
> *A fortress deep and mighty*
> *That none may penetrate*
> *I have no need of friendship, friendship causes pain*
> *It's laughter and it's loving I disdain*
> *I am a rock*
> *I am an island*
> *I have my books*
> *And my poetry to protect me*
> *I am shielded in my armor*
> *Hiding in my room, safe within my womb*
> *I touch no one and no one touches me*

I am a rock
I am an island
And a rock feels no pain
And an island never cries

As a matter of fact, however, we are not rocks. We are more akin to the fragile flower of the field, easily bent by the wind and quickly fading in its strength and glory (cf. Is. 40:6). Only God is a Rock (cf. Deut. 32:4); only God is unmoved by weather or circumstance.

The rest of us need to remember the biblical principle, *"Two are better than one...For if they fall, the one will lift up his fellow: but woe to him that is alone when he falleth; for he hath not another to help him up"* (Ecc. 4:9-10). Paul wisely surrounded himself with faithful friends, under the shade of whose fellowship, he found shelter and rest in his loneliness.

The next word of counsel we may glean from Paul's example as winter approaches: **remain active in the cause of Christ**. Even though he was confined, Paul was still engaged in the work of promoting the gospel of the grace of God. He knew that Crescens was ministering in Galatia and Titus in Dalmatia (2 Tim. 4:10b), and he had dispatched Tychicus to assist Timothy in Ephesus (v. 12). The limitations of his physical circumstances had not diminished in the least Paul's zeal and interest in the spread of the gospel.

Thirdly, Paul models for us the priority of **continuing a daily, personal walk with the Lord Jesus Christ**: *"The cloke that I left at Troas with Carpus, when thou comest, bring with thee, and the books, but especially the parchments"* (2 Tim. 4:13). Of course, he asked Timothy to bring his coat because he was cold. But why did he ask for his books, and especially his copies of the Old Testament manuscripts? Paul knew that the noblest ambition to which any believer may ever aspire is to be an authentic Christian.

Even when he is no longer useful in the public capacity of formal ministry, he may still *"grow in grace and in the knowledge of Jesus Christ the Lord"* (cf. 2 Pet. 3:18). He may still pursue the goal of Christian discipleship, i.e. to "know him and the power of his resurrection" (cf. Phi. 3:10a). He may still "press toward the mark for the prize of the high calling of God in Christ Jesus" (cf. Phi. 3:14).

In the fourth place, as winter approaches, Paul counsels Timothy and us by example to **let go of the heavy burden of past hurt**. Even though he mentions three separate episodes in which he had suffered personal pain, it is evident that Paul has turned these cases over to the Lord. Erwin Lutzer, pastor of Moody Church in Chicago, corrects a popular misconception concerning forgiveness: "When you forgive," Lutzer says, "justice doesn't evaporate — you ask God to take care of it."

Paul mentions the disappointment he experienced because of the defection of Demas: *"Demas hath forsaken me, having loved this present world, and is departed unto Thessalonica"*[1] (v. 11). Paul's words in 2 Corinthians 11:29 (*"Who is weak, and I am not weak? Who is offended, and I burn not?"*), mean "Who has stumbled into sin and I am unmoved by it?" We can be sure that Paul was deeply agitated in his soul by Demas' love of the world.

He also mentions the personal harm he had suffered at the hands of Alexander: *"Alexander the coppersmith did me much evil: the Lord reward him according to his works: of whom be thou ware also; for he hath greatly withstood our words"* (v. 14). Notice that Paul has turned the situation over to the Lord for any retribution the case demanded. He refuses to seek vigilante justice on Alexander, leaving vengeance to the Lord (cf. Rom. 12:19). In forgiveness, as Lutzer said, justice doesn't evaporate, but that is the Lord's business alone.

---

1   The fact that Demas had been with Paul during his first Roman imprisonment (cf. Col. 4:14) but was not with him now is a legitimate argument that Paul experienced at least two imprisonments in Rome.

But neither does forgiveness automatically equate to a restoration of trust. Trust must be rebuilt by evidence of genuine repentance (cf. Mt. 3:8). So wisely, Paul shares his experience with Timothy to let him know that unless Alexander has repented, he may continue his campaign to sabotage Timothy's gospel labors.

That Paul observed and practiced this balanced approach of true, biblical repentance is evident by his words concerning Mark in verse 11b: *"Take Mark, and bring him with thee: for he is profitable unto me for the ministry."* John Mark, of course, was the nephew of Barnabas who had deserted in the middle of the initial ministry effort in Galatia. Later, when Paul and Barnabas purposed to revisit these churches, Barnabas wanted to take Mark again, but Paul did not trust the young man (cf. Acts 15:36-41). The disagreement between the two preachers over Mark was so intense that they dissolved the ministry partnership.

The fact that Paul now urges Timothy to bring Mark with him when he visits is evidence that Mark had, in the meantime, displayed signs of spiritual growth to maturity. He had proved himself dependable, and *profitable for the ministry*. Paul makes no mention of the earlier lapse, but speaks words of affirmation and acceptance.

Letting go of past hurts involves forgiveness of those who have deserted (like Demas and Mark), damaged (like Alexander), and disappointed us, like the saints at Rome had disappointed Paul at his initial hearing before Caesar: *"At my first answer, no man stood with me, but all men forsook me: I pray God that it may not be laid to their charge. Notwithstanding the Lord stood with me, and strengthened me; that by me the preaching might be fully known, and that all the Gentiles might hear: and I was delivered out of the mouth of the lion."* (vs. 16-17).

The church members at Rome had likely promised Paul that they would be present to offer moral support and perhaps, speak as character witnesses, when his trial date arrived. Paul says that when that day arrived, no one showed up.

It would be easy to harbor hard feelings against the brethren for letting him down like that. He might have said, "I am very disappointed in you; you told me you would be there; you let me down." Instead of words or even an attitude of recrimination, however, Paul models the spirit of Christ who prayed on the cross for his persecutors: *"I pray God that it may not be laid to their charge."*

Such magnanimity derives from a mindset that places expectation only in the Lord, not in man (cf. Ps. 62:5). Paul knew that other people will disappoint, for he had likely let others down at some point in his life. People, like us, are dust (cf. Ps. 103:14). We each have feet of clay, and though we may have the best of intentions, sometimes we fail to follow through with our promises. Yet Paul is not bitter, for the Lord stood beside him, gave him strength, and delivered him from the jaws of death (cf. v. 17). When a Christian is conscious of Christ's abiding presence, he can afford to be indifferent to the disappointments of life.

Finally, Paul's mindset as he approaches the coming winter provides one further word of exemplary counsel: ***Keep your focus on heaven and the glory to come***. The faithful apostle departs from the scene of history with this ringing cry of confidence on his lips: *"And the Lord shall deliver me from every evil work, and will preserve me unto his heavenly kingdom: to whom be glory for ever and ever. Amen"* (2 Tim. 4:18).

The God who had been his help in ages past was also his hope for the future. Paul joyfully anticipates the heavenly kingdom and concludes this especially personal epistle with doxology. He is confident that God will *preserve*[2] him, that is, that he will never fall from grace. The doctrine of eternal security, or the Divine preservation of the saints, is a sure foundation for his hope.

As winter approaches, therefore, Paul encourages us to lean on godly friends, stay involved with the church, draw closer to Christ

---

2   The Greek word *tereo*, meaning "to safeguard," is also used in 1 Thessalonians 5:23 and Jude 1.

in daily fellowship, release the past to the Lord, and maintain focus on the finish line. Soon, after the cold blast of many earthly winters in this world, the everlasting springtime of heavenly bliss will blossom with all of its verdant fragrances and songs.

Verses 19-22 include salutations and greetings. The greetings he sends are likely from of the members of the church at Rome.[3] Some of the people mentioned appear nowhere else in the New Testament, teaching that every true follower of Jesus is not a public figure. In fact, the majority are people that, as far as the world is concerned—and as far, even, as the professing church is concerned—are unknown. But thought they are *unknown* by men, *yet* they are *well-known* by God (cf. 2 Cor. 6:9a).

Over and again in this passage, Paul hints at how lonely he is. It is impossible to read without pathos and tender empathy his request for Timothy's company, his revelation of Demas' desertion, his review of other ministers and the field in which they were then laboring, his reflection of the loneliness he felt when he stood before Caesar, and his reminder of the conflict he had weathered with Alexander. Like John the Baptist who struggled with doubt in prison (cf. Mt. 11:1ff), Paul is evidently fighting hard to resist discouragement.

We can be glad that the Bible records not only the successes of the saints but also their struggles. It shows us that they were, indeed, men of like passions as us. And it reminds us that even though they faced adversity and difficulty, their faith in God was real. Paul, like many saints before him, was a man of faith and prayer. His focus was Christ. His trust was in the Lord. And God was faithful to honor the faith of this incredibly useful servant. May Timothy, as well as you and I, take courage from the attitude with which this old Soldier faithfully faded away.

---

3   Notice the Latin names: *Eubulus, Pudens, Linus, Claudia*

The
Epistle
to
Titus

1
Introduction to Titus

L ike *1 Timothy*, Paul's epistle to Titus was written in *circa* 63-64 A. D., during his first imprisonment. Titus was Timothy's contemporary in gospel ministry, serving God on the island of Crete while Timothy was ministering at Ephesus. It is interesting, however, that there is no mention of Titus outside the epistles of Paul (cf. 2 Cor. 2, 7, 8, 12; Gal. 2; 2 Tim. 4:10; Titus 1:4). He is never referenced in the *Acts of the Apostles*.

Titus the Man

From the brief references to him in these passages, we may learn a little concerning this relatively obscure servant of God. First, he was a Gentile (cf. Gal. 2:3), making him one of the few ministers in the early church without some background in the Jewish faith. When some of the apostles and elders compelled him to be circumcised, Titus stood firm and resolute against this abuse of Christian liberty.

Second, he was Paul's traveling companion for a time (cf. 2 Cor. 8:23). His friendship was comforting to Paul (cf. 2 Cor. 2:13) and Paul trusted him to serve as his envoy (cf. 2 Cor. 8:6; 2 Tim. 4:10). Paul's confidence in Titus is especially evident in the fact that he left him at Crete to *"set in order the things that were wanting,"* i. e. lacking, there (Titus 1:5).

The Cretan Environment

The need for strong spiritual leadership in the church on the island of Crete was great. Cultural influences were taking a heavy toll on the Christians. Morally speaking, the church was in disarray.

The influence of the world continues to be a primary threat to the church of Jesus Christ. Because Christians are "in the world," they cannot escape the challenges posed to their high calling by the surrounding environment. And the environment on the island of Crete posed a significant threat to the early church there.

Crete was a crossroads in the Mediterranean world linking three continents—Asia, Europe, and Africa. Travelers on their trade routes frequented the island, each bringing with him his own cultural influences. Two thousand years before Christ, the Minoan Civilization inhabited Crete. They built a very structured society with a code of laws founded on the just basis of liberty and an equality of rights. The mighty empire of Greece rose from the Minoans. Historians concur that this little island was the cradle of Western Civilization.

By 200 B.C., the Cretan society had greatly degenerated from its ancestral nobility. Epimenides, a sixth-century B.C. teacher from the capital city of Knossos, is credited with the quote Paul cites in Titus 1:12—a quote that stereotypically labels the Cretans as "*liars, evil beasts, and slow bellies.*" This description of the Cretan moral character is clearly less-than-flattering and suggests the level of dishonesty, unrestrained indulgence, and general laziness that characterized the citizens there.

Paul's Epistle

The external threat to Christianity in such an ungodly environment is significant and, evidently, the church on the island was struggling to maintain a faithful testimony. Paul left Titus there to complete some unfinished work and to oversee the lives of believers. No doubt, the very presence of Titus would serve to deter some of the negative influences of culture on the church.

Paul's letter to Titus, and through him to the church, would act as a further deterrent. It would embolden and encourage Titus as he ministered in such an ungodly environment, and challenge the church to respect the apostle's vote of confidence in Titus' leadership.

Three main subjects are addressed in the three chapters of this epistle: 1) The Christian Church (ch. 1); 2) The Christian Home (ch. 2); and 3) The Christian in Society (ch. 3).

Unlike Timothy who faced a predominately internal problem at Ephesus (false teaching), Titus was faced with a problem that was primarily external (influence of the world). Paul's antidote to the eroding spirituality and growing worldliness of the saints on the island of Crete was to remind them of their respective duties and responsibilities in the three main contexts of Christian living—the church, the home, and the world.

2
Doctrine & Duty

Paul, a servant of God, and an apostle of Jesus Christ, according to the faith of God's elect, and the acknowledging of the truth which is after godliness; in hope of eternal life, which God, that cannot lie, promised before the world began; but hath in due times manifested his word through preaching, which is committed to me according to the commandment of God our Savior; to Titus, mine own son after the common faith: Grace, mercy, and peace, from God the Father and the Lord Jesus Christ our Savior. (Titus 1:1-4)

Paul does not waste time with unnecessary verbiage in his greeting to Titus. The epistle is theologically "front-loaded," with some of the most sublime doctrines discussed in the first four verses. Such noble themes as the Everlasting Covenant, and the Purpose of the Gospel, are highlighted in this rich, introductory section of the letter.

All is discussed in lieu of his apostolic commission so that we get a glimpse into Paul's thinking about his ministry and the grid through which he interpreted his labors in the gospel. These great doctrines formed the very foundation and impetus for his sense of duty and responsibility as an apostle of Jesus Christ.

The Covenant of Grace

The first great theme of Paul's ministry is the Everlasting Covenant. That he dwelt on this sublime subject as the foundation of his life and labors is evident from references to the doctrine of election in verse 1 and the entire content of verse 2.

The Everlasting Covenant is the arrangement made by the Godhead before time began regarding the eternal destiny of a portion of Adam's race. The term *"everlasting covenant"* is actually employed in Hebrews 13:20, and Paul regularly speaks of this Divine contract and agreement in terms of God's *"eternal purpose"* (cf. Eph. 1:9, 11; 3:11).

References to Divine activity *"before the world began"* or *"before the foundation of the world"* are always clues that the writer is thinking of this Covenant of Grace (e. g. Eph. 1:3-4; 2 Tim. 1:9; Jno. 17:24; 1 Cor. 2:7), the first act of which was the choice or *election* of a portion of humanity as God's very own people (cf. Jno. 6:37; 17:2; Eph. 1:4; Rom. 8:29; Rom. 9:11).

What arrangements did God make regarding his *"elect"*? He *"promised [them] eternal life"* (1:2). When did he make this promise? He promised eternal life *"before the world began."*

That God, before the morning of time, loved and chose His people in Christ, and made all the arrangements for their consummate happiness and sinless existence with Him in glory was the bedrock for Paul's life and labors. He approached his apostolic calling in the confidence that God's eternal purpose would not be thwarted. He found comfort in the thought that God's plan of the ages would not fail.

This is precisely what he means when he says, *"In hope of eternal life..."* The Greek preposition *epi* (*"in"*) suggests the idea of "resting on." Paul rested his immortal soul, yea, his entire being, on the hope of eternal life.

But, someone objects, what if God breaks his promise? What if certain unforeseen events force him to retract his pledge? Such is impossible, says Paul, for God *"cannot lie"* (cf. Heb. 6:17-19). Unlike the Cretans who were notorious liars (1:12), God is not capable of lying (1:2). To do so would be to deny his very own character—an impossibility (cf. 2 Tim. 2:13).

The Purpose of the Gospel

The covenant God who arranged eternal life for the elect before the foundation of the world has *"in due times manifested his word through preaching,"* commissioning men like Paul to that work (1:3). In other words, God has not only formed a Covenant of Redemption, but he has also revealed, or as the text says, *"manifested"* that fact.

Over and again, Paul distinguishes between the *fact* of redemption and the *revelation* of redemption (see Eph. 1:8-9; cf. Ps. 98:1-2). He indicates that this revelation was not clear in other ages. Now, however, it is *"manifested"* — that is, publicly visible like an item on exhibit (cf. Rom. 16:25; Col. 1:26; Eph. 3:5).

How is it revealed or manifested? It is revealed *"through preaching"* (cf. 2 Tim. 1:9-10). It was to this task that Paul was called and in this capacity that he defined his task.

He calls himself *"a servant of God and an apostle of Jesus Christ"* (1:1). *"Servant"* (lit. bondslave) is a title of humility and *"apostle"* is a title of authority. He saw himself as one bought, owned, and obligated to God — a bondslave. He also understood that he could speak with the authority of Christ as his representative — an apostle.

For what purpose had he been so commissioned to preach this message of God the covenant-keeper? For the purpose of ministering to God's elect (*"...according to the faith of God's elect"*). Preaching is not intended for the non-elect or the unregenerate, but for God's people. The gospel serves and nurtures the faith of God's elect, so that they may grow from "little" to "great" faith (cf. 2 Ths. 1:3). Hence, we learn that the preached gospel is not the means by which a person receives eternal life, but rather, the means by which God's work of salvation is revealed so that the people of God may grow toward spiritual maturity.

Paul's preaching also aimed at bringing God's people to *"acknowledge the truth which is after godliness"* (1:1b). Notice that doctrine is intended to lead to duty — truth to godly living.

This emphasis on godly living and the Christian's duty will be dominant as we proceed in this letter. The believers in Crete needed this reminder, for ungodliness was so prevalent. They needed to know, as we need to know, that grace teaches us to deny ungodliness and worldly lusts and to live soberly, righteously, and godly in this present world.

3
The Priority of Godly Leadership

For this cause left I thee in Crete, that thou shouldest set in order the things that are wanting, and ordain elders in every city, as I had appointed thee: if any be blameless, the husband of one wife, having faithful children not accused of riot or unruly. For a bishop must be blameless, as the steward of God; not selfwilled, not soon angry, not given to wine, no striker, not given to filthy lucre; but a lover of hospitality, a lover of good men, sober, just, holy, temperate; holding fast the faithful word as he hath been taught, that he may be able by sound doctrine both to exhort and to convince the gainsayers. For there are many unruly and vain talkers and deceivers, specially they of the circumcision: whose mouths must be stopped, who subvert whole houses, teaching things which they ought not, for filthy lucre's sake. One of themselves, even a prophet of their own, said, the Cretians are alway liars, evil beasts, slow bellies. This witness is true. Wherefore rebuke them sharply, that they may be sound in the faith; not giving heed to Jewish fables, and commandments of men, that turn from the truth. Unto the pure all things are pure: but unto them that are defiled and unbelieving is nothing pure; but even their mind and conscience is defiled. They profess that they know God; but in works they deny him, being abominable, and disobedient, and unto every good work reprobate. (Titus 1:5-16)

Paul left Titus in Crete for two reasons. First, that he might "*set in order the things that are wanting*" (v. 5a). Secondly, that he might "*ordain elders in every city, as I had appointed thee*" (v. 5b).

The first order of business was to complete unfinished business in this newly established church. Though we are not told the nature of this unfinished business, we must assume that Paul has reference, at least, to this infant congregation's need for guidance and spiritual direction from a mature minister. So Titus was there for the *edification* of the church.

He was also there for an *evangelistic* purpose — to *"ordain elders in every city."* Paul's incessant passion for the spread of the gospel and growth of the kingdom of God is revealed in expressions like this. He was constantly thinking of expansion. Titus was not to focus merely on establishing those who were already believers, but reaching out to the neighboring communities to plant churches and appoint godly leaders there. It is in lieu of that objective that Paul gives Titus a picture contrasting the character of someone who is qualified for that office from one who is to be avoided (vs. 6-16).

True Elders (vs. 5-9)

In these verses, Paul highlights the conditions of eligibility for the gospel ministry. Like the parallel passage in 1 Timothy 3, the emphasis is predominantly on the minister's character.

Twice Paul mentions the priority of *blamelessness* (vs. 6a, 7a). The word means "irreproachable, unimpeachable, of unquestioned integrity." This basic qualification for the pastorate is important because the ministry is such a public office. Since the reputation of the church and her Lord is at stake, an unblemished reputation among those who occupy such a visible role in the life of the church is essential.

Hence, Paul says, *"A bishop must be blameless, as the steward of God"* (v. 6a). It was critical for the Old Testament steward to be trustworthy, for he dispensed food to the household of his master. Likewise, the gospel minister is entrusted with heavenly manna for the people of God; consequently, personal integrity is the highest priority for eligibility.

Paul specifies three particular areas of the minister's life that merit examination. The first is *his leadership at home*, for if he cannot manage his own family, he will have difficulty managing the church (v. 6). He is to be thoroughly committed to his wife alone, and in control of his children (the Greek word *tekna* translated "children" speaks of minor, not adult, children — cf. Eph. 6:1,4; Col. 3:20-21).

The second area has to do with *his personal attitude and deportment* (vs. 7-8). The list given might be summarized by the synonyms in verse 8 — "*sober*" and "*temperate*." Both terms suggest the thought of self-mastery, self-discipline, and self-control. In regard to pride, temper, liquor, conflicts, and money (v. 7), an elder must be the master of himself. In place of these vices, he must demonstrate the virtues of hospitality, philanthropy, sobriety, honesty, piety, and self-mastery (v. 8).

The third area concerns *his doctrinal orthodoxy* (v. 9). God's message is described as a "*faithful word*," i.e. reliable, trustworthy. Since it is a trustworthy message, it demands a trustworthy messenger — one who will hold fast to it without the least deviation: "*...holding fast the faithful word as he hath been taught...*" Interestingly, the word "*taught*" means "tutored" and suggests an apprenticeship model for ministerial training. God's "seminary" model is not the popular academic approach of a professor and his students in a classroom. The apprenticeship model in which a "father in the ministry" tutors a potential candidate is the Biblical pattern for training preachers.

Why is such a tenacious commitment to a Bible-centered ministry so essential? Because it is by means of the word that the minister may fulfill the dual function of "*exhorting [believers] and convincing the gainsayers [lit. opponents]*" (v. 9b).

Someone once said that a pastor needs two voices in his teaching ministry — one to gather the sheep and another to drive away the wolves. It is by means of the double-edged sword of the Spirit, which is the word of God, that he will be able to accomplish both tasks.

Paul employs the conjuction "*for*" in verse 10 to express the reason that godly leadership in the church is so important: "*For there are many unruly and vain talkers and deceivers, especially they of the circumcision."* Titus is to make sure that elders are Biblically qualified to serve because false teachers are actively working to lead people astray.

Paul's words indicate that true teaching is the best antidote to false teaching. Error cannot stand against the brilliant light of truth; therefore, the multiplication of sound elders is Paul's prescription for the infection of falsehood.

In verses 10-16, Paul first identifies these false teachers (v. 10). Next he discusses their tactics (v. 11), and finally, he describes their character (vs. 12-16).

Who are They?

Paul identifies the proliferation of false teachers in Crete and the primary opponents to Titus and the apostolic gospel as Jewish people, probably the same stripe of Judaizers that were attempting to sabotage the gospel throughout the Mediterranean world: *"...chiefly they of the circumcision"* (v. 10b). Unbelieving Jews comprised the bulk of opposition to the early church, as the book of Acts demonstrates. It is remarkable that on this island so far from Jerusalem and these many years after the personal ministry of the Lord Jesus, Jewish opposition is still prominent.

In verse 10, Paul categorizes these false teachers as *"unruly"* (that is, rebellious and insubordinate), *"vain talkers"* (Their teaching lacked substance), and *"deceivers"* (They were deliberately trying to lead people astray). They were devoted to *"Jewish fables"*[1] (cf. 1 Tim. 1:4; 4:7; 2 Tim. 4:4) and the traditions of men designed to *"turn people from the truth"* (v. 14; cf. Mt. 15:9).

---

1   Likely a reference to a combination of pagan myths and extra-biblical traditions super-imposed on the Old Testament.

How do They Operate?

Had they merely kept their personal convictions to themselves, Paul would have no quarrel with them. But they were relentless in their efforts to sabotage the gospel of Christ and their influence was growing.

Hence Paul says that their *"mouths must be stopped,* [lit. muzzled, silenced]*"* (v. 11). A "live and let live" policy will not work in this situation, for they were attempting to proselyte others for financial gain: *"...who subvert whole houses, teaching things which they ought not, for filthy lucre's sake."* Entire families, and perhaps even entire house-churches, were being won by these men. By working behind the scenes to build support for their position, these false teachers were gaining momentum for their ideas and building a coalition of resistance to the church and its apostolic doctrine.

Interestingly, these same tactics, i.e. the proselytizing of a few at a time in a more informal setting like a person's own home, are employed by virtually every cult and non-Christian religion. Is it any wonder that John warns about receiving such people in your house (cf. 2 Jno. 10)?

What Kind of People are They?

Paul indicates that the motives of these false teachers are dishonest: *"...for filthy lucre's sake"* (v. 11b). That reference leads him to a more prolific description of their character: *"One of themselves, even a prophet of their own, said, The Cretians are always liars, evil beasts, slow bellies"* (v. 12). It is generally agreed that this quote originated with Epimenides in the 6th century B.C.

Paul charges the culture as patently dishonest: *"...always liars."* Further, he indicates that they live like wild animals: *"...evil beasts."* Epimenides even joked that the absence of wild beasts on the island was recompensed by its human inhabitants. Yet again, Paul indicates that the Cretans had a reputation for laziness and gluttony. *"Slow bellies"* means lazy gluttons.

Is Paul, by repeating the words of Epimenides, engaging in ethnic stereotyping? No, this is not an ethnic slur, but an ethical reputation. Paul quotes the famed Cretan to indict the false teachers as modern-day incarnations of the ancient reputation of the island. Their greed for financial gain coupled with their deliberate use of deception to lead people astray fits the pattern of Epimenides' caricature.

How should Titus respond, therefore, to the believers who have been influenced by these Cretan false teachers? *"Wherefore rebuke them sharply that they may be sound in the faith,"* says Paul (v. 13). Christian rebuke is not meant to humiliate or embarrass, but to recover one from error. The goal of this sharp rebuke is to stop the believers in Crete from listening to *"Jewish fables and commandments of men that turn from the truth"* (v. 14).

There is an allusion in verse 15 to the nature of some of these *"Jewish fables"* and *"traditions of men."* Evidently, the false teachers were emphasizing the need to keep the dietary laws of the Old Testament. Some foods were considered "clean" while others were labeled as "unclean." Paul says that those distinctions are no longer valid, for *"unto the pure, all things are pure "*(cf. 1 Tim. 4:4- 5).

Now this does not mean that there are no restrictions at all on Christian behavior, but rather that there is, as Albert Barnes puts it, *"no sanctity in eating one kind of food, and no sin in another."* The principle taught in this verse is that purity of mind and conscience exercises a controlling influence on a person's entire worldview. The depraved mind, however, uses and manipulates everything for sinful ends. A case in point would be the way godly people have used the internet for the spread of the gospel, while wicked people have used it for the promotion of all kinds of filth and wickedness. The thoughts of an unregenerate person are *"only evil continually"* (Gen. 6:5), while at the same time, *all things are pure* to those that believe.

Paul returns to his assessment of the false teachers in verse 16: *"They profess that they know God; but in works they deny him, being abominable, and disobedient, and unto every good work reprobate."* Strong words indeed.

He describes them as *abominable* (lit. detestable), *disobedient* (lit. rebellious to authority), and *unto every good work reprobate* (lit. void of judgment). Perhaps the most serious charge is the charge of hypocrisy, for *"they profess that they know God, but in works they deny him."* A dichotomy existed between the words and the deeds of these false teachers.

The character of the people on the island of Crete coupled with the momentum enjoyed by the false teachers made Titus' task of ordaining godly and qualified leaders in every city especially urgent. Even today, the best defense against error is a strong offense of truth. May those of us who care about righteousness pray deliberately that the Lord may be pleased to send laborers into His vineyard.

4
Christian Relationships in the Home

*But speak thou the things which become sound doctrine: that the aged men be
sober, grave, temperate, sound in faith, in charity, in patience. The aged women
likewise, that they be in behavior as becometh holiness, not false accusers, not
given to much wine, teachers of good things; that they may teach the young
women to be sober, to love their husbands, to love their children, to be discreet,
chaste, keepers at home, good, obedient to their own husbands, that the word of
God be not blasphemed. Young men likewise exhort to be sober minded. In all
things shewing thyself a pattern of good works: in doctrine shewing
uncorruptness, gravity, sincerity, sound speech, that cannot be condemned; that
he that is of the contrary part may be ashamed, having no evil thing to say of
you. Exhort servants to be obedient unto their own masters, and to please them
well in all things; not answering again; not purloining, but shewing all good
fidelity; that they may adorn the doctrine of God our Savior in all things.* (Titus
2:1-10)

Chapter two begins with the conjunction *but*: "*But speak thou the
things that become sound doctrine*" (v. 1). In contrast to the false
teachers who teach fables and traditions that undercut the faith of
God's elect (cf. 1:10-16), Titus is to be different. He is to teach the
wholesome and health-giving truth of apostolic doctrine.

The adjective "*sound*" derives etymologically from the word for
hygiene. It is the same term employed in the gospels to describe the
lame or the palsied who were "*made whole*." It suggests the thought
of "*good health*." The apostle's doctrine is healthful and health-

giving. The spiritual health of individual believers and the church as a whole is inseparably connected to the faithful, accurate, and consistent teaching of the word of God. There is no other recipe for the promotion of spiritual health in the church than the regular exposition of God's word.

The theme of this chapter is summarized by the phrase, *"become* [or adorn] *sound doctrine."* This thought of adorning the truth is repeated in verse 3 (*"becometh holiness"*), verse 5 (*"that the word of God be not blasphemed"*) and verse 10 (*"adorn the doctrine of God our Savior in all things"*). Paul wants the conduct of church members to adorn the doctrine they teach. Unlike the false teachers who fail to practice what they preach (cf. 1:16a), thus undermining their profession, Christian people must so live that their conduct becomes in itself an advertisement of the truth they believe.

With that objective in view, Paul now turns his attention to Christian ethics. His particular focus concerns various roles and relationships in the Christian home. Titus 2:1-10 is structured like a "domestic code," a document outlining rules for family groups in secular ethics.

The traditional home consisted of the five categories Paul addresses—*aged men, aged women, young women, young men,* and *servants.* His insights to each people-group prescribe the pattern of a truly Christian home.

The fact that Paul addresses individuals and stresses their respective responsibilities indicates that a Christian home, in an aggregate sense, is the product of Christian behavior on a personal level. His point is that the Christian church consists of Christian homes, and Christian homes of Christian individuals. The need to take personal responsibility for one's own conduct and behavior, therefore, is crucial to the health of both the family and the church as a whole.

And what does he say to each of these groups? In general terms, Paul emphasizes the need for self-control (vs. 2, 4, 6, 12). The repetition of the word *sober* (from the Greek root *sophron*) and its first cousin *temperance* (v. 2) suggest that personal discipline is basic and fundamental to Christian relationships in the home.

Aged Men (v. 2)

"That the aged men be sober, grave, temperate, sound in faith, in charity, in patience" (v. 2). Chrysostom wrote of the aged in the church: "There are some failings which age has, that youth has not. Some indeed it has in common with youth, but in addition it has a slowness, a timidity, a forgetfulness, an insensibility, and an irritability."

Indeed, the aged have a number of challenges that demand our patience and support. But they also have a very important role to fill in the family and in the church.

What are the responsibilities incumbent on the aged men? First, they must be **sober, grave,** and **temperate.** *Sober* means "serious-minded"; *grave* means "worthy of respect, dignified" (the popular term is *gravitas*); *temperate* means "self-controlled." Older men in the church should be distinguished by character traits that suggest the thought of dignity, level-headedness, and self-mastery.

Secondly, they are exhorted to be *"sound in faith, in charity, in patience."* In other words, they are to exhibit spiritual maturity. Paul emphasizes the importance of their personal walk with God, as well as their personal attitude and conduct.

Men who are mature in years should also be mature in *faith*, that is, in the matter of trusting in and depending on the Lord. Further, they are to be mature in *charity* (love) toward others, and *patience* (endurance) toward circumstances. Aged men should be dependable, steady, and generous-hearted men who love the Lord and walk closely with Him. Self-control and spiritual maturity should be the hallmarks of their lives.

Aged Women & Young Women

"*The aged women, likewise, that they be in behavior as becometh holiness, not false accusers or given to much wine, teachers of good things*" (v. 3). The exhortations Titus is to give to aged women are primarily concerned with the area of behavior. Their behavior is to "*become holiness.*"

It is significant that the Greek word translated *holiness* (*hieroprepes*) is not the usual word (*hagiasmos*) in the New Testament. In fact, this is its only use in the New Testament. It means "venerable, or that which befits what is sacred." John Stott writes, "They are to practice the presence of God and to allow their sense of his presence to permeate their whole lives."[1]

On a negative note, Titus is to warn against two moral failures which are sometimes associated with older women—gossip and alcohol addiction. They are not to be "*false accusers or given to much wine.*" Time on their hands without a family to raise may provide its own set of temptations in these latter years, and such moral lapses are to be avoided.

Finally, the older women are to be "*teachers of good things.*" Specifically, as verse 4 explains, they are to teach the younger women certain important things. It is interesting that Titus is to teach the aged men and the aged women, but the aged women are charged with the important task of teaching the younger women.

There is a great need in the church and in the home for mature women to convey their wisdom and insights to younger women. The voice of experience with which they speak is powerful. I believe that the importance of this role in the life of the church and in the Christian home cannot be exaggerated. The home where grandmothers are silent and the church where mature sisters are tentative in fulfilling this role is sorely impoverished.

Christian women who have moved past the years of child-rearing occupy a very important role in the life of the church. Although it is

---

1   Stott, *The Message of 1 Timothy & Titus*, p. 188.

an unofficial role, it is nonetheless a God-given responsibility.

What is this important ministry to which mature Christian women are called? They are called to be *"teachers of good things"* (2:3b). We might ask several pertinent questions about this job description. First, who are they to teach? Verse 4 answers *"the young women,"* i.e. those who are still in the child-rearing years, as well as unmarried teenagers. They have already taught their own children, and now are equipped by reason of experience to communicate their wisdom to those who are in the throes of family life. If the more mature sisters in the church would assume the responsibility of communicating the wisdom gleaned from many years of experience to the younger sisters, more of our youth would be saved from the snares of worldliness.

Secondly, how are they to teach them? What form should the teaching take? Obviously, they are to teach by example. But the text seems to indicate even more than that. The Greek word *tagma* (*"teach"*) means "to put in category, or order" and suggests the thought of structure and sequence.

It seems obvious to me that this is not a hint that the early church practiced formal classroom instruction in which aged women schooled the youths, for the New Testament says nothing about such auxiliaries in the life of the church. The teaching took place, rather, on a more informal level—a "one-on-one" tutelage, similar to the apprenticeship model for training gospel ministers, during the course of daily life.

It is not unrealistic to consider how a grandmother would be able to systematically communicate many life-lessons to her own daughter and grandchildren in the Christian home. Her godly Christian influence would be helpful in a variety of daily scenarios, from disciplining the children, to preparing meals, to finding the appropriate home remedy for an illness, to training the children in morals, to modeling an attitude of contentment concerning the circumstances of life, to verbally counseling family members when crises arise, etc. I fear that modem families have lost something very precious since those days when *family* was defined in terms of an extended, as opposed to nuclear, family.

Aged women in the church face a significant challenge in our day. It is the challenge of implementing this God-given commission to be *"teachers of good things"* even though the context for training is not as ready-made as it was in the first century church. The home and family, of course, is not nearly as tight-knit today as it was in previous generations. Today, some families are running in so many different directions that they don't even sit down together for a single meal in the course of the day.

Even in those situations in which it seems impossible to influence one's own family members, this calling to teach the younger women can still be met. Mature women can fulfill this responsibility by making a special effort to cultivate a relationship with the younger sisters in Christ in the church. Once the bond of friendship is established, opportunities to communicate the godly lessons you have learned in a way that is applicable to their lives (without, of course, being meddlesome) will be plentiful.

Thirdly, what are they to teach them? Paul answers, initially, in general terms. The older women are to teach the younger *"good things,"* that is, godly things. The purpose of establishing a Christian friendship with a younger sister in the church is the strengthening of her godly character, personal walk with God, and family relationships. Anything that might undermine the integrity of her home or contribute to disillusionment with her role should be relentlessly avoided.

Of course, the role of a home-maker is often unspectacular. It is certainly under-appreciated by the wider secular world. The temptation to discontentment, consequently, is significant. The influence and encouragement of a mature Christian woman, therefore, in the lives of those who are struggling to govern the affairs of daily family life can be tremendously beneficial.

More specifically, they are to teach them, says Paul, *"to be sober"* (v. 4). The word means, again, "self-controlled; able to master one's own thoughts, attitudes, and conduct." A mother in the home has many reasons to lose control, from a glass of spilled milk to crayon marks on the wall, etc. Sometimes the calm voice of reason that says, "Oh, I remember when my children did such-n-such..." goes a long way toward teaching self-control.

Next, they are to teach them *"to love their husbands...and to love their children"* (v. 4b). Paul speaks here, not of the love of emotion or eroticism, but of sacrifice and service. Young women can be trained "to love" in this sense. The aged women are to encourage the younger to be faithful to their own respective husbands, to be committed to their families, and to build the confidence that comes from the safety of love in their children. Few callings are nobler than the high calling of motherhood. Seldom will a person have greater opportunity to influence another individual for good than a mother has in regard to her children.

Third, mature women are to teach younger women to be *"discreet"* and *"chaste"* (v. 5a). The linguist Spiros Zodhiates says that *discreet* refers to "one who exercises proper restraints on all passions and desires." *Chaste* means "pure and undefiled."

In the fourth place, they are to teach them to be *"keepers at home, good, obedient to their own husbands"* (v. 5b). The expression *"keepers at home"* is intriguing. It means, literally, "to keep the home." Just as David "kept" the sheep, a Christian woman is to keep, or manage, her home. She is to be a home-lover and a home-worker, both of which thoughts are conveyed in the Greek word.

Proverbs 14:1 summarizes the thought: *"Every wise woman buildeth her house, but the foolish plucketh it down with her hands."* There is nothing more important to the Christian woman than her home, i.e. her family. Everything else takes a backseat to this. How important it is for older women to teach younger woman the importance of prioritizing the home and family!

The word *good* means "kind." The godly matrons in the church are to teach the young wives and mothers the importance of kindness. Nothing impacts the lives of others quite so positively and powerfully as kindness.

Finally, they are to teach them to be *"obedient to their own husbands."* The desire to revolt against the hierarchical structure that God has built into the fabric of his world is as old as Adam and Eve. But heartache alone is the result of any attempt to alter the Divine order for the family.

The decision to live in obedience to one's husband as an expression of a wholehearted, loving submission to God is a choice for genuine liberty. It sends a powerful message to the children regarding the authority of God's word in the family. It bespeaks trust, love, and respect to her husband. It models the relationship between Christ and his church before a watching world. And it promotes a closer personal walk with God.

Older women must be careful to train the younger sisters in each of these "good things"—whether in terms of domestic responsibilities, moral conduct, or personal attitudes—and to encourage them to please the Lord in every aspect of their lives.

Why is it so important? It is important so that *"the word of God might not be blasphemed."* Failure to implement this biblical model of godly femininity will give occasion for others to malign God's word. But Christian homes that operate by God's plan powerfully commend the gospel.

Young Men

Next, Paul instructs Titus regarding *"young men"*—those brethren, that is, who are still involved in raising a family and those young adults who may not yet be married. In general terms, this category could embrace people as young as thirteen and as old as fifty.

Paul highlights two basic priorities for young men. The first is *the need for sobriety*: *"...exhort young men to be sober minded."* Again,

Paul's use of the *sophron* root targets the importance of self-control and self-mastery.

John Stott comments, "...doubtless Paul is thinking of the control of temper and tongue, of ambition and avarice, and especially of bodily appetites, including sexual urges, so that Christian young men remain committed to the unalterable Christian standard of chastity before marriage and fidelity after it."[2]

Few virtues are more essential to young men than this mentality of self-discipline (cf. 1 Cor. 9:27). How many have ruined their lives and testimonies by unrestrained passion, addiction to drugs or alcohol, and explosive temper! The capacity to "look before you leap," to anticipate the consequences of an action, to keep attitudes in check, and to say "no" to oneself is a mark of Christian maturity in discipleship (cf. Pro. 16:32; 19:11; 14:29; 17:27; 25:28; Mt. 16:24).

The verb *exhort* means "to encourage." The fellowship of the church creates a context for developing loving relationships. When one brother compassionately and lovingly encourages a young man toward a disciplined-life, the results can be very positive.

Secondly, Christian young men need *godly examples*. Paul turns his attention in verse 7 to Titus himself: "*In all things showing thyself a pattern of good works...*"

Christian young men need godly role models. Like all of us, they need to see the truth modeled in life so that they will have a pattern to follow. The gospel minister is intended to be such a model of Christianity. He must be a person who not only proclaims the truth but also personifies it.

Hence, Paul could urge the Corinthians to *follow*, that is, imitate, *him as he followed Christ* (cf. 1 Cor. 11:1). Just as Timothy was charged to "*be an example of believers*" (1 Tim. 4:12), now Titus is charged to display an exemplary conduct and demeanor. "The young men of Crete are watching you, Titus," Paul says, "so do not let them down."

---

2 Stott, *The Message of 1 Timothy & Titus*, p. 189.

In what particular areas do young men need a living example of godliness? First, in terms of **doctrinal integrity**: *"...in doctrine showing uncorruptness."* Young men need sound, solid, and unadulterated doctrine, lest they succumb to theological fads and the temptation to innovate and experiment with the truth, a temptation that is very common among young people. There is a "Nadab and Abihu" spirit living in the heart of every young adult (cf. Num. 10). The desire to innovate and experiment is indigenous to the young.

I am thankful for the example in my formative years of brethren who were doctrinally sound and committed to the truth. Their theologically-oriented sermons coupled with their wise counsel to study the fundamentals of the faith have benefited me to this day.

Secondly, young men need a spiritual mentor to model *a serious Christian attitude*: *"...gravity, sincerity."* People will not take Christianity seriously unless those who teach the word exhibit a certain seriousness in demeanor. Serving Jesus Christ is not a game or a hobby, but a priceless privilege and way of life. Young men who witness an older Christian brother who is serious about his commitment to Christ and His word often find themselves compelled to follow that example.

Finally, young men need guidance in the area of **Christian speech**: *"...sound speech that cannot be condemned that he that is of the contrary part may be ashamed, having no evil thing to say of you."* To witness the example of a more experienced Christian brother who allows "no corrupt communication to proceed from his mouth" (cf. Eph. 4:32) is a powerful lesson in the discipline of the tongue for a young man.

Servants

The last group Titus is to exhort consists of **Christian servants** (or slaves): *"Exhort servants to be obedient unto their own masters, and to please them well in all things, not answering again: not purloining, but* *showing all good fidelity; that they may adorn the doctrine of God our Savior in all things"* (vs. 9- 10).

It is significant to note that Paul does not encourage servants to revolt against their masters because they are Christians. Just because they were spiritually free in Christ was not sufficient ground for demanding liberation from the civil yoke of servitude. Instead, Paul's rule is "Be a Christian where you are."

What does it mean to be a Christian in the less-than-ideal circumstance of slavery? It means that a Christian slave should strive to be the best servant his master has ever had. It means obedience with an aim to please. It means resisting the urge to talk back or to defend oneself. It means refusing to take advantage of one's master even in petty matters (*purloining* refers to "petty theft"), but faithfulness and trustworthiness in all things.

What is the motivation for such a willing attitude and cooperative spirit? Servants should do all of this in order to *"adorn the doctrine of God our Savior in all things."* Nothing makes the gospel more attractive than the Christian deportment of those who profess to believe it.

5

Grace Promotes Godliness

For the grace of God that bringeth salvation hath appeared to all men, teaching us that, denying ungodliness and worldly lusts, we should live soberly, righteously, and godly in this present world. Looking for that blessed hope, and the glorious appearing of the great God and our Saviour Jesus Christ; who gave himself for us, that he might redeem us from all iniquity, and purify unto himself a peculiar people, zealous of good works. (Titus 2:11-14)

Paul now identifies the motivation for each of these ethical matters he has addressed: *"For the grace of God that bringeth salvation hath appeared to all men, teaching us that, denying ungodliness and worldly lusts, we should live soberly, righteously, and godly in this present world"* (2:11-12). Why is personal godliness so important in the life of a believer? It is important because of God's saving grace.

Here we see another example in Pauline thought of the indivisible link between doctrine and duty. Paul characteristically explains the doctrine first, then applies that doctrine to practical life. He is fond, in other words, of the "therefore" argument (cf. Rom. 12:1; Eph. 4:1).

Here, however, he first insists on the various duties involved with being a Christian, then offers the doctrinal basis of those duties. We might call this the "because" argument: *"For* [i.e. *because*] *the grace of God..."* Whatever sequence he employs — doctrine then duty (as in Romans and Ephesians), or duty then doctrine (as in Titus 2) — Paul's point is the same. He wants people to know that grace promotes godliness. The grace that saves is also the grace that teaches the saved to live godly lives.

Grace the savior

Paul first states a fact—grace has appeared to all men. Which "grace" is he talking about? The same "grace" that brings salvation.

Two thoughts are here. First, salvation is by *grace.* Sinners are not saved by human works or self-will, but by Divine purpose and initiative. Elsewhere, Paul states the principle like this: *"[God] who hath saved us and called us with a holy calling, not according to our works, but according to his own purpose and grace which was given us in Christ Jesus before the world began"* (2 Tim. 1:9; cf. Eph. 2:8-9).

Grace is God's unmerited favor upon hell-deserving sinners. Because of man's native depravity, salvation by grace alone is a necessity if anyone will be saved.

> *'Tis not that I did choose thee,*
> *For, Lord, that could not be;*
> *This heart would still refuse thee,*
> *Had'st thou not chosen me.*

Secondly, God's saving grace has been revealed: *"grace...hath appeared to all men."* The verb *"appeared"* derives from the Greek word for *epiphany.* An epiphany is a visible manifestation.

What does Paul mean? How was "grace" visibly manifested? Obviously, Paul is thinking of the first coming of the Lord Jesus Christ who was *"full of grace and truth"* (cf. Jno. 1:14). Christ is grace personified—the very embodiment of grace. Hence, after talking about the fact of God's saving grace in 2 Timothy 1:9, Paul says in the next verse: *"But is now made manifest by the appearing of our Savior Jesus Christ..."* (v. 10).

But the language of Titus 2:11 suggests a further thought still. By including the prepositional phrase *"to all men,"* Paul refers to the revelation of God's grace not only in the person of his Son, but also in the gospel, a message that was then being circulated to both Jews and Greeks, bond and free, male and female, i.e. *all men*. The gospel is the revelation of God's gift of salvation through the Lord Jesus Christ.

So, Paul affirms both the fact of salvation by grace, and the revelation of that fact in the gospel. Then, in verse 12, he states yet a further truth. Not only does the gospel reveal what God has done by his grace in the stead of His people, it also instructs us how to live.

Grace the teacher

Grace as it revealed in the gospel, in other words, "*teaches us*." What lessons do those who are in the school of grace learn?

First, a negative lesson: "*...teaching us that denying ungodliness and worldly lusts...*" Grace teaches us to say "no" to sinful behavior and sinful passions. Far from being a license to sin, a true understanding of grace is a powerful incentive to holy living (cf. Rom. 6:1).

There exists no more powerful motivation to mortify the flesh, deny oneself, and turn from sin than an understanding of what Christ actually suffered and accomplished for sinners at the cross (cf. 2 Cor. 5:15). Is it any wonder that the Lord traced the cause of Israel's disobedience to the failure to understand the significance of His gracious dealings with them (cf. Deut. 32:29)? Even so, those who comprehend the love of Christ (cf. Eph. 3:18-19) have the information necessary to shun and avoid sinful conduct and attitudes. Grace teaches us to deny ungodliness.

Secondly, a positive lesson: "*...we should live soberly, righteously, and godly in this present world.*" The grace that God has demonstrated toward sinners is not only the impetus for renouncing the old life, but the catalyst for living a new life. In the place of self-indulgence, grace teaches its recipient the importance of self-control and self-discipline (to "*live soberly*"). In the place of disobedience and rebellion, they now long to live in obedience to

God's word (to *"live...righteously"*). And instead of carnal behavior, they now seek to conduct themselves with the kind of piety that would honor and glorify the Lord (to *"live...godly"*). Such is the curriculum inculcated to those who are students in the school of grace.

Grace, in summary, not only impacts our lives so far as the next world is concerned, but it also exercises a profound effect on our lives now — *"in this present world."* Grace is for heaven — praise God! But grace is also for living even now. This message of God's sovereign grace is good to die by, and it is also good to live by.

In verses 13 and following, Paul continues this theme concerning the motivation for Christian duty. Not only does past grace incite believers to godliness of life, but the future hope of Christ's glorious return does as well. A posture of anticipation — i.e. of *"looking for that blessed hope"* — will do much to promote obedience and holiness of life right now (cf. 2 Pet. 3:11-14; 1 Jno. 3:3). What Christian would want to be discovered in disobedience when Christ returns?

The 2nd Coming as a Motive

Paul employs two euphoric terms to describe the great doctrine of the Redeemer's Return. First, he terms it *"that blessed hope."* Hope — a desire accompanied by expectation — is the middle virtue in the triad of Christian graces that should characterize every believer (cf. 1 Cor. 13:13). By definition, it suggests the thought of a bright outlook on the future. Hope is faith looking forward. It signals an optimism that is rooted in the character of God (Heb. 6:18), the person and work of Christ (Col. 1:27), and the covenant promises of God (Titus 1:2).

Of all the future prospects on the distant horizon, the best and brightest is the second coming of Christ. The Savior's return is *"that blessed hope."* Hope for a loved one's recovery from illness, or for some obstinate sinner's conversion to the truth of God, or for a fresh outpouring of the Spirit of God upon the church in revival are all legitimate prospects; but each pales in comparison to that most blessed prospect of the Savior's second advent. Christian people, therefore, are instructed to maintain this long-range view and to orient their lives in the happy expectation of this momentous event (cf. 1 Ths. 1:10; 1 Cor. 1:7; Lk. 21:28).

Secondly, Paul terms it *"the glorious appearing."* The first appearing of the Lord was an epiphany of grace, but the second will be an epiphany of glory. Christ will *"appear the second time without sin unto salvation"* (Heb. 9:28) to judge every foe and ransom his own. We will behold his glory (cf. Jno. 17:24) and be glorified like him (cf. Phi. 3:20-21). Sin, Satan, death, hell, and the grave will be finally and ultimately destroyed, never to trouble the heir of grace again. Ah, what a blessed hope!

Who will appear? Paul answers, *"the great God and our Savior Jesus Christ."* The single definite article suggests that *"the great God"* is *"our Savior Jesus Christ,"* making this verse one of the most unmistakable references to the deity of Christ in the New Testament. Our Savior is indeed the great God. He himself is coming back for his own.

The Cross as a Motive

This mention of the second appearing of Christ prompts Paul to recall his first appearing—*"...who gave himself for us..."*—and thus to return to the thought with which he began this section in verse 11. Yet Paul is even more specific here, identifying the *"grace"* that promotes godliness as the substitutionary death of Christ on the cross.

"For us" means "in our place and for our benefit." This phrase is reminiscent of the Passover Lamb sacrificed to spare the Hebrew family from death. The clause *"redeem us from all iniquity,"* likewise, refers back to the deliverance from Egyptian bondage. *"Purify to himself a peculiar people zealous of good works"* also reminds us of the covenant at Sinai in which God consecrated the Israelites to himself

as his own servants.

Paul is saying that the death of Christ not only accomplished our redemption, but it also sets us apart as Christ's consecrated servants. We are not our own any longer, for we have been bought with a price; therefore, it is incumbent that we glorify God in our bodies and spirits, for they are God's (cf. 1 Cor. 6:19).

The cross, properly understood, is a compelling force for ethical holiness. With gratitude for his grace in redemption and hope for his glory at the Savior's second advent, the believer has the necessary motivation to spur him forward in a life of faith and obedience.

6

The Christian in Society

Put them in mind to be subject to principalities and powers, to obey magistrates, to be ready to every good work, to speak evil of no man, to be no brawlers, but gentle, shewing all meekness unto all men. For we ourselves also were sometimes foolish... (Titus 3:1-3a)

The epistle to Titus, as noted previously, is primarily concerned with the external threat of worldly influence on the church. These Christians on the island of Crete faced daily pressure to conform to the spirit of the age. But Paul urges them to live self-disciplined (*sober*) lives in this present world.

What does a life of Christian sobriety entail? Does godliness mean that we are supposed to isolate ourselves from the world? Since the world is an enemy to the church, should Christian people stage a political rebellion or seek to change the culture by protest or other forms of activism?

Paul's answer is "no." Instead of fighting the world as a foe, the believer must remember that he was once just like other people. The only thing that now distinguishes him from the ungodly world around him is the grace of God. The Christian's role in society, therefore, is not that of a warrior, but of a witness. He must not attempt to "take on" the world in battle, but to model an exemplary Christian life of personal integrity and godliness.

Hence, Paul exhorts Titus, "*Put them in mind to be subject to principalities and powers, to obey magistrates, to be ready to every good work, to speak evil of no man, to be no brawlers, but gentle, showing all meekness unto all men, for we ourselves also were sometimes foolish..."* (3:1-3a).

"Put them in mind" means "remind them." The Lord's people need to hear the same truths repeated again and again (cf. 2 Pet. 1:12-13; 3:1; Phi. 3:1; Heb. 2:1). The danger of forgetting God's word is amply illustrated in the history of the nation of Israel. Israel's rebellion to God is traced to their failure to remember the Lord's many mercies unto them (cf. Ps. 106:7, 13). A major part of the minister's responsibility might be summarized in this matter of putting God's people in memory of the things that they already know.

Responsibility to Authority

The first area of the Christian's ethical responsibility in society has to do with his relationship to rulers. Evidently, the Cretans were notorious for insubordination. They resented Rome's control and plotted revolution. It is important, therefore, for Paul to remind these believers of the Christian duty to obey the law.

Why is Christian submission to the state so essential? Because the authority of the government has been delegated to it by God (cf. Rom. 13:1). By submitting to authority, the believer takes away one of his persecutor's primary potential complaints against him, i.e. lawlessness and obstruction of justice (cf. 1 Pet. 2:13-15). Even Jesus "rendered to Caesar" the things that belonged to Caesar. When the Christian proclaims a message that emphasizes the priority of personal holiness and integrity while holding the law in contempt, his testimony smacks of hypocrisy.

So, submission to civil authority is the rule for Christian people. But are there any exceptions to that rule? Is "civil disobedience" ever warranted for a Christian? Indeed, it is. In fact, whenever civil laws contradict Divine laws, it is commanded (cf. Acts 4:18-19; 5:29). But as far as conscience will allow, the believer is to behave as a model citizen.

Christians are not only supposed to be law-abiding citizens, they should also be positive contributors to society: *"...to be ready to every good work."* They are to be eager to promote the public good, but are under no obligation to cooperate with society or government when its works are sinful.

Responsibility toward Other People

The believer also needs frequent reminders concerning his responsibilities toward other people. Paul focuses on three areas of social relationships.

First, the believer has a responsibility to watch his words. He must *"speak evil of no man."* Care must be taken that his words are not slanderous toward others, whether they are high-ranking government officials or the neighbor next-door. Insulting or disparaging comments about other people are unbecoming to the gospel of Christ, and often prove to be a stumbling block to those who might inquire into this way more perfectly.

Secondly, Christians have a responsibility to avoid fights, as much as is possible. The believer must *"be no brawler."* Of course, it is impossible to avoid all conflict, for Christian discipleship is fundamentally antithetical to the way this fallen world system operates. But the believer must not be quarrelsome, or naturally argumentative. A peaceable spirit is a powerful advertisement for the gospel of Christ.

Finally, a believer has a responsibility to keep a good attitude. Christians, Paul says, should be *"gentle."* The word Paul employs speaks of a spirit of clemency, graciousness, and consideration of the capacities of another. A believer must never be bellicose. The next clause, *"showing all meekness unto all men,"* suggests a parallel thought. The aggressive attitude so typical of this fallen world must never be mistaken for the spirit of Christ.

Hence, Paul could challenge the Corinthians to unity on the basis of these two virtues, i.e. *"the meekness and gentleness of Christ"* (2 Cor.

10:1). The use of these terms in Titus 3 illustrate just how important it is for professing Christians to maintain attitudes such as humility, kindness, consideration, and courtesy to other people.

The reason given for this kind of Christian behavior in society is that the believer was once, himself, like everyone else: "*For we ourselves also were sometime foolish...*"

Interestingly, the Greek term translated *foolish* means "anti-social." Just like others, we also once treated people with disdain and contempt (i.e. "*...full of malice and envy; hateful and hating one another*"), but the grace of God has wrought a change in our hearts.

Paul's point is simply, if God can change people like us, then he can change other people too. Christians should strive, therefore, to behave themselves in such compellingly winsome ways that if God is pleased to change them like he changed us, they may be open to the gospel we proclaim.

7

Paul's Doctrine of Salvation

For we ourselves also were sometimes foolish, disobedient, deceived, serving divers lusts and pleasures, living in malice and envy, hateful, and hating one another. But after that the kindness and love of God our Saviour toward man appeared, not by works of righteousness which we have done, but according to his mercy he saved us, by the washing of regeneration, and renewing of the Holy Ghost; which he shed on us abundantly through Jesus Christ our Savior; that being justified by his grace, we should be made heirs according to the hope of eternal life. (Titus 3:3-7)

P aul now gives the reason behind his insistence that the believer maintain a godly Christian testimony in society: "*For* [lit. because] *we ourselves also were sometimes foolish, disobedient, deceived, serving diverse lusts and pleasures, living in malice and envy, hateful and hating one another; but after that the kindness and love of God our Savior toward man appeared...*" (Titus 3:3-4).

The believer in Jesus Christ is obliged to model a changed life, with patience and understanding toward others, because he was once just like the rest; therefore, he/she (of all people) should be able to understand what it is like to live in bondage to the flesh. The Christian must never exhibit an attitude of superiority toward others, looking down contemptuously on them, but rather of empathy for their plight and humility that arises from the realization that the only difference now between he/she and them is the grace of God.

This passage outlines Paul's doctrine of salvation in very concise terms. Yet it is arguably the most comprehensive statement of salvation in the entire New Testament. From these verses, we may extract five important thoughts regarding the doctrine of salvation: (1) the need of it; (2) the motive of it; (3) the means of it; (4) the ground of it; and (5) the outcome or result of it.

Total Depravity — the Need of Salvation

First, Paul addresses man's native sinfulness, including himself in the dismal description: *"For we ourselves also were sometimes* [i.e. at one time] *foolish, disobedience, deceived, serving diverse lusts and pleasures, living in malice and envy, hateful and hating one another..."* The language is reminiscent of a similar statement to the Ephesians: *"Ye were sometime* [i.e. at one time] *darkness..."* (Eph. 5:8).

Paul has not resorted to hyperbole. This disagreeable picture is the real story of mankind apart from grace. By nature, people are *foolish* — the word conveys the idea of "thoughtlessness." According to Titus 1:15, man's *"mind and conscience is defiled"* in his natural state; consequently, the thoughts are the natural man are *"only evil continually"* (cf. Gen. 6:5). In the sum total of his thoughts, God is not considered (cf. Ps. 10:4). His *"understanding is darkened"* (cf. Eph. 4:18) because his *"carnal mind is enmity with God"* (cf. Rom. 8:7). Intellectually, then, man by nature is depraved.

Further, he is *disobedient*. The word means "obstinate, stubborn, unwilling to be persuaded." It speaks of an inward aversion toward God. It teaches that the unregenerate person possesses a moral bias and antagonism toward righteousness.

Further, he is described as *"deceived, serving divers lusts and pleasures."* Both Greek verbs are in the passive voice, indicating that the natural man is really the victim of forces beyond his control. Paul makes the same point in Ephesians 2:2: *"Wherein in time past ye walked according to the course of this world, according to the prince of the power of the air, the spirit that now worketh in the children of disobedience."* In this verse, Paul teaches that by nature, people are the devil's pawns and slaves, living with one and only one concern, i.e. to fulfill the lusts of the flesh and of the mind.

Finally, man needs salvation because he instinctively lives *"in malice and envy, hateful and hating one another."* His social relationships are marked by a spirit of ill-will and resentment toward others, which inevitably leads to reciprocal animosity and hostility.

God's Amazing Love—the Motive of Salvation

Against this dark backdrop, Paul proceeds to discuss the motive for salvation: *"...but after that the kindness and love of God our Savior toward man appeared, not by works of righteousness which we have done, but according to his mercy he saved us..."* Salvation, says Paul, is *"of the Lord"* (cf. Jon. 2:9). It originated in his sovereign will and purpose. Motivated by nothing except his own loving heart, God our Savior intervened to rescue miserable sinners.

He was not induced by any inherent goodness in man, for, as the preceding catalog of depraved characteristics suggest, there was no inherent goodness in the natural man. Salvation, therefore, is *"not by works of righteousness which we have done."* Nothing prompted such kindness but his own good pleasure. Love—love alone—moved the Creator to condescend to the low estate of such wretched and unworthy sinners.

The Holy Spirit—the Means of Salvation

Thirdly, Paul defines the means or instrumentality of salvation: *"...by the washing of regeneration and renewing of the Holy Ghost."* Obviously, Paul is thinking here of what we might call the *vital*[1]

---

1   *Vital*, of course, refers to "life." It is a wise practice to draw fine lines of theological distinction for the sake of clarity in biblical interpretation. One such helpful distinction is between justification, a legal concept, and regeneration, a vital concept. Justification by the Lord Jesus Christ on the cross concerns a person's legal status before God. It is something done *for* (or *on behalf of*) a human being. Regeneration by the Holy Spirit, on the other hand, is a vital work of grace. It is something done *in* the heart of (and *to*)

phase of salvation. He here terms this work of grace *regeneration*, meaning "new birth." Elsewhere in scripture, it is referred to as a *quickening*, a *drawing to Christ*, a *new creation*, a *translation*, a *passing from death to life*, and an *effectual calling*.

The two words *washing* and *renewing* describe the effect of God's gift of grace called *regeneration*. A "cleansing" takes place in the inner man (cf. Jno. 13:10)-an inward sanctification, if you will (cf. Eph. 4:24) — in *"the washing of regeneration."* Further, a moral transformation (*renewing*) occurs, so that sinful behavior can no longer be practiced without the inward tension of conviction in the conscience.

Notice that this work of *washing* and *renewing* happens by means of *"the Holy Ghost."* No subordinate agent is mentioned—not the gospel preacher, a religious tract, or even a Bible—indicating that the Holy Spirit works directly and immediately (i.e. without the use of external means or media) in the saving work of regeneration.

Justifying Grace — the Ground of Salvation

Next, Paul mentions the ground, or basis, on which the this vital work of regeneration is performed in the heart of a sinner: *"...that being justified freely by his grace..."* The legal work of the Lord Jesus Christ on the cross is the basis on which the vital work of regeneration takes place in the individual's heart. All for whom Jesus died will be quickened into divine life at some point between conception and death.

Eternal Inheritance — the Outcome of Salvation

Finally, all of this that God has done will lead to this glorious outcome: *"...that we might be made heirs according to the hope of eternal life."* Everyone who was loved by the Father, redeemed by the Son, and called by the Spirit, is in possession of an inheritance that consists of eternal life. Presently we stand *"in hope"* of receiving that

---

one of God's elect.

inheritance (cf. Titus 1:2), but one day, we will enter into the very enjoyment of it forevermore.

8
Final Admonitions

This is a faithful saying, and these things I will that thou affirm constantly, that they which have believed in God might be careful to maintain good works. These things are good and profitable unto men. But avoid foolish questions, and genealogies, and contentions, and strivings about the law; for they are unprofitable and vain. A man that is an heretick after the first and second admonition reject; knowing that he that is such is subverted, and sinneth, being condemned of himself. When I shall send Artemas unto thee, or Tychicus, be diligent to come unto me to Nicopolis: for I have determined there to winter. Bring Zenas the lawyer and Apollos on their journey diligently, that nothing be wanting unto them. And let ours also learn to maintain good works for necessary uses, that they be not unfruitful. All that are with me salute thee. Greet them that love us in the faith. Grace be with you all. Amen. (Titus 3:8-15)

Paul concludes his epistle to Titus with several, last-minute injunctions. The first three admonitions are of an ecclesiastical character. He enjoins him to *affirm* certain things, *avoid* others, and *reject* still others. The last three are of a more personal nature: *"Be diligent to come unto me;" "Bring Zenas...and Apollos on their journey;"* and *"Greet them that love us in the faith."*

Insist on Good Works
First, Titus is to emphasize the necessity of good works: *"This is a faithful saying and these things I will that thou affirm constantly, that they which have believed in God might be careful to maintain good works.*

These things are good and profitable unto men" (v. 8). Paul emphasizes the subject again just prior to his benediction: *"And let ours also learn to maintain good works for necessary uses, that they be no unfruitful"* (v. 14).

The importance of good works in the life of a Christian is axiomatic. Each of the "faithful sayings" in the Pastoral Epistles speak of an axiomatic truth—a Christian maxim, or truism. This basic emphasis of the Christian gospel is no different. The duty incumbent on every believer to practice righteousness and love is a "given"—a non-negotiable. Every one who professes to believe in Christ should be able to agree at this point.

Then why is there such disagreement concerning the subject of good works among people who profess to believe in Jesus Christ? The differences that exist regarding this subject generally have to do not with the importance of good works, but with their purpose. Are good works instrumental in or necessary to eternal salvation, or do they give evidence of salvation? Are good works, in other words, the root or the fruit of salvation?

The fact that Paul addresses this subject after his comprehensive statement on the doctrine of salvation in verses 3-7 indicates that good works *flow from*, not *lead to*, salvation. To this agrees the language of Ephesians 2:8-10. After laying down the principle of salvation by grace alone in verses 8-9, Paul says, *"For we are his workmanship, created in Christ Jesus unto good works, which God hath before ordained that we should walk in them."* The Christian, then, does not work *for* salvation, but *from* it.

Paul wants Titus to *"constantly affirm"* the obligation of good works. The word means "to stress; to insist upon." Evidently, the gospel minister cannot exaggerate the importance of good works in the life of the believer, nor stress the subject too frequently.

Interestingly, *"good works"* is a major theme in the Pastoral Epistles. The expression occurs fourteen times, demonstrating just how important the preaching of practical matters was to the apostles. An examination of this topic in the Pastorals provides us with several important, summary points.

First, the purpose of Christ's death on the cross was to *"purify unto himself a peculiar people, zealous of good works"* (2:14). His redeeming grace has not only purchased and cleansed us from our sins, but it should also incite and motivate us to godliness.

Second, the Lord has provided the necessary means to equip his people to perform good works (cf. 2 Tim. 2:21; 3:17). Those who have been "created unto good works" *should* walk therein. It is a duty incumbent upon them. Hence, God has given his inspired word to *"throughly furnish"* (or equip) the regenerate person *"unto all good works"* (2 Tim. 3:17).

Third, the Lord expects his people to be *"ready"* (or eager) to practice good works (Titus 3:1). The believer should look for opportunities to minister and serve. He should be zealous to pursue every open door.

Fourthly, it is by good works that the gospel is adorned and commended to others (cf. Titus 2:9-10). Here the faith we preach is practiced. Here the verbal gospel is visually proclaimed.

What kind of good works does Paul want Christian people to practice and maintain? Scripture answers this question when it employs the imperative mood, i.e. the language of command. First, no doubt, he wants them to "believe on the Lord Jesus Christ," for believing is a work that God requires (cf. Jno. 6:28-29; Acts 16:31; 1 Jno. 3:23). Also, he wants them to repent of their sins and be baptized (cf. Acts 2:38). He also wants them to love God supremely, and love others as themselves (cf. Mt. 22:37-39; 1 Jno. 4:21; Jno. 13:35). Good works also include activities such as prayer, giving, evangelism, bearing another's burden, ministering to the needy, helping the helpless, encouraging the downcast, resisting temptation (cf. Ps. 17:4), attendance on public worship, etc.

May we provoke one another to love and good works (Heb. 10:24), and exhort one another daily, while it is called today.

Instruction Concerning Controversies

On the island of Crete, Titus' challenges came from within the church as well as from the external, unbelieving culture. Because the culture presented threats to personal godliness, Titus must be diligent to remind believers of the need to maintain good works. But because the devil relentlessly attempts to sabotage the unity and peace of the church, Titus must also assume a courageous Biblical posture toward conflict and those who promote it: *"But avoid foolish questions, and genealogies, and contentions, and strivings about the law; for they are unprofitable and vain. A man that is an heretic, after the first and second admonition, reject; knowing that he that is such is subverted, and sinneth, being condemned of himself"* (3:9-11).

"Foolish questions" refers to pointless controversies. Titus is to keep his distance from unnecessary arguments and quarrels. Of course, not all controversies are pointless, and not all arguments are prohibited. Sometimes it is necessary for the pastor to stand firm for the sake of the truth. Even the Lord Jesus himself, as John R. W. Stott notes, "was a controversialist, in constant debate with the religious leaders of his day. Paul himself was also drawn into controversy over the gospel and could not avoid it...So, then, not all controversy is banned, but only 'foolish' controversies."[1]

"Foolish" translates the Greek noun *zeteseis*, meaning "speculations." That these speculative controversies in Titus' sphere of ministry had a Jewish flavor is indicated by the reference to *"genealogies."* Paul is simply advising Titus to make a judgment whether or not a contentious matter is a substantive and credible threat to the integrity of the gospel. If not, he is to *"avoid"* the conflict.

How vitally important it is for God's servants to know when to *"silence"* and *"rebuke"* false teachers (cf. Titus 1:11, 13), and when to keep their distance from conflict! No true servant of God enjoys controversy and the large majority of it, because it is *"foolish,"* i.e.

---

1   John Stott, *The Message of 1 Timothy & Titus*, p. 210.

based on sheer speculation, should simply be avoided.

What about cases when it cannot be avoided? What is Titus to do when the peddler of controversy is causing division among God's people?

Paul answers that Titus is to warn the divisive person repeatedly: *"...the first and second admonition..."* Labor is to be expended in an attempt to reclaim the schismatic individual.

The word *"heretic"* (Gr. *hairetikos*) is not used here as a term of insult (like it is frequently employed today), but as a description of a person's activity. The original word is used in *Acts* (cf. Acts 24:14) to speak of a sect or school of thought, like the Sadducees or Pharisees who had their own respective schools of thought.

It describes an individaul who embraces an idea that is foreign to the true gospel, then sets out to influence others to embrace his views. Just because a person holds to some unorthodox idea, then, does not make him a *"heretic."* He may become a heretic, however, when he uses those unorthodox ideas to divide people into factions. A heretic, then, might be defined as a factious, schismatic, or divisive person.

How should Titus deal with such schismatic people? Again, he should "admonish," i.e. warn, them. Not just once, but twice, which probably means that he should make repeated efforts to bring them to repentance.

What if they refuse to repent after a brief period of intensive labor? He should *"reject,"* that is, have nothing to do with, the unrepentant person. Notice, he is not to seek to persecute or malign the individual. He is simply to *"withdraw"* (cf. 2 Ths. 3:6-15), *"avoid"* (cf. Rom. 16:17), and assume an overall passive posture, leaving the schismatic individual to himself.

Contrary to popular opinion, there is nothing unkind or unloving about such a biblical approach. In fact, great love has already been demonstrated in the multiple attempts to reclaim the erring soul. The fact that the subversive individual refuses to listen to repeated admonitions indicates that he is himself "*subverted*," that is, under the control of a different spirit. The bottom line is that, in the words again of John Stott, Titus must give the "offender successive opportunities to repent; repudiation is to be the very last resort."[2]

Personal Matters

Next, Paul indicates his purpose to relieve Titus of pastoral responsibility and urges him to diligently attempt to come to Nicopolis (v. 12). Paul longed to see this dear brother and faithful minister, and hoped Titus would make the effort to arrange a personal visit. In the meantime, Zenus and Apollos would need whatever help and supplies Titus could give them after they completed their mission of delivering this epistle (v. 13).

Finally, Titus is urged to "*greet them that love us in the faith*" (v. 15). Because the truth of the gospel is a "common faith" (cf. Titus 1:4), it tends to bind those who share a conviction for it in love and fellowship (cf. 3 Jno. 1). Paul wants Titus to convey his personal greetings to these people. Paul concludes the letter with his classic benediction, expanded to include all the saints on the island of Crete, "*Grace be with you all. Amen.*"

Summary

The letter to Titus has taught us how Christian people who live in an ungodly environment are to conduct themselves. Motivated by the great gospel truths of salvation by Christ alone, they are to practice godliness, so that they may adorn the doctrine of God our Savior in all things. This is true in relationships within the church itself (ch. 1), relationships in the home (ch. 2), and relationships in society at large (ch. 3).

For those of us who live in an environment not unlike the one in which Titus lived and ministered, the practical instructions of this epistle speak with up-to-the-minute relevance. May God bless us to

---

2   Ibid. p. 211.

study it, to personally heed it, and to implement it into our respective situations, so that we too may "adorn the doctrine" we hold dear by authentic Christian lives of daily discipleship.

www.ingramcontent.com/pod-product-compliance
Lightning Source LLC
Chambersburg PA
CBHW031234090426
42742CB00007B/190